WOMEN
Who
TRI

WOMEN who TRI

A Reluctant Athlete's Journey into the Heart of America's Newest Obsession

ALICIA DIFABIO

VELO press

BOULDER, COLORADO

▼velopress®

3002 Sterling Circle, Suite 100
Boulder, Colorado 80301-2338 USA

VeloPress is the leading publisher of books on endurance sports. Focused on cycling, triathlon, running, swimming, and nutrition/diet, VeloPress books help athletes achieve their goals of going faster and farther. Preview books and contact us at velopress.com.

Distributed in the United States and Canada by Ingram Publisher Services

A Cataloging-in-Publication record for this book is available from the Library of Congress.
ISBN 978-1-937715-58-8

This paper meets the requirements of ANSI/NISO Z39.48-1992
(Permanence of Paper).

Art direction by Vicki Hopewell
Cover illustration by Karolin Schnoor
Handlettering by Molly Jacques
Photograph on page 295 by Bridget Horgan Bell

17 18 19 / 10 9 8 7 6 5 4 3 2 1

For my girls—
Carlie, Sophia, Madelena, and Ariella.
Never underestimate the gifts you bring to this world.

Contents

If you can't fly, then run. If you can't run, then walk.
If you can't walk, then crawl. But whatever you do,
you have to keep moving forward.

—DR. MARTIN LUTHER KING JR.

༄

Even if you fall on your face, you're still moving forward.

—VICTOR KIAM

Greater Than the Sum of All Fears

I had as many doubts as anyone else. Standing on the starting line, we're all cowards.

—ALBERTO SALAZAR

I stand on the bank of a lake in the calm of morning, bare toes tickled by the sparse grass. The 7:00 a.m. sun has not yet warmed the fresh summer air, but it makes the lake's surface shimmer like a diamond. To my left, a growing group of spectators aligns the overpass bridge. To my right is the finish line I hope to cross in less than two hours. Directly ahead is my biggest fear and greatest weakness—the quarter-mile open-water swim. The first of three events comprising the Queen of the Hill Sprint Triathlon. Surrounding me, over 300 women of all shapes and sizes, ranging in age from 14 to 75. Despite the diversity of the group, little distinguishes us from one another, clad as we are in matching black-and-pink tri suits, hair tucked beneath swim caps, faces free of makeup. In our caps, color-coded by age groups, we look like a moving rainbow. Some women in the crowd are confident and focused; others are tearful and nervous. The quiet buzz among us contains everything from excited, giggly chatter to softly whispered prayers.

Today is race day. For some, this is just one of many races on their schedule this season. For others, like me, today is our very first triathlon. Today is bucket list day. It's the day when our dreams will prove to be just a little bit greater than the sum of our fears.

Cheers erupt as the first age group wave is called to the water's edge. Instead of the chaos of a "mass start" typical of most triathlons, the Queen of the Hill Sprint Triathlon avoids the fury of splashing arms and legs by bringing each of the nine waves of competitors out to the water and letting them jump into the lake one at a time. Timing chips strapped around our ankles will take care of the rest. It's all quite civilized, and newbies like me appreciate anything to keep the anxiety level down.

First to go are the orange caps. As I watch them parade down to the water, I feel my stomach churning. I hug my arms across my chest to stop from shaking. My eyes wander out across the lake. Glassy and expansive, Lake Gilman is beautiful and placid, yet somehow today it seems more formidable than serene. I note the final buoy marking the turnaround for the quarter-mile swim. It seems so far. Too far. Did it look that far in my practice swim weeks ago? I know the water will be cold and dark and deep, and I'm a novice swimmer. I know this first leg of the race will be my greatest challenge, not so much physically as mentally. I remind myself that if I just keep my head together, I can do this.

I scan the crowd of onlookers, hoping to catch a glimpse of my family. I can't find them, so instead I picture their faces—four sweet little girls and my husband, who I know is already proud of me before I've even started the race. Who believed I could do this long before *I* believed it. Even as I try to draw strength from all the people who have supported me on this triathlon journey, I have reached that point where no one else can do this *for* me. Right now, there is only one person I can count on. It's up to me, and me alone.

There are only white-capped women left on the shore. I stand anxiously among them. We are the final wave of the nine age groups—the 45- to 49-year-olds. Though we are not the oldest age group competing, the race directors have put us last in the lineup. The lake is now alive with the splashing arms and bobbing heads of 300 women who have already started their journey. Some of them are already exiting the water and running up the hill to jump on their bikes. Meanwhile, the white caps are only now filing down the slope of the bank. It's showtime.

As the women in front of me begin systematically disappearing from the tiny dock, my position advances. I'm alive with adrenaline, my head spinning with every fear and doubt I've until now held at bay. I steel myself, filling my head with positive mantras, reminding myself of my sole goal—to finish. Just swim. Then bike. Then run. One thing at a time. One stroke, one step, one mile at a time. I *got* this.

"Call out your number before crossing the timing mat, then jump in," a race official instructs. I glance at my arm where a volunteer body-marked me with thick black marker earlier this morning. "One-O-six!" I call in a thready voice as I step across the blue-and-orange timing mat. With that one step, my race officially starts.

The worn planks of wood have all but disappeared under my bare feet. I'm at the edge, the splash of the woman in front of me rippling the water. The heat of the woman directly behind me urges me forward. There is no time to hesitate, to panic, to waver, to choose. There is only this heartbeat of a moment.

The words of Eleanor Roosevelt nudge me with a gentle whisper. *You must do the things you cannot.* So I jump.

In an instant, I am swallowed whole and the world goes cold, dark, and quiet. The voices in my head clamor, then hush.

I rise. I breathe. Then, I do the only thing left for me to do.

I begin.

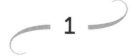

A SPANDEX REVOLUTION

*Never underestimate the power of dreams
and the influence of the human spirit.
The potential for greatness lives within each of us.*
—WILMA RUDOLPH

I t's February 1982 and I'm glued to my 20-inch tube television—the kind with rabbit ears and a round dial that clicks loudly when you turn it to one of five stations. An obscure event called the Ironman Kona® is being broadcast on ABC's *Wide World of Sports*. I have never heard of the Ironman, but because I'm a cross-country runner, my dad figures I'd be interested in watching the marathon leg of this three-part race. So I tear myself away from the impossible act of trying to tape my favorite songs off the radio without the DJ talking over the entire ending, and join my parents on the couch.

My dad read about the Ironman in *Sports Illustrated* a few years ago, so he fills me in. It's something called a triathlon, which strings together three athletic events. First, the competitors swim 2.4 miles in the ocean, then bike 112 miles, and finish up by running 26.2 miles . . . all in a row. *As if!* Even I know, at the tender age of 14, that this Ironman thing is completely nuts. My mother corroborates my thoughts by muttering, "These people are completely nuts." Naturally, we're riveted.

The competitor of most interest to us is a young woman named Julie Moss. Julie, a 23-year-old graduate student, is embarking on the Ironman for the first time. She is a non-elite athlete—an unknown, regular, "ordinary" competitor—who somehow has secured the female lead during the final leg of the race. Julie is one of only 47 women competing in the Ironman this year, and since she is the underdog and a girl, we are rooting for her. She's in the lead, and it looks like she'll have no trouble keeping the elite athlete Kathleen McCartney, trailing her by a good distance, at bay. Victory seems firmly in Julie's grasp as she closes in on the finish line.

But something happens to Julie in that final mile. After 10 hours of continuous swimming, biking, and running under the unrelenting Hawaiian sun, her body starts to break down from immense fatigue, poor nourishment, and serious dehydration. In the final mile of this nationally televised, 140.6-mile race, Julie Moss seems to hit a wall. She staggers and sways, her legs turn to jelly, and her body collapses into a heap on the ground.

My mother, father, and I stop fidgeting. Stop talking. Stop breathing. We suck in one collective breath and hold it. My initial fear is that Julie may have suffered a massive stroke or heart attack. Or, perhaps someone from the sidelines shot her because that's how suddenly she went down. Confused and then concerned, we watch Julie rise on shaky legs. She is like a rag doll, head bobbling, her physical being relinquished to a twisting, uncooperative pile. Yet on her face there is intense focus and unrelenting determination. Despite her heroic efforts to propel her body forward, she collapses again. The tremendous effort it takes for her to rise again is heartbreaking.

I can't understand how someone could be so healthy and strong one moment and so utterly broken the next. I'm too young to fathom the incomprehensible distance of an Ironman race, the physical pain the body endures, and the mental fortitude required to press on. Confused, I barrage my parents with a string of questions, scared we were watching this girl die. "What's wrong with her? Why does she keep falling? Where's the ambulance? Why isn't someone helping her? Why doesn't she just *quit*?" My mom loudly shushes me, eyes fixed on the screen, mouth covered in shock and concern.

Julie is moving forward. In fits and spurts, she stumbles and staggers closer to the finish line. A steeled mind inside a crumbling body. The finisher's tape is illuminated by bright lights, flanked by hundreds of cheering fans who have fallen into a collective silence at her struggle. She knows she will be the first female to cross the finish line and win Ironman Kona . . . if she can just make it those final measly yards. She is inching her way there, slowly, painfully. In my living room, we are rooting for her. We found out later that an entire nation was rooting as well.

Julie had been managing an inebriated-looking stumble, but then she breaks into a light jog. The crowd erupts into cheers. Just as my heart soars for her miraculous recovery, she collapses to the ground again, and the crowd's roar quiets into a concerned hush.

This is the part where she stays down, I think to myself. I wait for her to succumb, for the stretcher to come from the sidelines and whisk her away because there is no way she can carry on. Besides, why on earth would she want to? Anyone would just pack it in at this point. Anyone, apparently, but an Ironman.

When Julie Moss can no longer stagger or stand, she does the only thing she can manage—she crawls. It's more of a drag, really. Slow and purposeful, in spasmodic motions, she crawls those final 10 yards down Ali'i Drive, fueled by nothing but sheer, invincible will.

Yards—*yards!*—from crossing that coveted finish line, the elite athlete who had been chasing Moss for miles sails by Julie's crawling form and breaks the tape. Twenty-nine seconds after Kathleen McCarthy is crowned the overall female winner, Julie crosses the finish line on hands and knees. First-time Ironman competitor and amateur athlete Julie Moss covered 140.6 miles in an impressive 11 hours, 10 minutes, and 9 seconds. The only thing I could do for that long was sleep.

Though she came in second place that night, in the eyes of the nation Julie Moss was the true victor. She was a regular girl who became a hero, and remains an icon in triathlon history. After Julie crawled across that finish line, Ironman would never, ever be the same.

❧

That was my first glimpse into the world of triathlon. Yet, as powerful as it was watching Julie Moss in the 1982 Ironman Kona, I never thought much about triathlons after that. Sure, Julie's dramatic Ironman finish made her an international symbol of determination. It is still considered one of the most inspirational race finishes in televised sports history. Even so, while Julie was being embraced as America's sweetheart, I was hanging up my cross-country shoes for good, convinced I loathed the sport. And just like that, my lackluster running career and Julie's inspirational Ironman finish faded into the primordial stew of my subconscious where I was content to keep them.

Thirty-five years and four children later, I found myself confronted by triathlon once again. Only this time, it wasn't on a rabbit-eared television. This time, it was right in my own backyard. And instead of one young Ironman competitor with a fire in her belly, there were hundreds of them—the young and old, the couch potatoes and fitness junkies, soccer moms, working moms, stay-at-home moms, teenagers, and grandmothers.

I could see the influence of triathlon in my town simply by watching the transformation of minivans in the grocery store and school parking lots. Once unadorned, cars now sprouted bike racks from the rear and were emblazoned with the pink triathlon club car magnet that proclaimed membership in one of the hottest social scenes in southern New Jersey—the Mullica Hill Women's Triathlon Club (MHWTC). What began as a handful of tri-curious women had grown into an army of weekend warriors, peaking at more than 900 tri-zealots, making it the largest all-female triathlon club in the country. No matter where I went or what I did, I couldn't escape "those girls in pink."

Dressed in the club's signature colors of pink and black, they could be found biking and running on every back road, swimming in the local lakes and pools, organizing charity functions, and being quoted in local newspapers. My Facebook newsfeed was flooded with sporty status updates of every mile run, biked, and swum with friends. I'd scroll through reels of photos of sweaty, happy groups of women, smiling post-race next to their $2,000 pimped-out road bikes, finisher medals gleaming on their chests. As I watched friends and neighbors bond through this shared obsession, I started to feel a tad left out. Although I was a grown 40-something-year-old woman, I felt sort of like that new girl who can't find a seat at the cool crowd's lunch table. But if the cost of admission was to actually *do* a triathlon, I wasn't at all sure that I was ready to pay that price.

I comforted myself with the knowledge that trends in fitness come and go. This whole triathlon craze was probably just a flash in the pan. After all, I remembered when step aerobics, Zumba, P90X, and kickboxing were all the rage. They were soon replaced with hot yoga, barre, TRX, and CrossFit. I was certain triathlon was just another passing fad. Like jeggings, extreme couponing, and ombre hair color, this too would pass.

But triathlons not only stuck, they snowballed. Turns out, my little New Jersey town was simply a microcosm of a far bigger phenomenon. In 2013, approximately 2.3 million Americans competed in a triathlon, representing an all-time high following a decade of unprecedented growth. In 2015, estimates were well over 4 million. Triathlon's popularity has been on a meteoric rise across the nation and women have been leading the charge, representing more than half of the newcomers to the sport. Once an obscure sport for the elite, recreational and subelite triathlon participation is rising among youth, seniors, and women of all ages, sizes, fitness levels, and body types. In fact, it's the female triathlete "weekend warriors" who are the driving force behind the sport's overall growth.

Triathlons have become more than a one-off bucket list goal. More than a fitness fad, weight loss tool, pre-midlife, post-motherhood, or empty-nester rite of passage. Triathlons are a fitness regime turned passion. A dream turned lifestyle. A bona fide obsession. A new religion. A female revolution clad in spandex.

Although a slew of celebrities, like Jennifer Lopez, Teri Hatcher, Jillian Michaels, and America Ferrera, have been taking on triathlon, the real drivers of the sport's burgeoning popularity are neither the rich and famous nor the elite pros.

A new breed of triathlete is taking the sport by storm. Women between the ages of 35 and 55 are flocking to this sport by the thousands. Most are not the sinewy, chiseled, competitive athletes featured on Nike commercials. The large majority actually look a lot like the regular people you see in the mall or a PTA meeting. They are the young mothers changing diapers and chasing toddlers, and the seasoned mothers chauffeuring their preteens to a million activities while juggling a career. They are the women working 60 to 70 hours a week, and the stay-at-home moms who put their career on pause. They are girls as young as 8 and women as old as 80. They have survived cancer, battled depression and anxiety, and lost spouses, mothers, fathers, and siblings. They have found sobriety, lost weight, let themselves go, and found themselves again. These women come to triathlons as new mothers, veteran mothers, and grandmothers. They may be single, married, widowed, or divorced. They may be out of shape, unable to swim, or recovering from a major injury or illness. They may be competitive collegiate athletes or self-proclaimed couch potatoes. They come filled with both anxiety and determination. They come in every age, shape, size, athletic experience, and fitness level, yet they all share some common bonds—the desire to do something slightly outrageous, to push themselves further, to face their fears, to dig deep and test their mettle. They are "ordinary" women who want nothing more and nothing less than to swim, bike, and run in between the heaps of laundry, the crying babies, the piles of dishes, and the long days at the office. They pledge their new fitness sorority insecure and daunted, but they emerge empowered and addicted. *They* are the newest faces of triathlon.

As I watched my own town's triathlon club morph from a little spark into a blazing white-hot sun, I could no longer ignore the phenomenon occurring right before my eyes. Sure, it felt like the women in this town had lost their marbles, but it also felt like magic was happening.

Given my front-row seat to all of this, you might think I would be one of the first to catch the tri-bug. Yet, while tri-fever burned all around me, I remained largely immune. But although I had absolutely no desire to *do* a triathlon, my cerebral interest in the topic was piqued. The psychologist in me was fascinated by the seductive lure of triathlon among women. I was intrigued by the popularity and addictive nature of the sport, the personalities of the women who loved it, and the subculture they created. Mostly, I was curious to uncover the greater meaning triathlon held in their lives.

This book was born out of that curiosity. As I watched triathlon seduce hundreds of women around me, I wondered: What makes them so willing to invest their limited time and discretionary income into this sport? What makes them want to plunge into cold oceans and lakes, spend thousands of dollars on racing bikes, and get up to train before the sun even cracks the sky? After all, there were no cash prizes waiting for them at the end of the race, no date with Ryan Gosling or a brand new car. From what I could tell, there was nothing waiting at that finish line except immense exhaustion, high fives, and some Facebook bragging rights. And yet, clearly there was something that held these women captive and fed their passion. Whatever it was, I was determined to understand it. Even if it meant that I might have to do the unimaginable. Even if it meant that to truly understand their hearts, lives, and minds, I would (somewhat reluctantly) have to become one of them.

SO IT BEGINS

We must be willing to get rid of the life we've planned
so as to have the life that is waiting for us.

—JOSEPH CAMPBELL

I never thought I'd be writing a book about triathlons. But then, I also never thought I'd end up in South Jersey or find happiness again. Yet, here I am, happy in New Jersey and writing a book about a topic I didn't even know existed until recently. Like most good things in life, it all just snuck up on me when I wasn't looking.

Let's start with an introduction. Meet me—well, the 2009 me. Back then I was a minivan-driving, harried, tired, out-of-shape wife of a busy executive and mother of four small children, trying to survive each day with sanity intact. I was a walking stereotype—that mom in stained yoga pants and messy ponytail, with too many kids to fit in the shopping cart, all of them sucking on bribery lollypops and dropping goldfish crackers in the aisles of Target. The one with a big diaper bag slung over her shoulder and even bigger bags under her eyes. The one who lived off three cups of coffee by day and a glass of red wine at night, who fantasized about when she could go back to bed the moment she opened her eyes in the morning. The one who was deep in the weeds, but if you asked her at any point if she was happy, she would say yes.

I was in my late thirties at the time, on hiatus from my professional life where I had worked in the field of psychology, and up to my elbows in children and mayhem in my new gig as a stay-at-home mom. My husband, Anthony, and I had recently moved to South Jersey, two hours away from friends, family, and my former career. I was in a new town making a new life with a new baby, a 2-year-old, and a 3-year-old. It was a deeply gratifying time of my life, but it was also physically exhausting and often emotionally draining. The physical nature of that stage of motherhood was all consuming, to the point where these little beings felt like extensions of my own body. I didn't know where I began and they ended. My peanut gallery accompanied me everywhere from the grocery store to the gynecologist's office. As the saying goes, I couldn't even pee alone. Or shower alone. Or sleep alone. Or manage to have an uninterrupted thought in my head without some little being needing me desperately in some way, shape, or form.

Now, I did say I had four young children. Three were age 3 and under, and my eldest was 12 years old. However, her severe and multiple disabilities required round-the-clock supervision and total assistance for all self-care and basic needs. Unlike my other three, Carlie's dependence on me would be always and forever. Her uncontrolled seizure disorder, autism, severe cognitive impairments, and scoliosis (along with her knack for getting into everything from her dirty diaper to the contents of the fridge at 4:00 a.m.) all kept me on my toes. Let's just say that caring for my 12-year-old was akin to having 18-month-old triplets. At that point in my life, it was safe to say there was never, ever, a dull moment.

To save my sanity and make new friends after our move from northern to southern New Jersey (which, by the way, is like moving across state lines), I joined a few social groups where other moms mingled. A monthly book club was one of my favorite activities because it involved an assortment of mid-priced wines, chatter, chocolate, and no children. Oh, and occasionally discussing books.

In the winter of 2009, it was my turn to be book club hostess. Key responsibilities included selecting a book, downloading discussion questions from the Internet, engaging in the Sisyphean act of cleaning my house, and providing an array of finger foods and alcoholic beverages. I rushed through putting four kids to bed just as my company was ringing the doorbell, giving me scarcely a moment to remove my hair scrunchy, douse myself in hand sanitizer, and pull on a fresh shirt.

While it was stressful preparing for company in the midst of kiddie-palooza, once the evening got going and the wine started flowing, I collapsed in an oversized chair among friends who, by some black magic, had made it out of their homes showered, wearing clean, trendy clothes and makeup, with their hair blown dry. I was used to being the lone unwashed, raggedy woman in the mix, so I did a mental shoulder shrug and filled my wine glass. I knew one day I'd be out of the weeds, smelling like honeysuckle, wearing lip gloss and shaving my legs more than once a month. After all, as they say, the days are long but the years are short.

As the evening progressed, I relaxed even more and enjoyed talking about everything under the sun but the book. (Book club, as it turned out, was less of a deep literary discussion and more about legitimizing a night of drinking and laughing with friends until 1:00 a.m.) It was that night, right there in my family room, when I heard the word "triathlon" for the first time in forever.

Lydia DelRosso started the tri-talk. That figured, because Lydia was the person in our group who usually said something completely random, hilarious, shocking, or a combination of all three. That's why we loved her.

"So, I'm training to do a triathlon," she announced, smiling broadly over the rim of her wine glass. Heather S., the group's southern belle, squealed in delight. Heather was a marathoner and started every morning at the gym, so her enthusiasm made sense. The rest of us furrowed our brows. "Wait, what's a triathlon again?" I asked. I had a vague recollection but couldn't remember the specifics. All I knew was this: It involved three sports and you'd never catch me doing one.

Lydia explained the event she was training for, which involved swimming in a river, biking, and then running some number of miles that made our mouths hang open in shock. Who on earth would sign up to do all of that? *On purpose?* I listened politely with some feigned interest, but honestly, I couldn't wait to change the subject to something that wasn't about fitness classes, gyms, or working out. I guess you could say I wasn't interested in sports. Well, except air hockey. That was pretty fun, as was the unofficial collegiate sport of beer pong. Now, that takes some mad skills.

"It's a sprint tri," Lydia continued, as if (1) we knew what that was and (2) it made any of it sound less ridiculous. "So, it's short."

Oh, sure, the short kind, I laughed to myself, stifling a smirk as I took another sip of wine.

"And it's SheROX, so it's all women." I had no idea what SheROX was, but the fact that it was all women didn't necessarily make it sound any easier or better.

"It's going to be fun! I'm obsessed!" Lydia gushed. "Plus, the outfits are cute. I'm already planning what I'm going to wear when I cross the finish line." We burst into collective laughter because we all knew Lydia's love of style would be present even when she was swimming in a dirty river and sweating her ass off on a bike and run. Between her love of working out and her terrific fashion sense, this triathlon thing seemed a perfect match.

> *I believe that every human has a finite number*
> *of heartbeats. I don't intend to waste any of mine running*
> *around doing exercises.*
>
> —NEIL ARMSTRONG

Each time I saw Lydia after that, she filled me in on her new endeavor, eyes sparkling with excitement. She described buying her new road bike with shoes that clipped into the pedals, shopping for tri-wear, and stocking her kitchen with "recovery smoothies." She was most excited about finding three other women who were also into triathlons. As far as I was concerned, she was lucky to have found even one partner in crime. I didn't know who these ladies were, but I was a little surprised anyone else would willingly agree to this nonsense, cute outfits or not.

Yet, as I listened to her enthusiasm over the next several months, I allowed myself to consider it. It's only natural to at least *consider* something when a friend is on such a giddy high about it. Perhaps there was something fun about doing a triathlon, perhaps something compelling in the challenge. I searched my soul for any inkling of interest. Something . . . anything?

Nada. Zilch. Zip.

Some people have a love-hate relationship with exercise. My relationship with exercise was much less labile. I simply hated it. Well, hate might be a strong word. Loathe would be stronger and more accurate. I loathed running, loathed the gym, loathed fitness classes and treadmills, and even loathed wearing anything Lycra. I did have a gym membership and used it off and on (mostly off), but forcing myself to go felt like a form of water boarding. I generally steered clear of all things athletic, my definition of which was breaking a light sweat on level 2 of the Stairmaster or hiding in the back of a Pilates class. Every once in a while, I'd dig a little deeper to try to lose the baby weight I had accumulated after each of my four pregnancies. But those half-hearted attempts at exercise never really worked, which made me loathe exercise even more because, ultimately, it duped me. So, I'd give up and resume the junky diet and exercise-free lifestyle to which I had grown accustomed.

"You used to be a cross-country runner," my father would remind me when I joked about how winded I felt chasing my toddlers around the yard. What he failed to remember was that was 200 years ago, and that I was never really good at it. What I failed to tell him was that I had done it to make him happy, not me.

Even if I had a modicum of interest in triathlons (which I did not) the whole thing sounded far too difficult. There were these small stumbling blocks:

1. I hated running, in case you didn't catch that.

2. I didn't own a bike and wasn't planning on forking over hundreds of dollars for one.

3. I couldn't swim, and even if I learned how to swim, there was no way in hell I would be capable of swimming a quarter of a mile. But, the most important detail of all was . . .

4. I felt a surge of raw, primal panic at the mere thought of bobbing around in any type of lake or river. Forget the ocean. I saw *Jaws* during a very impressionable time in my youth. It ruined me for the ocean. It ruined me for waterskiing and skinny-dipping and sailing and going past mid-shin in the breaking waves. I've even had to remind myself that there are no sharks in lakes. Or my bathtub.

So, no swimming. No open water. *Ever.* Anyway, the whole thing sounded way too hard for a normal person. Which begged the question—why would anyone bother to do it?

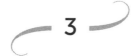

A TRI IS BORN

If God invented marathons to keep people from doing
anything more stupid, then triathlon must have taken
Him completely by surprise.

—P. Z. PEARCE

Triathlons are indeed difficult, but that seems to be the whole point. The appeal is the challenge; the challenge is the appeal. Certainly, no one was thinking of taking it easy on the few brave souls who stepped up to that original triathlon decades ago. That's right, just *decades*. Triathlon is a relatively young sport, or at least the Americanized version with which we are familiar today.

Every sport has a backstory, and triathlon's is certainly an interesting one. The story of triathlon not only explains the genesis of the sport but also reveals a great deal about its tribe. Ultimately, triathlon is *more than* a sport, *more than* a race. It's a distinct subculture that attracts a unique breed of individuals.

PARISIAN ROOTS

Triathlon's roots date back to 1902, when a race held in France strung together three events—running, cycling, and canoeing. (If you are thinking that canoeing seems random, I agree. Yet, if canoeing were still replacing the swim today, I'd be much more inclined to do it.) From that canoe-bike-run evolved a three-pronged race called, quite simply, "Les Trois Sports." It was most commonly advertised as a 3-km run, a 12-km bike, and a swim of an undocumented length across the channel Marne. Les Trois Sports remained relatively popular in certain regions of France throughout the 1920s and 1930s before it fizzled out.

Despite triathlon's roots, it's not the French who are given credit for orig-inating the modern-day triathlon. That very first race officially occurred on *American* soil . . . or, should I say, sand. The inaugural swim-bike-run took place on September 25, 1974, in Mission Bay, California.

MISSION TRI

In the early 1970s, multisport events were obscure to nonexistent. But, *one* sport was all the rage—running. Avid runners congregated in their satiny running shorts, tube socks, and thick terrycloth sweatbands and organized themselves into various running clubs. These clubs gave men and women an opportunity to run together, socialize, and enjoy the spirit of competi-tion by participating in locally organized races. One popular running club on the West Coast (still going strong today) was the San Diego Track Club. One of its members, Jack Johnstone, is credited with brainstorming a mul-tisport event that would become the first triathlon.

Jack was both a distance runner and a college swimmer, so naturally he wanted to design an event that would showcase his two talents. He had competed in a few biathlons, a new race at the time that combined a 4-mile run with a 200-yard swim. The swim-run biathlon debuted in 1972 as the first documented multisport held in America. (Today that race is known as a Splash and Dash or an Aquathon to avoid confusion with the Olympic Biathlon, a sport dating back to 1958 that combines cross-country skiing and target shooting.)

Inspired by his biathlon experience, Jack pitched a similar event to the San Diego Track Club's calendar chairman, Bill Stock. It turned out that another club member, Don Shanahan, was concurrently pitching his own idea for a multisport race. As the story goes, Bill Stock asked these two guys to collaborate and design *one* multisport race because he didn't want too many "weird" races appearing on the schedule. Don had taken up cycling because of an injury and suggested adding a cycling component to the swim and run. Reportedly, Jack was uncertain about adding a bike leg as bicycling wasn't a very popular sport at the time. But the verdict was some version of "What the heck, let's go for it."

From there, these two guys who had never directed a race in their lives got the Mission Bay Triathlon onto the San Diego Track Club calendar. Scheduled for a random Wednesday evening with two weeks' notice, the ad simply stated: "Run, Cycle, Swim: Triathlon Set for 25th." Little information about the race was included, other than the instruction to "bring your own bike" (just in case that wasn't obvious). The entry fee? A dollar.

Technically speaking, the Mission Bay Triathlon was more of a run-bike-swim-run-swim-run consisting of 6 total miles of running (broken up), 5 miles of continuous biking, and 500 total yards of swimming (also broken up). The race started out with a 3-mile run and then a bike loop of about 5 miles on Fiesta Island; followed by a 250-yard swim from the island to the mainland shore, a second leg of running down the coastline, a second swim leg across a little lagoon, another short run and short swim; and ended with a final crawl up a steep bank. Since there were no transition areas between each leg of the triathlon, volunteers collected the sneakers left along the shore after the swim portions and transported them in plastic baggies so they were waiting for the next leg of the run.

Unlike in today's triathlons, the swim was toward the end of the event. Since most participants were slower swimmers and the race didn't begin until evening, many ended up swimming in the dark. As an impromptu solution to the problem of nightfall, Jack and Don gathered some cars together to shine their headlights on the water and finish line for the final racers.

Surprisingly, this new, local, wacky event had a decent turnout. Word of mouth in a tight-knit community of avid runners and endurance athletes seemed to do the trick. Forty-six eager men and women showed up on September 25, 1974, to the relief of the race directors who worried that the bike leg would reduce the race's credibility, the short notice would not reach enough competitors, and the weeknight would deter participation.

Some of the racers had previous biathlon experience. Others were runners but weak swimmers. Because cycling was not in vogue, most didn't even *own* a bike, let alone cycle for exercise. The majority of the bikes used in the race were borrowed three-speeds and beach cruisers. A basic 10-speed Volkcycle was reportedly the fanciest bike there. But, the playing field was leveled by the fact that no one had any prior triathlon experience. As this was the very first triathlon ever, *no one* was a triathlete. No one knew how to train for one. There were no books to read, no YouTube videos to watch, no tri-clubs or coaches or online communities to learn from. In fact, the term "triathlon" didn't even officially *exist*. As one story tells it, when Jack Johnstone ordered the trophies, the engravers called and asked how to spell "triathlon." Apparently, they could not find it in any dictionary. Jack winged it, using the spellings of "pentathlon" and "decathlon" as his guide.

The race was considered a success, despite some logistical challenges that can be chalked up to inexperience and a limited budget. The winner was 44-year-old Bill Phillips, who finished with a time of 55:44. Of the 10 women racing that evening, Eileen Water was the first female to cross the finish line—the *very first* female finisher of the *very first* triathlon—placing 23rd overall with a time of 71:43.

After the race, it's said that almost everyone went out for pizza and agreed that it was all great fun. Triathlon's initial success was not so much about the race but about the positive vibe and enthusiasm of the people involved. Without the passion, adventurous spirit, and camaraderie of that original group, that first triathlon might well have been the last.

The Mission Bay Triathlon attracted a certain type of personality. It beckoned to them with the promise of a challenge that they could no longer find in their single sport of choice. This was certainly the case for

US Navy officer John Collins; his wife, Judy; and their two children, 13-year-old Michael and 12-year-old Kristin. The whole Collins family participated in the Mission Bay Triathlon and loved it. Their experience stayed with them and ended up inspiring another race, years later, that would put triathlon on a worldwide stage.

Sometimes the road less traveled is less traveled for a reason.
—JERRY SEINFELD

FORGING IRON

Some time after competing in the Mission Bay Triathlon, officer John Collins received his orders to transfer to Hawaii. The Collins family were very athletic and had a long history of involvement in sports and races. So, naturally, they hooked up with a community of endurance runners and swimmers once they relocated. And, naturally, they participated in two of the most challenging endurance events Hawaii offered—the Honolulu Marathon and the Waikiki Rough Water Swim.

The most well-known version of the Ironman story goes like this: John and Judy attended the awards banquet for the Oahu Perimeter Run one evening, and John and his military buddies started arguing about who was the better athlete—the swimmer, the cyclist, or the runner. This animated debate ended in a friendly bet. They decided the only way to settle the argument was to hold a race that put all three athletes to the test. However, there have been several interviews in which Judy and John make some important amendments to the story. In one article, Judy's version clarifies that there wasn't an actual wager. Instead, it was more like a few military buddies who, in her words, were "middle-aged and slow," trying to design an event in which they could beat the really fast people. As they brainstormed this new type of race at the banquet, some lively conversation ensued about whether runners or swimmers were the better athletes. Apparently, when John referenced something he read about a champion cyclist who had "the highest oxygen intake," that got the gang riled up. All that talk about swimming, biking, and running reminded John of the good time he had had at the Mission Bay Triathlon in California. So he proposed a race that would put swimmers, bikers, and runners to the ultimate test. This gang of passionate endurance athletes thought it was a great idea. But how would they do it? Easy. Just combine three of the largest endurance races in Hawaii at the time: the Waikiki Rough Water Swim, the Oahu Bike Race, and the Honolulu Marathon. The obvious conclusion!

Once the idea was hatched, John apparently didn't need any time to sleep on it. He announced his race idea over the microphone right there at the banquet. To John's credit, he didn't wake up the next day backpedaling. Those who egged him on that night hadn't lost interest either. The race was on. Now, it just needed a name. That name came from John Collins's historic quote: "Whoever finishes first, we'll call him the Ironman."

However, the name "Ironman" (and even the term "triathlon") took a while to stick. The "three-part thing," as most people called it, was set to take place on the island of Oahu. It began with a swim of 2.4 miles (the distance of the Waikiki Rough Water Swim), continued with a bike race of 112 miles (a few miles shy of the 116-mile Oahu Bike Race, which circumnavigated the island), and ended with a full marathon of 26.2 miles (the distance of the Honolulu Marathon). These three continuous events added up to a grand total of 140.6 miles. And this was 140.6 miles in some of the most challenging race conditions you could conjure. The Waikiki Rough Water Swim was aptly named; no further explanation was needed. Following that death-defying swim, exhausted athletes would bike and run for over 100 miles in the beautiful yet treacherous island terrain, contending with extreme heat, unrelenting steep hills, and terrific crosswinds.

On February 18, 1978, the day of the big "three-part thing," a whopping 18 people showed up to compete. A marketing budget of nil coupled with the obscurity of this new event weren't working in Ironman's favor. I would imagine most were rightfully daunted and chose self-preservation over adventure. Of those 18 registered competitors, three backed out that morning, leaving 15 Ironman pioneers. John Collins passed out some papers on the beach that explained the rules. At the bottom of the last page was a simple proclamation: "Swim 2.4 miles, ride 112, run 26.2, brag for the rest of your life." Unlike the hefty purse that can be won today, bragging rights, a T-shirt silk-screened by Collins in his garage, and a statue made of literal nuts and bolts were the only swag. Not too shabby for a $5.00 entry fee.

The men on the beach were certainly brave. They also possessed physical strength and athletic ability. Yet, what really seemed to distinguish them from the general public were their personalities. Competitive and daring, these guys didn't seem the type to back down from a thrill or worry too much about all the "what ifs."

Among the motley crew were Herculean exercise junkies like Gordon Haller and strong endurance athletes like Tom Warren and John Dunbar. There were also colorful characters like Ken Shirk, a.k.a. Cowman, who wore a cow-horned headpiece throughout the race. (He was ahead of his time with the whole personal branding thing.) Then, there were those who were a tad ill-prepared. One competitor was barely able to tread water. Another had borrowed a bike and learned how to ride it less than 24 hours before the race. Another had to scramble to borrow a pair of shorts after emerging from the swim because, I guess, he forgot his. All that seems pretty hilarious when you think about the high-tech expensive gear and equipment that triathletes have today and the race preparation they do. Back in the day, there were no premier carbon road bikes with clip-in pedals, aerobars, and tiny handlebar computers. No energy drinks, energy gels, body glide, and Kinesio tape. No moisture-wicking fabrics, compression socks, and tri-suits. No Garmin watches, triathlon coaches, and training manuals. People just showed up in their 1970s Speedos and brought along a ragtag bike, a pair of goggles, basic running shoes, and a cotton T-shirt and shorts for the bike and run (or just went shirtless). Maybe they ate an orange and a bagel for breakfast before hitting the race, and little else (including water, as there were no water stations along the way) during the 11 to 24 hours it took to finish. It was nothing like the finely tuned machine you see today. Back in the day, it was a bona fide, hard-core, pure grit adventure. It's a wonder anyone finished. Or survived.

Only 12 of the 15 competitors who started the race that morning finished the inaugural Ironman. Two quit, and the other crashed his bike. Miraculously, no one was hospitalized, which was astonishing given that most were not properly trained, hydrated, nourished, or competing with the kind of safety measures and knowledge we have in place today. With no real aid stations along the course, dehydration was a serious problem. Competitors provided their own water, and when that supply ran dry there weren't many opportunities to hydrate. One racer reportedly ran into a McDonald's to grab a soda along the marathon route. Some of the locals took pity and offered sustenance to the fatigued souls staggering through town. John Collins (who was both race director and competitor) was offered a bowl of chili and a beer by a local spectator. John Dunbar, who was vying for the win, ran out of water during the marathon leg. All his crew had were two beers, which Dunbar gulped down. This proved to be his undoing. To his credit, he still managed to place second, even while staggering into parked cars, incoherent and drunk. Apparently, severely dehydrated people should not drink alcohol.

It wasn't a pro athlete who won the first Ironman. It was a 28-year-old taxi driver named Gordon Haller. He won, even after emerging from the ocean swim 20 minutes behind John Dunbar, showering and changing in a nearby hotel after the swim, and switching bikes midway through the bike course. He was the very first Ironman, finishing with a time of 11 hours, 46 minutes, and 58 seconds. Without the 17-hour cut-off enforced today, some racers continued straight through the night, finishing after sunrise. Even in this very first race, the tone was set. Ironmen don't quit. (Well, except for those two guys who quit.)

At this point you might be thinking: *Isn't this book supposed to be about women in triathlon? Why are we only hearing about the dudes?* Well, there were no women at that first Ironman. They weren't prohibited or discouraged; they just didn't sign up.

But fear not. There would be a second Ironman (despite the modest turnout for the first), and there would be a woman.

There are far better things ahead than any we leave behind.
—C. S. LEWIS

IRONMAN, THE SEQUEL

The weather was exceptionally dicey on the morning of the second Ironman, causing the race to be postponed one day. Unfortunately, the weather still sucked the following day. That small detail did little to dissuade the participants. Many of the original cast from Ironman I came out for Ironman II. There was John Dunbar (the previous year's second-place finisher, who'd accidentally become inebriated during the marathon), who this time arrived not in an expensive streamlined tri-suit but in a hand-sewn Superman costume, hell-bent on beating his nemesis Gordon Haller. There was Cowman dressed in caveman pants and his signature cow-horned hat. These regulars were joined by several newbies for a grand total of 28 racers—27 men and *one badass woman.*

The conditions were more dangerous than usual, thanks to a storm that had dumped 5 feet of rain the week prior. The ocean was choppy and roiling with 6-foot waves, and 40-mph winds pummeling the shore. When the rescue boats couldn't even get out into the water, the race directors had to make an executive decision. They had already postponed the race from Saturday to Sunday, so the only thing left to do was cancel or continue. They deferred to the athletes.

Of the 28 racers, 15 decided to brave the conditions and just go for it. Among them was 27-year-old Lyn Lemaire—who was the very first female Ironman competitor.

The 1979 Ironman went a lot like the first, with the extra bonus of a perilous ocean swim that whooped everyone's ass. Despite the long-anticipated rematch between rivals Dunbar and Haller, it was a dark horse who clinched the Ironman title that year. San Diego bar owner Tom Warren became the new Ironman, finishing in 11 hours, 15 minutes, and 56 seconds to the cheers of about 20 spectators. He had been stung by a jellyfish, was half blind from the saltwater, and apparently ate merely a roll and an orange the entire day. Dunbar, second place once again, finished 48 minutes later.

Lyn Lemaire had been holding *second* during the bike leg. I don't mean second female. Remember, she was the *only* female in the race. I mean *second overall*. That woman was lightning on a bike (she held the American women's 25-mile cycling record at the time). Lyn finished in fifth place overall with a time of 12 hours and 55 minutes.

Only 12 competitors finished that year's race. Three dropped out due to injuries and mishaps. The last runner finished at 8:30 a.m. the following morning, to the cheers of one proud father. That proud father was John Collins, who waited straight through the night for his 16-year-old son, Mike, to become an Ironman.

Ironman might have remained an unconventional, maverick race with a small cult-like following, but as luck would have it, *Sports Illustrated* journalist Barry McDermott happened to be in Hawaii covering a popular golf event at the same time. While there, he stumbled upon the Ironman when he heard some talk at a local bar the night before. His curiosity piqued, McDermott showed up race morning to see the shenanigans. Like most people witnessing such a mind-boggling concoction of three challenging sports, he was enthralled with both the race itself and the colorful people drawn to it. He introduced the country to triathlon, and the incredible people who tackled it, when his iconic article appeared in *Sports Illustrated* on May 14, 1979. It was titled simply "Ironman."

Thanks to the free advertisement in *Sports Illustrated*, the third Ironman welcomed 108 competitors from various countries in 1980, an almost 10-fold increase in participation. That year also saw two big changes. One was that the race moved from the island of Oahu to Hawaii, the Big Island. The second was that ABC's *Wide World of Sports* began its national broadcast of the Ironman, bringing the little-known sport into the living rooms of millions of viewers. The spotlight was suddenly shining on triathlon, though it was still far from mainstream. Also, when people thought of triathlon, they thought of the Ironman, a race reserved for a small subset of the population. The extreme amount of training, sacrifice, and athleticism necessary to compete in a race of that distance made triathlons interesting to watch but virtually unattainable for the average person.

But that would soon change.

STILL TIME

"I just decided early on that I could be really depressed about this or I could live my life and make something positive about this crappy situation."

ANDREA PEET was the last competitor to cross the finish line of the Ramblin' Rose Sprint Triathlon, nearly an hour after the second-to-last competitor finished. Assisted by two trekking poles and the supportive arms of both her best friend and her husband, she approached the finisher's chute expecting it to be pretty desolate. Instead, it was lined with nearly 100 people cheering and teary-eyed as Queen's "We Are the Champions" blared over the loudspeaker. They had heard Andrea's story and stuck around to cheer this strong and courageous woman home.

❧

Andrea was a young professional just out of graduate school, living in Washington, D.C., when she took up running. "I never went to the gym growing up or was active in sports," she says. When Andrea discovered running in the spring of 2010, she enjoyed the ability to explore the city, relieve stress, and get in shape. Running also allowed her to set goals, and as a Type A person, she was pretty goal-oriented. First, she trained for an 8K and then worked her way up to a marathon. When someone told her about triathlon, she thought it sounded fun. "I liked big goals and big challenges," says Andrea, so "triathlon" was added to her list. In the fall of 2011, she checked that box and quickly signed up for several more races over the next two seasons.

"In 2013, I decided I needed more balance in life. So, that translated into a half-Ironman," Andrea laughs. "It was a great experience." Although her race went well, her body didn't seem to want to recover. "I was tripping over my toes," she says. "I also noticed when I was walking, my hamstrings were really tight. . . . I thought it was a race injury." Andrea consulted a physical therapist who seemed confused by her level of muscle weakness, given that she had just successfully done five triathlons, including a half-Ironman, that year alone. When Andrea raced a portion of a marathon as part of a relay team in November 2013, she was surprised at how often she had to stop and walk, particularly on the downhills where she felt she was falling uncontrollably forward.

Her symptoms were not improving, and no one understood why. Eventually, Andrea was referred to a neurologist and ran through a battery of tests, including MRIs, blood work, and an electromyography (EMG). The EMG, she would later discover, was a test for amyotrophic lateral sclerosis, or ALS.

"Everything came back normal," she says. "So, ALS was ruled out early on." That was a relief, but she still didn't have answers. "They were looking at rare diseases . . . sending me down a specialized road." Although they had ruled it out initially, Andrea was sent to a doctor specializing in ALS to revisit this disease as a possibility. "They sent me [there] as a last stop," she says.

In May 2014, after almost a year of uncertainty, appointments with numerous neurologists, and multiple tests, Andrea finally received a diagnosis of "probable ALS." "While I was worried, I assumed 'probable' meant there was a chance it could be something else," she says. When she returned to the specialist in August 2014, her doctor explained that she had not met the clinical criteria for a definite diagnosis, because the disease had not shown up in enough regions of her body yet. An ALS diagnosis required weakness in three areas; she only had two. "When I asked [the doctor] point-blank if it could be anything else, she said 'no.' That's when I finally understood what 'probable' *really* meant."

Andrea was 33 years old. She had been married for five years. She and her husband had recently bought a home and were planning on starting a family. They had a lifetime of plans, none of which included ALS and its sobering, life-changing prognosis.

Also known as Lou Gehrig's disease, ALS recently gained widespread attention when the ice bucket challenge stormed social media. It's a rapidly progressive degenerative disease in which the brain loses the ability to communicate with the muscles of the body, slowly taking away a person's ability to walk, move, talk, eat, and eventually swallow and breathe. The only thing that isn't affected is the mind, which stays sharp, present, and fully intact through it all. There is no treatment and no cure: 90 percent of individuals diagnosed with ALS will die within two to five years.

Although Andrea had received the worst possible news, she had no plans to stop living, hoping, and contributing to the world. Inspired by Jon "Blazeman" Blais, who became an Ironman at Kona in 2005 only five months after his own ALS diagnosis, Andrea decided two things: (1) this disease wasn't going to stop her from doing another race, and (2) she wanted to use that race to raise money for the Blazeman Foundation for ALS research. She knew if she wanted to do another triathlon, it had to be soon. "Who knew what I'd be like by the spring?" she says. Andrea chose the Ramblin' Rose Super Sprint in Chapel Hill, North Carolina (a 250-yard swim, 9-mile bike race, and 2-mile run). It was all female, had a pool swim, and was only six weeks away. Her friend Julie, who had never done a triathlon before, would be right by her side.

"My body was different," Andrea explains, and that required a few modifications. The first thing she did was buy a recumbent tricycle, or what she refers to as her "trike." At this point, she was using a cane to walk so, for the run, Andrea used two trekking poles for support. She could still swim without much adjustment, but getting her breathing down was challenging.

"The race director, who has since become my very good friend . . . said 'Whatever you need, we'll do.'" Andrea didn't know how the day would go, or how her body would cooperate during the race, but she did know one thing. She. Would. Finish.

The swim went well, and she enjoyed the bike leg, but the run was exceptionally difficult. Her toes were curling, her feet were dragging, and her knees kept locking. Julie, her friend since age 2, literally held onto her arm for those final miles. The bond of that friendship, coupled with Andrea's unrelenting will, got her to the finish line.

Many people approached Andrea that day saying she inspired them, but Andrea says it was the other way around. The compassion and support that enveloped her during that race reflected what she calls "the best of humanity" and inspired her to make this bigger than herself.

Team Drea was officially formed in 2015. It began with about 30 people and a collective goal of raising $9,000 for ALS research and awareness. Today, the Team Drea Foundation is a 501(c)(3) organization with more than 100 team members across the country and in Europe who have collectively raised $150,000. But Team Drea goes beyond fundraising. It's about inspiring people to live fully. The heart of Team Drea? Challenging yourself to do something you never thought possible, whether it be a 5K or an Ironman. It's about the journey—learning about yourself, connecting with your inner strength, and making a difference in your own life while helping to support those living with ALS and their caregivers.

Andrea was thrilled at the response to Team Drea but wasn't sure how long she could actively race with the team. "I assumed I'd be on the sidelines in 2015," she says. "I was basically waiting for the decline." But as she waited, she kept training on her trike and found that she could still keep up. Instead of being sidelined, Team Drea's namesake was going strong. She did the Walk to Defeat ALS in Washington, D.C., and then triked a local 5K, a half-marathon, and a full marathon. "I thought, 'I'm done with ALS running the show here. I'm just going to do what I want to do.'"

Andrea's "brand" of ALS leads to muscle tightness and weakness, but her nerves are still communicating with her muscles. "What they're finding is that ALS is probably an umbrella term, like 'cancer.' Some people can talk normally but are paralyzed. For others, it's the opposite. Most are somewhere in the middle," she says. Andrea's speech is considerably slowed, as are her hand movements. However, she is fully ambulatory with the support of a walker, and is training on her new hand cycle (courtesy of the Challenged Athletes Foundation). She keeps up her inspiring *Team Drea* blog, is writing a book, and still drives a car. "They tell you not to overuse your muscles or push them to the breaking point because they don't recover normally," Andrea says. "But what I find is I'm so much more mobile when I'm active. It helps me keep my muscles loose."

At the close of 2015, Andrea had a big idea. She was intensely interested in people like Jon Blais, the first and only person with ALS to finish a full Ironman unaided, and Chris Rosati, who created an organization awarding small grants to kids who aspire to make a difference in the world. "These are the kinds of [ALS] stories that are inspiring to me," she says. So, she set a goal for 2016— complete 12 races in 12 months each in honor of 12 inspiring people with ALS. She has documented her journey, and the 12 lives of those who inspire her, on her blog. "The biggest reward and inspiration is just doing it. . . . realizing that I still can do it," she says. "[It's about] coming from a place of gratitude and not fear."

Andrea will be participating in 12 races for ALS again in 2017, as long as her body and health cooperate. They will be mostly 5Ks and half-marathons, with a few sprint triathlons peppered in there. In addition, Team Drea has added two new programs—a Kids Virtual Race, allowing kids to fundraise through running, and the MedALS program, in which athletes can donate their finishers medals to someone living with ALS.

Like her hero Jon Blais, Andrea keeps her own spirit blazing bright no matter the threat of darkness ahead. "This diagnosis doesn't mean you have two years to live. I have lived with the disease long enough to learn the huge differences between people," Andrea says. Though she intimately understands the gravity of ALS and its implications for her future, Andrea chooses to focus on what she *can* do, what she *can* contribute, and *how* she wants to live: hope in the place of despair, action in the place of complacency, and gratitude in the place of fear. "It was never something I set out to do, but I so appreciate [that] my story can make something positive out of ALS."

The ALS diagnosis may have taken a great many things from the life Andrea Peet had intended to lead, but it hasn't taken the best of what's inside her. In choosing to live her life on her terms, she brings out the best of what's inside all of us, too. "I just decided early on that I could be really depressed about this or I could live my life and make something positive about this crappy situation," she says. "Just because you have this diagnosis, your life isn't over. You still have time to make a difference."

4

THE LONG AND SHORT OF IT

No road is too long with good company.
—TURKISH PROVERB

Triathlon has been dubbed "the new marathon" by the Sporting Goods Manufacturers Association. Cervélo's Phil White has called it "the new golf," and ESPN describes triathlon as having graduated "from maverick to mainstream." Indeed, triathlon participation in the United States has hit record highs in the new millennium, after years of steady growth. According to the Sports and Fitness Industry Association's 2015 Report, on-road and off-road triathlons rank among the top five sports experiencing the most percentage growth. Glide Slope lists triathlon as one of the five fastest-growing sports around the world, rubbing elbows with mixed martial arts, stand-up paddleboarding, rugby, and cycling.

FROM MAVERICK TO MAINSTREAM

One way to view the growth of triathlon is to look at USA Triathlon membership numbers over the past several decades. USA Triathlon (USAT), the national governing body of the sport, was formed in 1982 when the US

Triathlon Association and the American Triathlon Association merged. In 1999, USAT membership was 127,824. After the triathlon debuted in the 2000 Olympic Games held in Sydney, there was a notable increase in triathlon interest and participation. By 2005, membership more than doubled to 262,703. Two years later, it climbed to 336,356, and two years after that to 441,060. Membership in 2014 was over half a million, following a year in which the numbers of USAT-certified coaches, race directors, and clubs broke records. More than 4,000 USAT-sanctioned events were held across the United States in 2015, nearly triple the number held in 2007.

Look beyond USAT membership statistics at total triathlon event participation, and the numbers are even more staggering. In 2010, triathlon participation was reported at 2.3 million. By 2015, it reached 4.24 million.

There has also been a concerted push to support, encourage, and remove barriers to triathlon so that all individuals can participate. A special focus has been on attracting more girls and women, as well as expanding opportunities for kids, teens, and college athletes at the elite and recreational/club levels. Title IX's announcement of triathlon as a "new and emerging sport for women" started triathlon's journey toward being a full-fledged, NCAA Championship sport. And in 2016, at long last, the Paratriathlon debuted in the Paralympic Games held in Rio de Janeiro. (By the way, the American women cleaned up!)

While triathlon is growing most rapidly among 35- to 44-year-olds, it is also becoming a sport of choice for seniors, kids, and teens. Why has the playing field become so diverse? Both the variety of race distances and the diversity of race types have ushered in a whole new group of athletes. Now, more than ever, there is truly something for everyone who wants to give the tri a try.

We cannot become what we want to be
by remaining what we are.

—MAX DEPREE

SIZE MATTERS

The most popular distances for traditional (or "on-road") triathlons are sprint, Olympic, half-Ironman, and full Ironman. A whopping 78 percent of USAT members participate in sprints. In comparison, 58 percent of its membership race Olympic distances, and 39 percent race half-Ironmans. Only 17 percent have tackled full Ironmans.

Ironman continues to be the most recognizable triathlon. However, there are non-Ironman-branded races of the same distance. Ah, but just because a race totals 140.6 miles does not mean you can technically call yourself an "Ironman." In the triathlon community, this is a hot button issue and a ticket to a heated debate. If you have finished 140.6 miles in 17 hours or less in an Ironman-branded race, you can call yourself an Ironman and get the "M-dot" tattoo without causing waves. It might seem like a technicality, but whether you agree or not, it is definitely a rookie mistake to trip over these distinctions.

In 2006, the folks at Ironman cut the 140.6 miles in half for a new race series called the **half-Ironman**. Competitors swim 1.2 miles, bike 56 miles, and run a half-marathon of 13.1 miles for a grand total of 70.3 miles. Often, you will hear the race referred to as a "70.3," and the same issue accompanies the Ironman-branded versus non-Ironman-branded races. The reaction to the half-Ironman has been very positive, as evidenced by its skyrocketing popularity. In its first year as an official race distance, 17 official half-Ironman events were held worldwide. Now, there are 42 official half-Ironman events held across 22 countries. Most sell out faster than it takes to bake a batch of cookies.

A lesser-known distance dubbed the **Tinman** was created in 1979 by four athletes living in Kona who wanted the triathlon experience without the huge training commitment of a full Ironman. They pared things down to a 750-meter swim, 40-km bike race, and 10K run—still challenging, but far less time-consuming. The Tinman was piloted and met with such enthusiasm by local athletes that the event was officially launched the following year. Three hundred competitors signed up. Today, the Tinman Kona boasts 1,200 participants. The distances of these Tinman triathlons vary from 400 to 1,000 meters for the swim, from 13 to 19 miles for the bike, and from 3.1 to 7 miles for the run.

The **Olympic** distance triathlon is a close cousin to the Tinman, but while the Tinman distance can vary, the Olympic is standardized at a .9-mile swim (1,500 meters), 24.8-mile bike ride (40 km), and a 6.2-mile run (10K) for a grand total of 31.9 miles. The Olympic distance got its name when it appeared in, you guessed it, the 2000 Olympics. Many consider the Olympic distance the "perfect" triathlon because it gives athletes a hearty challenge without the monumental training commitment that comes with the half- and full Ironmans. If the distances are tweaked a little, the race will be referred to as either an "international distance" or a "classic distance" triathlon.

The Olympic might be considered "the most perfect" and the Ironman the most prestigious, but the sprint holds the title of most *popular*. Sometimes called a "mini-tri," the sprint was a game changer for the sport, opening up the playing field to everyone and anyone who dreamed about being a triathlete. The **Sprint Tri** is often the entry point for triathlon virgins because it is much less daunting but still challenging. Seasoned triathletes love them because the training regimen is not as time-consuming, making it easier to balance life, family, career, and (gasp) other hobbies. (Wait, other hobbies?) Longer-course triathletes also love the sprints, using these "shorter" races as part of their training for longer distances.

The distance of a sprint is not as standardized as the full Ironman, half-Ironman, and Olympic. The swim tends to be about a half-mile. The bike distance hovers somewhere in the 12- to 14-mile range, and the run is typically a 5K (3.1 miles), though it can be as short as 2 miles or as long as 4. Finally there's the **Super Sprint**, which typically consists of a quarter-mile swim, 6- to 10-mile bike ride, and a 1- to 2-mile run. Depending upon the race, sprint and super sprint distances will vary, and often the line between the two categories is blurred.

SHAKE IT UP

It isn't just race distances that have varied over the years. The world of multisport has expanded greatly, giving athletes more choices and new ways to raise the bar. Whether you are looking to create something more extreme, to have more fun, or just to avoid one of the three triathlon legs, there is a multisport race out there just for you.

The **Duathlon** cuts out the swim altogether with a run-bike-run, appealing to the person who wants no part of that swim. (That would be me.) Those who *do* feel like fish in the water can select an **Aquathon,** a race based on early-20th-century ocean lifeguard competitions. Aquathons typically involve a 2.5-mile run, a 1,000-meter swim, and then another 2.5-mile run. The **Aquabike** (also known as an Aqua Velo) was sanctioned by USAT in 2006 and pairs swimming with biking, perfect for those who either hate running or have an injury preventing it. The Aquabike is typically a 1.2-mile swim followed by a 56-mile bike ride.

There are also more obscure triathlon events, like **Equilateral Triathlons** (in which each leg takes an equal amount of time), **Indoor Triathlons** (a pool swim, stationary bike ride, and treadmill run), **Winter Triathlons** (cross-country skiing, running, and mountain biking in the snowy terrain), and the **SupBikeRun** (stand-up paddleboarding, mountain biking, and trail running). You gotta give props for the creativity.

Of course, in the multisport world of Go Big or Go Home, we have to make something that's already extreme even *more* extreme by taking it out of the box and off the road. **Off-road triathlons** are the second-fastest-growing market in the sports and fitness industry and appeal to those who love things like adventure racing, mountain biking, trail running, and muddy obstacle races. The basics of off-road triathlons are the same as traditional triathlons—swim, bike, run—but they forgo the blacktop, swapping it for "roads less traveled" through woods, valleys, hills, and canyons.

Like Ironman, off-road triathlons began in Hawaii, but on the island of Maui. The first known off-road event was held in 1996, when mountain bikers and triathletes challenged each other in a friendly "battle of the fittest" in a race they named Aquaterra. (Hawaii? Friendly wager? Battle over which athlete was the fittest? All that sounds vaguely familiar. What is *with* these people?) After swimming, mountain biking, and running along the beautiful Hawaiian trails, both mountain bikers *and* triathletes were hooked, and the off-road triathlon was born.

GOING ROGUE

The **XTERRA** race series is almost synonymous with off-road triathlon, in the way that we say "ping-pong" more often than we say "table tennis." XTERRA shakes up the triathlon world by taking the race deep into nature, like something out of *Swiss Family Robinson*. The open-water swim (typically 1.5 miles) is followed by mountain biking (typically a 30K) through wooded, hilly terrain complete with steep inclines and rocky descents. Then, the racers hit the trails for a run (typically an 11K) along muddy, uneven paths full of gnarled roots and steep inclines. You end up sweaty, muddy, and often bleeding from somewhere.

If all that isn't enough adventure for you, fear not.

Behold: The **Ultra-Triathlons**. They make Ironman and XTERRA look like a casual jaunt through a field of buttercups.

ULTRA-TRIATHLONS

In the world of ultraracing, there are **Double Irons** (281.2 total miles) and **Triple Irons** (425.8 total miles). Child's play? No worries. Let me introduce you to the **Quadruple Ultra**, the **Quintuple Ultra,** and **Deca Ultra** (which sound a little like awesome burgers, but aren't).

But wait, there's more. The most extreme of the extreme are the **10-Days Triathlon** (a 7.5-km swim, 200-km bike ride, and 50-km run every day for 10 straight days), the **Double Deca Ultra-Triathlon,** and the **Triple Deca Ultra-Triathlon.** (You will have to do the math on those because I'm suffering from exhaustion just thinking about it.)

Clearly, there are many choices in the big, wide world of multisports. Perhaps these choices explain the USAT's 600 percent growth rate since

2000. All of triathlon's success has grown from that original Mission Bay Triathlon, the indelible mark it left on John and Judy Collins, and the incredible success of the Ironman.

It was undoubtedly the Ironman that put triathlon on the map. It also gave triathlon its reputation—an extreme sport appealing primarily to male, elite, and subelite athletes. Men hailing straight from Mount Olympus, chiseled from Plutonian rock and capable of supersonic speed, strength, and stamina that no mere mortal could ever possess.

That is, until 1982, when one *woman* changed Ironman forever.

5

WHO'S DRINKING
THE KOOL-AID?

We lose ourselves in the things we love.
We find ourselves there, too.

—KRISTIN MARTZ

Julie Moss's Ironman finish is widely considered a defining moment in sports history. Before Julie, triathlon was all about the competition, all about the winners. After Julie, just finishing was not only enough—it was everything. Instead of freaking everyone out, her collapse and dramatic crawl actually inspired the masses, as evidenced by a marked rise in female participation in triathlons, which continued into the new millennium.

I sure as heck didn't know anything about it, though. Triathlon was not on my radar. That is, until decades later, when I moved my family across New Jersey and right into the epicenter of a TriathaStorm.

ANYTOWN, USA

Let me introduce you to a speck on the map called Mullica Hill, population 3,982 and home to one of the largest all-female triathlon clubs in the country. What makes this town so significant? Well, it's not. *That* is its significance. Mullica Hill could be "Anytown, USA." It isn't a thriving metropolis, buzzing with activity. And unlike athletic hotbeds such as San Diego, Boulder, or Tucson, southern New Jersey has no vibe whatsoever that would make you think it would be swarming with triathletes, or more specifically *female* triathletes.

As Anthony and I researched towns in which to plant permanent roots, we were attracted to Mullica Hill's large wooded lots, open spaces, cute downtown, friendly community, and great school system. It has too many farms to feel suburban, and it's a little too developed to be considered truly rural. It has, as far as I'm concerned, the best of both worlds—a small town feel along with close proximity to civilization (which I loosely define as a 10-minute drive to Target). A charming winery with acres of grapevines planted along the winding roads, loads of orchards and cornfields, horse farms, gingerbread boutique shops down a picturesque Main Street, and a fair trade, organic coffee shop with the best cup of Joe this side of the Schuylkill River define this sweet, quiet town.

Around the time we were settling into our new home, the Mullica Hill Women's Triathlon Club (MHWTC) was transforming from bud to bloom. It was subtle at first—a bike rack on a minivan here, a pink tri-club shirt running through town there. At time went on, however, I saw more and more of them, hitting the blacktop in earnest on two feet and two wheels. I tried to ignore it at first, but "those girls in pink" (as they were known around town) were everywhere you looked, reminding me of how out of shape I was. Reminding me of what I was missing. Perhaps even beckoning me to join the so-called fun.

Lydia, one of the four MHWTC founding members, kept encouraging me to join, if only for the T-shirt. But as much as I loved a cute pink shirt, my excuses abounded, and always ended with "I can't." Not to be daunted, she continued to assure me with boundless enthusiasm that I certainly *could* do triathlon if I really wanted to. But that was the glitch. You see, I *wanted* dessert. I *wanted* to sleep through the night. But *wanting* and *triathlon*? Those two didn't belong in the same sentence.

I vowed to remain on the outside of this rapidly expanding phenomenon. The story I told myself was that I was a maverick who wouldn't succumb to peer pressure, wouldn't follow the lemmings, wouldn't do it just because "everyone else" was. Hey, I didn't need to sit at the cool kids' lunch table. I didn't need to go for a bucket of Margaronas after a group bike ride, no matter how fun it all looked (the drinking part, not the biking part). But as time went on, I realized the story I told myself was a flimsy stand-in for the real story. The real story involved copious amounts of fear, self-doubt, some guilt, and a resistance to change or challenge.

While their powers of persuasion failed to work on me, Lydia and Company were doing a great job convincing just about every other woman in their sphere of influence. One evening, I found myself perched on a barstool right in the center of that sphere. It was a rare night out with new friends at a local hangout. I ordered a seasonal pumpkin beer with a cinnamon sugar–rimmed glass and settled onto one of the stools at a long table filled with chatting, smiling women from town.

Just about everyone there, except me, had been recently inducted into what I had started to think of as the Triathlon Sorority. Not surprisingly, conversation quickly turned to running and triathlon. Instead of drooling over a designer handbag or hot pair of stilettos, these women were gushing over the latest Garmin watch or indoor bike trainer. It was clear that everyone at the table was in some phase of training for something, whether it was a 10-mile race, a half-marathon, or a triathlon. I finished an entire beer trapped between two women painstakingly comparing the routes of their 8-mile run, complete with olfactory descriptions of a cow farm. I hailed our waitress and ordered another beer, because that conversation seemed like it was going to take a while.

As enjoyable as it was to get out and socialize, I felt a bit like the odd girl out. I couldn't even make it around the block without collapsing (not that I ever tried). My big exercise that day had been hoisting an overflowing laundry basket up a flight of stairs and pushing a grocery cart with a bum wheel and zero turning radius, filled with 60 pounds of children and an additional 47 pounds of groceries. I was perplexed at how anyone found this topic so fascinating and even *more* perplexed that I seemed to be the only one who didn't. I mean, seriously, how long can people talk about running? You run. You finish running. You're tired. The end. Is there really so much to say? Apparently there is: where you buy your shoes, any injuries or lost toenails you have incurred, the debris and roadkill you leapt over, the feral dog that chased someone you knew, the races you've done and plan to do, a brief history of the size and slope of all hills within 10 square miles, the supportiveness of sports bras, and the chafing of inner thighs. I ask you, did I really need to get the inside scoop on the pain of bouncy boobs and the miracles of body glide?

Although much of this conversation left my mind glazed as a donut, I had to admit to also feeling rather fascinated. They were just so enthralled. You know how you get excited about something and you want to talk about it all the time? They were like that . . . but with *exercise*! These women were committed. Passionate. Alive. There was an undeniable sizzle in the air around them as they conversed. Training seemed to be invigorating instead of the drain and drag I imagined it to be. Clearly, it was also binding them together. These friends and neighbors had graduated from relationships based on their kids' activities and mutual schedules to more meaningful friendships based on shared, grown-up interests and quality adult interactions.

The night left me wondering: Who exactly were these triathletes? Like the psychology geek I am, I couldn't resist pondering the motivations and mind of a triathlete. What made them tick? Were people with certain personality traits more drawn to triathlon than others? What made me so different from them? A little investigation was in order.

Squats are a form of torture designed by people
who don't need to do squats in the first place.
—NORA ROBERTS

TRIATHLETES: WHAT MAKES THEM TICK?

Triathlons have been around for over 30 years, yet research on the psychology of the triathlete is practically nil. Scientists like to study triathletes to see what happens to the body under strenuous activity, how the body adapts to acute trauma, responds to training, and recovers from exertion. But the psyche of the triathlete remains largely unexplored. This is partly because it's a softer science. Objectively measuring things like motivation, compulsiveness, addiction, and drive have their methodological challenges. Some curious researchers have given it their best shot with some pretty interesting studies using surveys and questionnaires. After crunching the data, some of what they found confirmed the triathlete stereotypes, to a certain extent. Like most research in the early stages, however, the conclusions sometimes *raise* as many questions as they answer.

MIND OVER PAIN

If you know a triathlete or are one yourself, the list of typical attributes won't surprise you: perfectionist, driven, goal-oriented, stubborn, curious, persistent, thrill-seeking, fearless. In 2008, a *Forbes* article profiled the mind of the endurance athlete and confirmed these aforementioned traits. In addition, the author found that endurance athletes seemed obsessed with seeking out bigger and bigger challenges, much more so than the average person.

Studies also suggest that triathletes have significantly higher pain tolerance and more effective modulation of pain than non-triathletes. In other words, triathletes can endure pain at higher levels than most non-triathlete folks. They are also more willing to endure the pain.

A study by Jeffery Kress and Traci Statler found that endurance athletes viewed the intensity of their pain as a function of their own perception, which was something they believed was within their control. For them, pain was simply physiological proof of their dedication to their sport. Rather than viewing pain as something negative to be avoided, it was viewed as an affirmation of the hard work they had been putting into training. Pain meant you were pushing yourself to your maximum potential, while avoidance of pain meant underperformance, an act of treason against oneself. (For me, pain avoidance is totally acceptable. I see "No Pain, No Gain" not as a motto but a multiple-choice question, and I check the box next to "No Pain.")

Interestingly, it's not just that triathletes can endure more pain. Some research suggests that they *seek out* the pain and suffering. In his 2008 article, "Triathlon: Suffering and Exciting Significance," Michael Atkinson makes a strong case for suffering as the primary reward in triathlon. For Atkinson, the term "suffering" isn't defined as some type of masochism. It has to do with the feeling the athlete gets during the most difficult moments of a race, when she wants to quit but instead somehow digs deep and keeps going. Suffering is about hitting that wall of pain and pushing through it into the mystery of what lies beyond. Atkinson describes this concept of "suffering" much better than I can:

> In the hardest moments of a long race, the athlete's entire conscious experience of reality boils down to a desire to continue pitted against a desire to quit. Nothing else remains. . . . The desire to continue versus the desire to quit—the athlete is this and this alone until he chooses one or the other. And then the choice is made and he briefly becomes either persevering or quitting until, after he has stopped at the finish line, or God forbid, short of it, the stripped-away layers are piled back on and he becomes his old self again. Only not quite. He is changed, for better or worse.

A psychological sketch was starting to come into focus for me. Clearly, triathletes were driven. They were persistent. They liked to set bigger and bigger goals. They were tough with pain, even sought out the suffering. But it all begged the question, did people seek out triathlon *because* they were inherently tough, or did triathlon make tough guys out of regular people? I couldn't find anything about the directionality of this correlation. But I found plenty of anecdotal evidence of triathlon building a sense of confidence and inner strength in women who formerly felt they had none.

Ability is what you're capable of doing.
Motivation determines what you do. Attitude
determines how well you do it.
—LOU HOLTZ

MOTIVATION

Motivation is the force that drives us into action. Without it, we probably wouldn't do much of anything. It influences our behavior and pushes us to set and achieve our goals. Keeping the house clean, studying for exams, meeting work deadlines, cooking dinner, volunteering, exercising—none of it would happen without some type of internal or external motivation.

Generally, motivation can be derived from the following broad categories of desire: for power or self-improvement, for reward or for avoidance of punishment, to socialize with others, or to control the things and people around us. The root of our motivation is unique to each of us and varies depending upon the task at hand.

When it comes to what motivates a triathlete, researcher David M. Lovett found significant gender differences. Females appeared to be more motivated by what he calls "affiliation, life meaning, and personal goal achievement" than men. In other words, females had more desire to socialize with others and bring peace and meaning to their lives, and they emphasized inner competition over external competition.

Alexis Waddel also examined the motivation of elite female triathletes. She too found intriguing gender differences. Motivation fell within three predominant themes among the women surveyed: "competency" (after meeting a challenge), "passion for the sport," and "togetherness."

Affiliation and togetherness. I was certainly seeing this in action with the Mullica Hill Women's Tri Club. And as I sat sipping my pumpkin beer amid the excited triathlon chatter, I had to admit I was starting to see the appeal of it.

Whatever you're meant to do, do it.
The conditions are always impossible.
—DORIS LESSING

AN IDEA IS HATCHED

My cerebral interest in this topic was mounting. As I watched the impact the tri-club had on both the community and individual lives, I began to flesh out an idea for a book. As this idea started expanding and taking shape, something I never thought I would consider wriggled its way into my mind.

"Maybe I should add a memoir part to my book where I train for and compete in a triathlon," I blurted out to Anthony one night, thinking out loud. He looked at me as if I were speaking in tongues. *He* was the lifelong athlete, a star soccer player who went to college on a sports scholarship, and has stayed pretty buff by going to the gym and eating healthful foods. I mean, he still has a six-pack without really trying (while my abs have become a party ball). I'm not going to lie; it's super annoying.

"Really?" he asked carefully. This was dangerous territory for him. If he got too excited, I might wonder why he was so thrilled I wanted to exercise. If he stayed too nonchalant, I might accuse him of not caring about my hopes and dreams.

"Yeah, well, I don't mean right *this moment,*" I snapped. Part of me wanted to backpedal, but a bigger part of me realized the importance of doing something like this. Not just for the book, but for me. "I mean, maybe I should start running at some point. You know, get my old ass in shape so I can play with my future grandkids without breaking a hip. All I have to do is learn to swim, get a bike, and do that Queen of the Hill race."

To his credit, he didn't laugh, but he looked at me as if he knew I probably didn't mean it.

And maybe I didn't. The thought of doing a triathlon scared the hell out of me. But somewhere mixed in with that fear was also a little bit of excitement. Excitement about my book project or about my own personal growth, I couldn't yet discern. All I knew was that for the first time in a very long time, the walls of my comfort zone felt a little too confining.

FOR CECILIA

"This is not about me; it's about her."

DEBBIE NIEMANN and her eldest daughter Cecilia have been racing together for three years. By the age of 12, Cecilia had already amassed an assortment of medals, from 5Ks to half-marathons to triathlons. She sacrifices her free time for training and endures discomfort and pain, all for the love of the sport. If you see her out on the racecourse, you'll notice two things about Cecilia. One is her smile. The second is that she needs someone else to act as her arms and legs.

Diagnosed with cerebral palsy secondary to complications during a premature birth, Cecilia is dependent on a wheelchair. Some might think that a person who can't independently swim, bike, or run wouldn't be able to experience a triathlon. But for her mom, Debbie, those were minor details. From the time Cecilia was diagnosed, Debbie's motto was that her daughter wasn't going to miss out on anything in life. Yes, Cecilia might have to do things differently, but that didn't mean she couldn't do them. To get her daughter off the sidelines and into the race, they'd just have to get creative.

Running has always been a focal point in Debbie's life. To say she comes from a family of athletes is an understatement. "My whole family tris. . . . My dad has been doing triathlons since they started the sport. He is 68 now. . . .

He has done one every year since the sport started," explains Debbie. Racing, running, triathlons; it's in their genes. In their soles and souls. Debbie began running at the age of 8 and has never stopped. Racing together was a big part of her family life. It still is. "That's how we bond," Debbie says. She didn't want Cecilia, the eldest of her three children, to miss out.

Born weighing 1 lb., 12 oz., and only 13 inches long, Cecilia spent the first 12 weeks of her life in the neonatal intensive care unit. The fourth day after birth, she contracted methicillin-resistant *Staphylococcus aureus* (MRSA), resulting in septic shock and scalded skin syndrome. Debbie couldn't even hold her daughter for the first 10 days of her life, and then had to do so for only 10-minute increments wearing sterile gloves.

"The kid is a fighter," Debbie says. And that fight guided Debbie's philosophy toward her daughter's life from those early days.

"When I found out she had cerebral palsy, I read about the Hoyts," Debbie says. Dick and Rick Hoyt are living legends, an inspiring father-son team who have competed in over 1,100 athletic events all over the world, including six Ironmans and 31 Boston Marathons. Dick Hoyt swims, bikes, and runs while pulling his (now adult) son, who was diagnosed with spastic quadriplegia cerebral palsy at birth. "I thought, 'I want to do this one day, but I don't do triathlons and I don't want to swim in the lake,'" Debbie laughs.

She did run, however, and where Debbie ran, Cecilia came too. "I started running with her at 6 months old. I loaded up the oxygen tank and went. And she loved it!" After Debbie's second daughter, Lucy, was born, she upgraded to a double jogging stroller and pushed them both along.

Years later, Debbie's friend suggested they do a triathlon together. Debbie already had the running thing down. She was also swimming twice a week and taking Spin classes. But she had three small children and was going through a divorce. Still, Debbie agreed. "We signed up, and she bailed!" she laughs. "But I did it anyway." She did it, and she loved it.

A few years later, Debbie was working for the United Cerebral Palsy (UCP) of Greater Kansas City. The organization needed a fresh idea for a new fundraising event, so she suggested triathlon. Not only would the event be a great fundraiser and awareness campaign, but Debbie planned to do it with a then 9-year-old Cecilia.

Convincing a race director to add a Challenged Athlete Division to their triathlon proved to be nearly as difficult as the triathlon itself. All the race directors she contacted threw up their hands, claiming "Liability risk!" and slamming the door on the idea. Frustrated, Debbie could have given up, but she persisted. She was fueled not by her own personal agenda, but by a deep passion for inclusion. "You can't discriminate against a whole group of people because they need to do things differently," Debbie says. "[Cecilia] just wants to participate with the community." Finally, Debbie found a race director who was willing to go to bat for her. It was the Shawnee Mission Triathlon, the oldest tri in Kansas City, with much notoriety and prestige. The staff agreed to work with Debbie and the UCP of Kansas City by offering the opportunity for challenged athletes to participate in the race. One huge hurdle down. Unfortunately, a larger hurdle loomed in the distance, one that was not only a threat to Cecilia racing, but a threat to her very life.

In the spring of 2013, Cecilia began lapsing into unconsciousness for periods ranging from 10 minutes to 10 hours. During these episodes, her temperature would plummet into the 80s, her oxygen level dropped below 70 percent, and her heart rate would dip into the 40s. Initially, doctors thought she was having seizure activity, which an EEG confirmed. However, seizures couldn't explain the dramatic temperature and heart rate fluctuations. Cecilia was admitted to the hospital, where she spent three weeks being monitored and tested up, down, and sideways. Nothing was conclusive.

Cecilia remained a medical mystery until her doctors reached out to international colleagues. It was determined that she was having a rare autoimmune reaction, an autonomic dysfunction involving her hypothalamus, a region of the brain responsible for all basic survival functions. The hypothalamus was basically on the fritz, misfiring like crazy. The condition was rare; according to Debbie there were only about 50 known, documented cases in the world. It was also grave. "We took her home and planned her funeral," Debbie says.

Team Cecilia's first triathlon was scheduled for July, but Debbie had little hope that her daughter would live to see the starting line. She arranged "a backup," in case she needed to push another child with cerebral palsy in the race. She promised herself that she'd either run the race *with* Cecilia, or in Cecilia's honor if that's how fate played out.

But fate was smiling on Cecilia and she made it to the starting line. Her episodes had lessened in frequency in the weeks leading up to the triathlon, perhaps due to medication changes. They might never know. All Debbie knew was that her daughter was alive and well enough to participate in the Shawnee Mission Tri in July 2013.

Debbie assembled a team of three athletes, one for each leg of the race. A friend volunteered to do the 18-mile bike leg, pulling Cecilia in a bike trailer. Debbie's stepmom would do the 4.5-mile run, pushing a special jogging stroller. "But I wouldn't let anyone else swim her," Debbie says, so she swam tethered to a raft, pulling Cecilia along for the 500-yard open-water swim. When Team Cecilia crossed the finish line, cheers erupted from the inspired crowds. "I've never had so much fun," Debbie says. "It was the beginning of us doing triathlons every year."

In 2014, Team Cecilia finished three more triathlons. Debbie was now doing both the swim and the run legs. The bike remained her biggest challenge since the weight of Cecilia and the bike trailer combined were about 120 pounds. As Cecilia grows, the total weight will only increase. Debbie is petite and admits she isn't a particularly strong cyclist, so she's grateful for her fellow triathletes who volunteer to bike and serve as handlers in the transition areas. By 2015, Debbie was pulling Cecilia through all three legs of the race. "It was such a great bonding experience for me and my daughter."

When Debbie suffered from her own autoimmune reaction and a foot injury and couldn't race for months, the triathlon community made sure that Cecilia kept competing. Debbie's heart was warmed by the support. Serious, competitive triathletes and runners clamored to be part of Team Cecilia. "These are elite athletes who have qualified for Ironman Worlds, who want to race with her because they feel it is an *honor* to race with her," Debbie says.

"She's a local celebrity. We go to running races and tris and everyone knows her. The triathlon community is so welcoming and loving." Even the pro athletes at the front of the pack, vying for a spot on the podium, take the time to find Cecilia and give her words of encouragement during a race. For Debbie, that is what it's all about. Instead of being pitied, ignored, or discounted, Cecilia is treated as a true competitor. She's one of the tribe. "Here's this kid that from birth was told she could never do anything. She can barely talk, and she's able to be this inspiring."

Team Cecilia has helped change the perception of disabilities in the community. "Instead of talking to *me* about her, they now come up and address *her*," says Debbie. The message of Team Cecilia is clear and far reaching. "The decrease in ignorance is amazing."

Just as important, Team Cecilia also benefits its namesake. "This is not about me, it's about *her*," Debbie says, reflecting on how her daughter has blossomed thanks to the racing experience. "She loves doing sports. For years we were hearing what she couldn't do. Racing has built up her self-esteem."

Cecilia and Debbie aren't the only inspiring ones in this family. Younger sister Lucy has been training with her mom and Cecilia since she was six, waiting for the day she was strong enough and old enough to pull her big sister in a race. When Debbie first started training for open-water swims, she'd put Lucy and Cecilia in the raft and pull them both. Soon, Lucy was in the water swimming alongside her mom. "By the end, she was swimming as much as I was," Debbie remembers. "Lucy is an amazing swimmer."

Lucy began by helping her mom in the transition area of races, reconfiguring the bike trailer and providing support. Finally, at the age of nine, Lucy pushed her big sister as the runner on Team Cecilia. When they crossed that finish line together, Debbie says there wasn't a dry eye in the crowd. "I've never seen so much determination. That was the proudest I've ever been."

Debbie's son Loren is the youngest of the three but is already a great runner. When he is old enough, Debbie believes Lucy will do the swim and Loren the run for Team Cecilia. "It will happen in the next two years," Debbie predicts. Her pride in her three children is undeniable. "I'm blessed to have these amazing little people in my life. They're so compassionate."

Countless people approach Debbie at races to tell her how inspiring she is, but she immediately deflects their praise. "I'm not inspiring," she says with both humility and conviction. "I am an able-bodied person. *She* is inspiring. She's in pain every day [and] she chooses to fight. My daughter is literally trapped in her body. [When] I push her for a few hours, she's free. . . . I don't know any parent who, if all it took was to push your child, wouldn't do it."

For Debbie, it's Cecilia who inspires her to get her through the race, not the other way around. When a race starts getting tough, she sees Cecilia's little hand come up for a high five, or hears her cheering "Go, Mom!" and it makes Debbie dig a little deeper and smile through the pain. "I can do it because my daughter is there. You can't hear the voice in your head telling you that you can't do it when you see a kid looking up at you like that," says Debbie. "What better motivator is there? She's truly pulling me along."

6

NO NUTS, JUST GUTS

I'm strong; I'm tough;
I still wear my eyeliner.

—LISA LESLIE

The Mullica Hill Women's Triathlon Club was born over breakfast. Four women, carbs, caffeine, mutual passion, and one big idea.

Lydia and Michelle Powell were already good friends and training buddies. They had recently done a triathlon together and loved it. Michelle wanted to introduce Lydia to her friend, Colleen Fossett, who was a working mother of two and had a few marathons and triathlons already under her belt. Colleen's neighbor, Maureen Brigham, also a working mother of two, had started training with Colleen. None of them had a lot of triathlon experience, but they knew they loved the sport and wanted to introduce other women to it. When these four women sat down together at the Blue Plate restaurant in Mullica Hill, there were some introductions, lots of animated conversation, and one goal: Form a tri-club where women could also raise money for charity.

It should have been no surprise that these four women would bond immediately on that winter's day in 2009. Whether it was their love for triathlon and new challenges, their desire to empower other women, their philanthropic spirit, a shared Bruce Springsteen obsession, or a combination of all the above, the chemistry was palpable. There was infectious energy just waiting to be harnessed. It was as if they were destined to meet and start a phenomenon.

The happy chatter quickly organized around a central theme. They imagined the idea, developed a mission statement, and researched what would be involved in becoming a legitimate USAT-sanctioned triathlon club. In mere weeks, this newly formed club had a name, website, logo design, designated charity to support, fee structure, advertisement posters, and a date for the first informational session. Everything but a theme song and a secret handshake. They even had a brilliant tagline: "No Nuts, Just Guts." I was tempted to join just to wear that slogan on a T-shirt.

The MHWTC held its first informational session at a local coffee shop in February 2010. The founding members crossed their fingers, hoping someone—anyone—would come. I was invited multiple times, but had to wash my hair or something equally as dodgy. There was no way I was showing up and getting sucked into that nonsense. Next thing you knew, I'd be drowning in the Schuykill River at SheROX. No, thank you.

Somehow, the party went on without me. Nearly 80 women showed up to hear about the club and the sport of triathlon that night. "We thought maybe we'd end up with 30. It was more than we anticipated," Lydia recalls. I don't know what was said at that first Kick Off Meeting or what might have been slipped into those drinks, but it worked. Women were lining up to pay their club dues and become card-carrying members.

The MHWTC closed its inaugural year with 120 registered members, well beyond expectations. Whether this said something about the level of inspiration and support or the power of peer pressure, I couldn't yet be sure. Most of the women who signed up had no prior triathlon experience, but by the end of their first tri season, nearly all had one notch on their race belt. And once they crossed that first finish line, a crazy thing happened. They were completely, unabashedly hooked.

With the popularity of a sorority, the passionate following of a religion, and the influence of a political party, the Mullica Hill Women's Tri Club came out of the gate kicking asses and taking names. They were not just changing the fabric of our corner of society. They were not just changing bodies. They were changing lives.

What's more, these new triathletes were on a mission to invite more friends and neighbors. Passion will do that. Plus, a small, tight-knit community makes it virtually impossible to avoid a giant movement such as this. These girls in pink were walking billboards for the tri-club and the best advertisement around. And I had to give it to them—these ladies made it look pretty appealing. Of course, I wasn't fully buying that whole "fun" shtick, so I stayed on the periphery, watching from a safe distance, captivated by the subculture being created. The sport of triathlon was their new obsession, and intellectual curiosity about it was mine. My interest continued to grow with each new recruit. I still didn't understand this phenomenon, but the social scientist in me really wanted to. The best place to start, I figured, was to find the trail of breadcrumbs that led them here.

If there is no struggle, there is no progress.
—FREDERICK DOUGLASS

AN ENLIGHTENED SPORT

During triathlon's debut years, America was emerging from what I will call the Dark Age of Sports, an era when females were not only discouraged but actually forbidden to participate in any physical activity involving endurance. It is difficult to believe that only six years before the first Ironman in Hawaii, women had been banned from running in the Boston Marathon. *Banned!* The taboo against women in endurance sports, including concerns about its effect on women's health, can be traced back to misogynistic attitudes from ancient times when women were seen as inferior at best, property at worst. Lest you think I'm being overdramatic, the ancient

Olympic Games not only prohibited female participation, but forbade married women from attending the games on penalty of death.

After the Civil War, women were permitted to participate in sports that didn't involve physical contact or perspiration, which basically ruled out just about everything but golf, archery, and croquet. Women were allowed to compete in the Olympic Games during the early 1900s, but only in a handful of events deemed appropriate (by men, of course). Track and field were not on that short list, but golf, tennis, sailing, croquet, and equestrian events were. Almost 30 years later, in 1928, women could officially run in the Olympic Games, so long as the race didn't exceed 800 meters. Apparently, the mega-minds of the medical world had determined that anything exceeding 800 meters would cause irreparable harm to a woman, ranging from infertility to death.

Women's sports really started coming out of the shadows and into the light after the passage of Title IX in 1972. Title IX required schools receiving federal funding to provide females with an equal opportunity to compete in sports. And guess what? It worked. Before Title IX, it was estimated that 1 in 27 high school girls played a sport. Today, it's about 1 in 2.5. In other words, the number of girls in sports went from 300,000 to 2.7 million! Women comprise 43 percent of college athletes competing on more than 3,700 women's sports teams.

However, Title IX didn't change things overnight; no great social change ever occurred with the flip of a light switch. Case in point: It took over a decade after Title IX for the 3,000-meter women's track event to be included in the Olympic Games. That same year, the Olympics also debuted the women's marathon. That year was 1984—in my own lifetime! Either I'm really *that* old, or it took *that* long for women to have the opportunities they wanted and deserved in sports.

WOMEN IN TRIATHLON

Triathlon welcomed women from the very beginning. But despite its gender equality right out of the gate, female triathletes were a minority during triathlon's fledgling years. Now, women are credited with driving the over-all popularity of the sport. The millennium witnessed a virtual tsunami of women entering the sport. In 1990, only 9 percent of USAT member-ship was female, compared to 37 percent in 2015. In 1981, there were only 20 female participants in the Ironman, a mere 6 percent of the finishers. Now, female representation in North American Ironman events is about 34 percent.

Why are women and triathlon being drawn together with such magnetic force? There are several significant factors. One was triathlon's debut in the 2000 Olympic Games, held in Sydney. Millions were introduced to a sport about which they were probably clueless. Triathlon coverage that year made history as 111 million Americans tuned in, making it the most watched Olympic games outside the United States. The exposure did won-ders for the sport, placing it on a worldwide stage and sending a ripple of inspiration through the masses. In the post-Olympic vapor trail came a new group of tri-curious men and women. The excitement of a new chal-lenge trickled down from elite and subelite athletes to "regular folks."

Strong women wear their pain like stilettos. No matter how much it hurts, all you see is the beauty of it.
—HARRIET MORGAN

Another key factor was the introduction of a shorter distance triath-lon. The idea for a racecourse friendly to the amateur or beginner triath-lete came from Mark Aiton of Northern California. He wanted to entice interested-but-hesitant wannabe triathletes into the sport with a race dis-tance that actually felt doable for a first timer. So, Aiton created Tri-For-Fun in 1988, a non-competitive triathlon event that featured a 400-yard swim, an 11-mile bike ride, and a 3-mile run. Its popularity was undeniable. The sprint was born.

While the Olympics introduced triathlon to people across the globe and sprints made triathlons more accessible, other important factors led more *women* into the fold. These included the creation of women-only races, the fashionable gear, the charitable opportunities, and the sense of community formed by all-female triathlon clubs.

NO BOYS ALLOWED

For some women—especially those brand-new to triathlon—the idea of racing among men could be intimidating. Even a deterrent. Thanks to the creation of women-only triathlons, that is no longer a barrier to entry. Of course, there are many female triathletes who don't care about the gender composition of a race. But for those who might find a co-ed environment another reason to talk themselves out of it, all-female races are perfect.

There is more at play here than the absence of testosterone. Women-only events are known for having an altogether different vibe. They tend to be overtly supportive environments that celebrate the spirit of personal best and camaraderie. These events often attract women with unique stories—surviving cancer, losing a hundred pounds, celebrating a milestone birthday, or coping with the loss of a spouse, a divorce, or the diagnosis of a chronic health condition. For many of the women participating in these races, just finishing is winning.

FASTINISTAS

Forgive me if I sound shallow here, but workout clothes have gotten super cute. It's a thing now, active wear that is so hip and figure-flattering you might start exercising just to wear it. "Athleisure" has surpassed denim sales, redefining comfortable style.

There are zip-up hoodies with flattering ruching, thigh-slimming running pants, and coordinating running bras peeking out of racer-back burnout tank tops. The T-shirts included in your race swag have also gotten a makeover. Once boxy, crew-necked cotton tees that you stuffed in the back of your drawer, these shirts now offer fitted cuts, V-necks, high-quality materials, and trendy graphics that appeal to a female athlete's form and function. That means we can actually use them as something more than pajamas.

Though some might roll their eyes at running skirts and colorful arm warmers, others like to rock fun style options while they're kicking butt. There is even a name for these fashion-conscious racers—Fastinistas. In her 2011 *Runner's World* article, Sarah Bowen Shea, coauthor of the best-selling *Run Like a Mother*, coined the term "Fastinista" to describe fast and fashionable women runners who streaked through the racecourse in running dresses, brightly colored and patterned compression kneesocks, capris, tank tops, and headbands. Whether you are into it or against it, you have to appreciate this: The industry has come a long way.

Once upon a time, athletic apparel for women was quite dreadful. Males were running that show and did not always understand women's bodies, athletic needs, or style. Consider the sports bra. Or lack thereof. Unarguably, this is the most important piece of clothing a female runner will wear, and yet, for a long time, nothing even remotely functional existed. Who invented it? Women runners who were tired of those suckers bouncing around.

Designed and marketed by Lisa Lindahl, Polly Smith, and Hinda Schreiber in 1978, the first working prototype of our modern sports bra was fashioned out of two jockstraps sewn together. Eventually, they figured out how to manufacture it out of something *other than* jockstraps and sold their amazing creation, the Jogbra, through their new company called Moving Comfort. Initially, the Jogbra was sold primarily through mail order since most sporting goods stores resisted carrying such risqué merchandise.

As time went on, the industry couldn't deny the increasing demand for women's athletic wear, but its first response was to "shrink it and pink it." Sounds cute, but it didn't work out well. Women are far too complicated, multidimensional, and demanding as consumers. We have boobs. We have hips. We know what we want, how we want it to feel, and how we want to look in it. We don't want to sacrifice form for function or function for form. We are feminine. We are beasts. Some girls glisten; others flat-out sweat. We need athletic wear to compress us in some places and allow some give in others.

We also need it to be multifunctional because we are often piggyback-ing a workout onto 27,000 other things. That means our workout clothing can't be too embarrassing to wear to the grocery store or our child's school. Plus, let's face it. If you dress like an athlete, you feel like one. Or, at least you can fool people into thinking so.

CHARITY

"I did my first triathlon because my sister who had just survived Stage III breast cancer at age 40 asked me to do one with her," says Lori W. "I hadn't run or swum in over 10 years and had never been on a road bike. Doing this for her was by far one of the best things I ever did for me."

Charity races, run in honor or memory of a loved one, have been the cat-alyst for many people. Hitch a big race to an important cause, and it's like a huge call to action. Races connected with a cause can jumpstart the journey into triathlon or simply add a new dimension to a sport you love by making it bigger than yourself. I devote an entire chapter to the charitable aspect of triathlon later in this book, but it deserves mention here as a significant factor drawing women to the sport.

According to a significant body of research, the most consistent predic-tor of charitable giving is gender. Women spend more time volunteering and give more money to charity than men, which is most likely a func-tion of socialization. It's no wonder that women, triathlon, and charity go extraordinarily well together.

Team in Training (TNT) exemplifies this phenomenon. Heralded as the largest endurance sports training program in the world, TNT is not only the flagship fundraising program for the Leukemia and Lymphoma Society but also the only endurance sports training program that raises money for blood cancer research. Since forming in 1988, TNT has raised more than $1.4 billion for blood cancer research and patient services. It boasts over half a million race finishers. TNT coaches will help any interested partici-pant at any athletic level train for anything from half-marathons and mara-thons to century rides, hiking adventures, or triathlon.

Heather S. was inspired to join Team in Training in 1996 after her 18-year-old sister, Amber, was diagnosed with leukemia. Heather had never considered herself a runner, but she went to a local Team in Training meeting and signed up to run the Marine Corps Marathon. As she trained, something transformative happened within her. "The emotional part of it started to click with the running. I *felt* and thought during long runs," she says. As a single teacher, Heather was worried she wouldn't be able to raise the money for her team, but she was wrong. "Because of the personal connection, I had money pouring in." That experience with TNT turned Heather into a runner, something she once thought she hated. Some years later, she became a triathlete.

Three years after her diagnosis, Amber died. She was only 21. Decades later, Heather still runs and tris and inspires others to do the same.

After Colleen W. lost her mom to cancer in 2009, she joined TNT to train for her first marathon. "Those long runs on Saturdays were my therapy. I met wonderful people who I shared stories, laughed, cried, and celebrated every mile with. Everyone has an inspiration. Mine is my mom." For Colleen, the driving force behind these endurance races is to help find a cure for cancer. "I may never stop grieving for my mother, but I'll never stop believing that there's a cure out there. I'm still fighting right alongside of her and I'll never give up."

SOCIAL BUTTERFLIES

Though I kept hearing about the "fun" aspect, let the record state that triathlon isn't all fun and games. There is a lot hard work and sacrifice involved. Training can be tedious, grueling, demanding, tiring, and at times painful. Yet the scale quickly tips in favor of "fun" when there is a social component. Training and competing alongside friends is not only motivating and often practical, but also emotionally rewarding.

"I love doing tris and races, but I've never done one by myself," says Heather S. "For me, it's not just about running and biking. It's about connecting." Heather enjoys the company during training and on race day.

Her true reward, however, comes from supporting others on their journey, helping them do the things they thought they could never do.

Amy Dillon, president of Tucson Tri Girls (TTG) in Arizona, sees the support triathletes give each other every day. Amy stumbled into triathlon at the invitation of a friend. She figured she could run, swim, and bike well enough to at least give it a shot. But it took courage to finally join the Tucson Tri Girls. "I was nervous. I thought they'd be really professional and super fit. But everyone was very welcoming." With nearly 100 active members, TTG comprises women of all ages. Some are experienced athletes who stand on the podium and have completed ultradistance races, and some are novices seeking to jumpstart their long-neglected health. "Everybody is very supportive," Amy says. "It's a great way to stay inspired."

Champions are not made on the track or field; champions are made by the things you accomplish and the way you use your abilities in everyday life situations.
—BOB BEAMON

For some women, joining an all-female club is their golden ticket into triathlon and the reason they aren't "one and done" after their first race. Being part of a community of women who train, carpool, vent, laugh, cry, and embrace in a sweaty hug after crossing that finish line makes everything sweeter. I could see the positive influence of that camaraderie occurring in my own town.

Until this point, I had been peeping into the tri-club's little microcosm like a stalker, taking notes, and generally lurking about. But to move things forward with the book and my theoretical triathlon journey, it was time to stop standing on the outside and finally enter the fray.

VISIONARY

"What I get really inspired by are the people who can barely finish but never give up."

NANCY STEVENS is a world champion triathlete and three-time gold medalist in cross-country skiing. She has cycled 3,000 miles on the Race Across America and set a mountain climbing world record. She is an advocate, philanthropist, inspirational speaker, mentor, and musician.

Oh, I almost forgot to mention one small detail. Nancy has been blind since birth.

❧

Nancy's childhood was pretty typical. She grew up as one of seven children in a close, supportive, active, and outdoorsy family. She got a tandem bike at an early age, which she rode from childhood straight into adulthood. At the age of 11, Nancy started cross-country skiing with her family. Wearing bells on their poles, her siblings took turns as guides. Quickly, she developed both competency and a love for the sport.

Later, Nancy added downhill skiing. Her passion and skill on the slopes secured her a spot on the US Paralympic Ski Team as a cross-country skier.

She trained and competed with them for six years, winning gold three times in her division.

In 1997, Nancy heard about a duathlon from one of her training partners. Since she was already a runner and had really gotten into tandem cycling, she was excited to try something new. "I thought, *This could be kind of fun*," she says. It was indeed fun, and over the next few years she participated in several duathlons.

Now, Nancy was clearly an active, athletic, and adventurous person. The only limits to her dreams and goals were those of a practical nature. To participate in the sports she loved, like skiing, cycling, hiking, and running, she was dependent on a guide. Securing guides was sometimes easier said than done. First, you needed to find people who were willing to train for the event and invest their time and resources into the race. Second, they needed to be okay with it being Nancy's race, not theirs. They were the guide; Nancy was the competitor. Practically speaking, the guide also needed to be the right size for her tandem bike. Thankfully, she had a network of athletes to guide her, but then she relocated and had to start fresh.

"When I moved to Glenwood Springs, I didn't know anybody. I was turning into a couch potato," says Nancy. She could swim laps unguided, so she began exercising in the local hot springs pool to stay in shape.

Eventually, Nancy built a new network and, in 2002, registered for her first triathlon using three guides, one for each leg of the race. Weeks before the event, her running guide had to pull out, and Nancy was stuck. She'd have to find a replacement or be unable to compete. The race director put Nancy in touch with another Nancy—Nancy Reinisch of the Roaring Fork Women's Triathlon Team.

The two chatted on the phone, and Nancy R. agreed to think on it and call back with some recommendations for guides. The next day, Nancy S. received a call.

"I found you a guide," Nancy R. told her. "It's me. But I have a condition. I want to guide you through the whole triathlon." Nancy S. was ecstatic. "If my [tandem] bike fits you, we're golden!"

With only three weeks until the triathlon, the two Nancies began their training in earnest.

As Nancy S. explained to me, she runs with a tether about 18 inches long connecting her wrist to a belt worn by her guide. In tandem biking, Nancy S. is the "stoker," sitting in the rear seat, while her sighted guide acts as the "pilot" or "captain" in the front. But Nancy S. had never used a guide for open-water swimming. Conversely, Nancy R. had no previous experience guiding at all.

At first the two practiced swimming in open water without a tether. Their system involved Nancy R. periodically tapping Nancy S. as they swam. Ultimately, they opted to use a two-foot-long bungee cord to keep them together. While this required some alterations to their stroke technique, it seemed the safest option.

On the day of the triathlon, the weather was wet and horrible. "I thought, *This is gonna suck,*" Nancy S. laughs. However, rain wasn't going to dampen the positive, fun spirit of the two Nancies, who could find the humor in any situation. "That first tri, it was so cold and rainy, [but] we had so much fun together," she says.

In fact, the two Nancies worked together so well that they continued training regularly. "We kept working out together the next season and signed up for a few more [races]," Nancy S. says. They finished six triathlons as a "blind-and-sighted-guide" duo.

The dynamic duo placed third in their division after competing in a 2004 race in California, and, to her utter surprise, Nancy S. received an email informing her that she had qualified to compete in the 2005 Honolulu Triathlon World Championships (affiliated with the International Triathlon Union, or ITU). It would be her first Olympic-distance race.

Team Nancy headed to the Big Island to compete in ITU world's as the first all-female blind-and-sighted-guide duo. "We celebrated the whole time we were there," Nancy S. says. "It was so exciting." She can't say enough about the kindness and support she received from the other half of Team Nancy. "She had shirts made. She just really put her heart and soul into it." They had become more than athlete and guide. They were good friends.

Team Nancy made history when they became the first masters-level, all-female, blind-and-sighted-guide duo to win gold at the world championships in the visually impaired division. "We got to the finish line and I got so teary-eyed," says Nancy S. "I had no idea when we first did that tri in the pouring rain that all this would happen."

Nancy longed to share the empowering experience of triathlon with other women who were blind and visually impaired. She came up with the concept of the Tri-It Camp for the Blind, wrote a grant, recruited volunteers, and secured resources and sponsorship. The first Tri-It Camp was held in 2007. With the support of Nancy R., the Roaring Fork Women's Triathlon Team, and the Glenwood Springs community, the Tri-It Camp for the Blind was a phenomenal success. "The first year . . . I had six women who were blind from all over the country. I had tons of support . . . lots of volunteers," says Nancy. "Everybody in the community was behind this project. It was incredible." So much so that it ran again a second year.

Team Nancy raced together for a total of three years and remain close friends. Nancy Stevens continued in triathlon with other guides, qualifying for and winning gold in her age group at the ITU World Championships, in the visually impaired division, again in 2006 and 2007. She has raced in a total of 14 triathlons, the last of which was in 2013. "I'm not totally out of racing," she says, "but I'm not seriously racing."

Though she is on a triathlon hiatus, Nancy's active lifestyle has not slowed down. She continues to tandem cycle, ski, and hike and has run a few half-marathons. She became the first blind woman to climb the Grand Teton in 2012 at the age of 51. Her last big race was the US Bank Pole Pedal Paddle in 2014, a unique multisport race consisting of downhill skiing, cross-country skiing, a 22-mile bike ride, a 5-mile run, and kayaking. She keeps herself busy volunteering with Oregon Adaptive Sports, coordinating and training guides for hiking, kayaking, and indoor rock climbing. She recently presented at the Disabled Sports USA Adapt to Achieve Cycling Clinic, where she taught tandem cycling.

Nancy dreams of starting up another Tri-It Camp. "I would like to give back to the sport," she says. "I just want to see more women in triathlon." When she was actively racing, Nancy estimates that there were fewer than 10 blind female triathletes in the United States. She was a true pioneer, a trailblazer. When no road map existed, she created her own, and inspired others to follow. Her journey has been a spectacular adventure, and I have no doubt that it is far from over.

7

SIGMA TRI

If you want to go fast, go alone.
If you want to go far, go together.
—AFRICAN PROVERB

My little town was morphing into a triathlon mecca, and I had a bird's-eye view into the lives, hearts, and souls of these impassioned tri-athletes. Though I resisted the gravitational pull of the tri-club in 2010, by the winter of 2011 I was hard-pressed to conjure an excuse not to at least *attend* their second annual Kick Off Meeting. Half the women in my town were going to be there, the night promised to be a good time, and alcohol was being served. How could I resist?

Sure, my reasons were predominantly social, but I had been researching triathlon with a passion that surprised even me, and I felt determined to understand this phenomenon more intimately. What better way to experience the seduction, inspiration, appeal, and transformative power of triathlon than to be right at the beginning of a new season, smack dab in the center of it all?

When I arrived at the Mullica Hill Women's Tri Club's second annual Kick Off Meeting, I was surprised to see the line stretching down a long hallway and spilling out the front door. Once inside, roughly 300 women mingled, hugged, laughed, and snaked through the endless raffle tables, dropping their tickets like a trail of breadcrumbs. I seeded myself among them in the hopes of hearing their siren song. I went into the night as a sort of data collector, an observer, a fly on the wall (a fly with a glass of wine, of course. All good field research should involve wine).

After securing the all-important wine along with a fistful of raffle tickets, I worked my way toward the expansive maze of raffle tables, waving to familiar faces along the way. I skipped the table filled with the free race entries because, seriously, how is winning an entry into an Olympic-distance triathlon or a 10-mile race really *winning*? What I decided I really wanted was the premier raffle item propped up high above the crowds: A beautiful carbon road bike valued at over $2,000, donated by a local cycling shop. I was gunning for that bike. To clarify, I wasn't wanting this bike to take it cycling around town in spandex. I simply did not own a bike and liked the idea of scoring an expensive one for free. It also occurred to me that if I won that bike, maybe it was a sign that I should more seriously consider doing a triathlon. Of course, the converse would also be true if I did not win the bike. And I could definitely live with that.

I dropped my entire wad of tickets into the bike's raffle bag, already fat and overflowing with thousands of chances. Then I turned and followed the crowd to the neat rows of folding chairs in the main room.

"Alicia!" A petite brunette with a familiar face waved as we worked our way through the crowd. I recognized her as an old acquaintance, Jamie, whom I hadn't seen in years. We had belonged to the same group of stay-at-home moms years before, spending many mornings pushing our little ones on swings while squeezing in some adult conversation.

"Are you in the club? Have you done a triathlon yet?" she asked. I was always getting asked that. People assumed I was an obsessed TriathaMom because I was friends with so many of them. I laughed and answered, "Nope and nope!" Then I added politely, "Or, at least not yet. Maybe I'll get talked into it tonight," doubting the words even as they passed my lips. "How about you?"

Jamie said she had wanted to do a triathlon last year, but that it had not been possible, whereupon she nonchalantly explained how she was diagnosed with breast cancer and the surgery derailed her training.

And here I was afraid of swimming in the scary lake water?

"Wow," I gasped, stunned. She was probably in her mid-thirties, with two girls around the ages of my own kids. I couldn't wrap my head around it, but Jamie seemed nonplussed. "Maybe this will be my year," she said, shrugging casually.

"I *know* it will be," I replied as a moving wall of people parted us.

We shouted goodbyes across a sea of bobbing heads, and I went to find a seat for the presentation. Suddenly, inside, I was totally rooting for that girl. *Yeah, she's gonna do it. I really hope she does that triathlon. She's got this. . . . You go, Jamie, you go!* In mere seconds, I progressed from thinking triathlon was so time-consuming and a bit ridiculous to wanting Jamie to totally rock it because that would mean something big. And wanting it for her made me get a little bit jazzed about it in general.

I found an empty folding chair next to one of my newer Mullica Hill friends, a skeptical, slightly belligerent, non-triathlete like me.

"So, are you going to actually *do* this?" she asked, raising an eyebrow. We had shared our mutual confusion about the whole craze months ago. It had been a bonding moment for two gals on the outskirts of the in-crowd. Neither of us had caught tri-fever, nor were we planning on it.

"Hell, no!" I laughed, quickly over my momentary lapse of triathlon excitement. "I'm just here for the raffle and the wine."

"Yeah, me too," she laughed in return. We quietly joked about how this presentation would do nothing to penetrate our armor of resistance. We'd be the last two mavericks standing in all of Mullica Hill, the lone survivors of a triathlon pandemic! You would never see us getting into that cold lake or spending the equivalent of a week's vacation on some Tour de

France–quality bike just to ride around town as if our 40-year-old asses were going to the Olympics or something.

As we chuckled, happy throngs of women settled around us, and the educational portion of the evening commenced.

All right, ladies, I thought to myself. Make me want to do this. Bring your A game.

The four founders of the MHWTC took their places at the front of the room, where a makeshift stage was outfitted with a microphone and large screen. Colleen, Lydia, Michelle, and Maureen were local celebrities at this point. The statuesque Colleen, with her mane of auburn hair and athletic build, was the grand matriarch of the triathlon club. This 40-something, working mother of two tween girls was a force of nature. She possessed boundless energy, tons of drive, an unrivaled attention to detail, and the ability to multitask beyond that of a normal human being. If Wonder Woman lived in Suburbia, she would come in the form of Colleen.

The most impressive thing about Colleen was that she knew almost everyone by name. Not only that, she remembered their likes, dislikes, and fears and the details of their personal story. She was a mama bird who considered every little chickadee in the club an extension of her family.

As Colleen gave her opening remarks and an overview of the club, the energy in the room became palpable. She had us at hello. She knew how to sell triathlon. She knew all the ways you would talk yourself out of it, every excuse you would make. She knew you didn't believe in yourself, but she believed in you already. Honestly, truly, wholeheartedly believed. You didn't just hear it; you felt it.

Standing next to Colleen was Lydia, whose passion for triathlon equaled her passion for supporting charitable causes. Lydia headed the club's charity branch and was committed to using the club as a vehicle to promote change in the community and beyond. Though Lydia didn't consider herself an athlete growing up, this 30-something working mother had quickly amassed a record of several triathlons and road races. It wasn't a hobby; it was a lifestyle. She was all in—mind, body, and soul.

Alongside Lydia was Michelle, an avid runner, part-time graduate student, and 40-something mother of two. Michelle was that friendly face in the crowd, that warm, encouraging, nurturing spirit who would do anything for you. Although a quiet "behind-the-scenes" person, she was a true force as the race director of the MHWTC's new sprint triathlon, the Queen of the Hill.

Finally, there was Maureen. A working mother of two teens in her late 40s, Maureen had a dry, quick wit and a wonderfully self-deprecating sense of humor. She talked about her messy house and finishing races dead last. She had the audience cracking up during her speech and made triathlon less intimidating . . . at least momentarily. Maureen was in great shape, but she confessed her nickname was "Slo Mo." When it came to racing, she was all about the fun and the friendships. She kept it real. "If I can do it, you can do it," she encouraged. Since most of us probably related to Maureen the most, we hung on her every word.

Each of the founders discussed a different aspect of the tri-club, including the sport of triathlon, the training programs, the club benefits, and the charitable initiatives. In doing so, they painted a vivid and welcoming picture. It was a picture of you (yes, you, the one who doesn't believe you can do it) running across that finish line with fists raised in the air and eyes glassy with tears of joy. Together, they were funny, realistic, nonjudgmental, convincing, supportive, and encouraging. Something special happened when those women stood together in front of the room and let their passion shine. It may sound cheesy, but I must confess—it was magical. Infectious. Empowering. Their energy was so positive and their stories were so relatable that by the end of the night I think that most women there believed they could truly complete a triathlon.

For a fleeting moment, even me.

Awards become corroded,
friends gather no dust.
—JESSE OWENS

OUT CLUBBIN'

The simple act of joining a tri-club may be the single most important thing a newcomer to the sport can do. The encouragement, instruction, and guidance that a club offers are invaluable. But clubs aren't just for the newbie. The confident and seasoned triathlete thrives in a group that supports her as she pushes herself toward new goals. She can also learn new techniques and training tips, and build friendships with like-minded women along the way.

There is an undeniable correlation between the rising number of clubs and the increase in triathlon participation. In 2000, there were only 50 USAT-sanctioned triathlon clubs in existence across America. A decade later, that number had grown to 831. Today, there are more than 1,000 triathlon clubs registered with USAT, and counting. From California to Maine, Michigan to Texas, tri-clubs are cropping up like dandelions. They range from the largest coed club, located in southern Florida, to one of the smallest, on the island of Nantucket. Whether they include serious Ironman competitors, casual weekend enthusiasts, or some combination of both, tri-clubs make the same promise to their members. They offer training, support, and camaraderie for individuals intent on unlocking their inner athlete.

"Before the tri-club, I went to races by myself," Megan H. says. She was disciplined about working out but fumbled through her triathlon training alone and without much support. At her first races, she'd be so nervous she couldn't even speak. Then, at one race, she saw a few women with matching pink shirts. It was those girls in pink! That's when she learned about the MHWTC, and it was just the support she needed.

No matter their gender composition, triathlon clubs serve two main purposes. The first purpose is what I'll call the Practicalities. That includes things like training plans, group workouts, and sometimes professional coaching. Many clubs offer fitness-related workshops on topics like injury prevention, open-water swim technique, and nutrition for athletes. They may also hold how-to clinics, like how to fix a flat or shift gears on your road bike, or how to reduce panic during open-water swims. Supplemental workouts (such as boot camp or yoga), discounts to local fitness stores, mentoring, and invitations to exclusive club-only parties round out the list of tangible club benefits. By creating a forum for members to ask questions, learn from each other, find training buddies, carpool to races, and receive advice on a multitude of triathlon-related questions, a triathlon club cultivates a rich environment of training opportunities, advice, and education.

"The thing I liked most of all about joining the tri-club was the opportunity to meet over 100 new women," Heather S. says. "It's hard to make friends sometimes as an adult, and this club gave me a chance to meet some great people."

Heather S.'s sentiment is shared by many, which leads me to the second purpose of a triathlon club, arguably even more powerful than the first. Tri-clubs offer what I call the Intangibles—friendship, inspiration, belongingness, and emotional connectedness. Although triathlon is an individual sport, clubs create a sense of being on the same "team," of belonging to the same tribe.

Bridget S. trains regularly with a group of tri-club members who have become her closest friends. "When you race with someone and share that experience, you have so much more in common," she explains. These women not only bond through training, but push each other to achieve their personal bests. "I never thought I had it in me to be able to run quickly," she says. "I never pushed myself before. I did not push myself until I started running with them."

Triathlon is a race, and a race involves competition. For many triathletes, especially at the recreational level, that competition lies within. It's about beating that little voice in their head that fills them with doubt and angst. For a select group of triathletes gunning for a spot on the podium, there's no denying they need people to eat their dust. Yet many triathletes, even very competitive ones, are often less focused on beating someone else than on besting their own personal time. Winning is simply a byproduct of being their best. When a community's entire paradigm shifts from competing *against* to competing *within*, racing takes on a different vibe. Club triathletes seem to truly celebrate each and every tribe member's personal victory while pursuing their own.

CLIMBING THE PYRAMID

Can motivation to tri come from a sense of community and friendship? Let's get psychological for a moment. Humanistic psychologist Abraham Maslow is best known for his theory of human motivation, which he developed back in 1943. The crowning jewel of this theory was his Hierarchy of Needs. The diagram seen in all Psych 101 textbooks depicts this hierarchy in the shape of a pyramid, neatly subdivided into five stacked, color-coded sections representing each stage. Essentially, Maslow theorized that all human beings are motivated by unsatisfied needs. As we work toward satisfying them, we work our way up the pyramid toward the tiny triangle at the top. That top, the peak of the pyramid and that which we all strive to embody, is called Self-Actualization. It's a state of complete self-fulfillment, where the "ideal" self meets the "real" self—the embodiment of a human's full potential. In other words, it is when you become your best self.

Sounds easy enough, right? Well, to summit this pyramid, one must fully satisfy all the lower needs along the journey. If a need is left unmet or partially met, that person remains stuck at that level, striving to fill that void. The most basic needs are at the pyramid's base: food, drink, warmth, sleep. Every human being requires these things for survival, and if deprived, she can't even begin to work toward anything more existential. Above the Physiological needs are the Safety needs for shelter, security, stability, law, and order. Once those two sets of needs are met, the next step toward self-actualization involves the Belongingness needs: love, friendship, intimacy, affection, and relationships. Theoretically, without those needs being satisfied, an individual will not be able to advance into the two top tiers of Self-Esteem and Self-Actualization.

That intrinsic drive to find caring, reciprocal, healthy, supportive relationships is the very thing that helps people achieve their higher goals and dreams. Belongingness fortifies self-esteem, which paves the road to self-actualization. In this respect, triathlon clubs make a lot of sense. And, if you think about it, triathlon by its very nature is a self-actualizing endeavor. Let's face it, no one "needs" to do a triathlon to survive, to eat, to stay safe and warm. In fact, triathlon is the *opposite of* staying safe and warm. It was doctored *by* those and *for* those who want to challenge themselves. Therefore, it makes perfect sense that securing basic belongingness needs via a triathlon club helps make the journey to the top of Maslow's pyramid, or the finish line of a triathlon, a reality.

Research supports this notion as well. Social factors, group identification, and belongingness are powerful motivators for people participating in endurance sports. Nearly 40 percent of endurance sport competitors enter these races at the encouragement of friends or family. This suggests that people can be talked into a great many things in the name of friendship.

A perfect example of this is Megan H. After a brutal swim in freezing cold water, Megan crossed the finish line of her first 70.3 and promised herself to never, *ever* race that distance again. Enter friends, stage left. Next thing she knew, she was signed up for another 70.3 with her buddies. When I asked her if she caved because of friendship, Megan laughed and admitted, "Yes!"

Jenny Thullier of the Transcend Racing Triathlon Club in California confesses that triathlon legitimizes spending time with her friends. "There's a lot more justification to say we're going away together for a race," she laughs. Training and racing become fun social events. When those events are broadcast on social media, people get a serious case of FOMO (fear of missing out). "You get caught up in the energy," Jenny explains. "You don't want to miss anything!"

Triathlon clubs use friendship, fun, fitness, and a dash of good old-fashioned peer pressure to pull others in. But I didn't need to read a bunch of research to figure that out, being a woman myself. There are exceptions to every rule, but a large majority of women aren't eager to sign up, train for, and travel to their first triathlon alone. Especially after we've spent our adolescence going to the bathroom in packs. Seriously, women make just about *anything* into a social opportunity: the PTA, girls' nights out, book clubs, Bunco, and even the gaggle of bridesmaids at our wedding. Many of us find comfort in numbers. We find comfort in friendship. And when we feel there is a high risk of embarrassing ourselves, we like to travel with a human shield.

While there is no way to definitively know whether female-only tri-clubs lure a subgroup of women who might normally shy away, it might well be a tipping point for those on the fence. Certainly coed tri-clubs offer the same mentoring, support, and guidance, but many women, especially those new to the sport, are simply more comfortable with a "No Boys Allowed" policy. Particularly for someone feeling past her prime, who hadn't shed that baby weight, never played a sport in her life, or was insecure about her fitness level and conspicuous about her body in Lycra. One could see where a dude-heavy environment might be intimidating and even a deterrent for some . . . even if the stereotype of the ultracompetitive, testosterone-ridden male isn't always true.

Both coed and all-female tri-clubs can provide a safe atmosphere where women can thrive. The MHWTC chose to follow a women-only philosophy, and it has worked well. They attract every type of athlete: the sub-7-minute milers who podium at races and the easygoing, recreational triathletes who walk the entire run. There are those who have conquered the Ironman, those who do only one sprint a year, and those who just stick to running races. There are Type A obsessives and Type B socializers, those who crush the course and those who can be found reapplying lip gloss before hopping on their old beach cruiser bike with a basket on the front. Megan H. says she's one of those people applying lip gloss during the swim-to-bike transition. "I don't try to PR," she laughs. "I try to FI—*Finish Intact*. You get the same medal as everyone else as long as you finish."

Megan sums up the dynamic of the MHWTC perfectly: "The club is challenging people to step outside their comfort zone. But the key is you're not doing it alone."

If you only do what you know you can do,
you never do very much.

—TOM KRAUSE

I arrived home from the Kick Off Meeting after 11:00 p.m., tiptoeing into each of my girls' bedrooms to kiss their sleeping faces. Then I crept quietly into my own bedroom, where my husband was only partially awake.

"How was your first cult meeting?" he mumbled. Truth be told, I was feeling a little overwhelmed, a little inspired, but mostly tired. I had gone into the evening expecting to observe how *others* were moved into action. I certainly wasn't expecting to feel motivated myself. After all, I detested all forms of exercise, and triathlon was just exercise cubed.

"It's not a cult," I corrected indignantly, insulted by his insinuation that I would be so easily brainwashed. "It's a sorority." I slipped off my impractical shoes and peeled off my too-tight jeans in exchange for comfy sweatpants.

"What's the difference?" he yawned.

"Cults marginalize you and don't serve alcohol. Sororities make you popular and get you drunk."

"So are you drunk enough to *tri*?" he chuckled.

"I don't think there is enough alcohol in the world for that," I replied wryly as I slipped into bed. Yet my words didn't seem to hold the same conviction. There was some deeper meaning than just the act of swimming, biking, and running. There was something about this club that went beyond a mere "sorority." While I wasn't coming down with tri-fever, I was certainly feeling something. Maybe it was a sneeze coming on. Maybe a tickle in my throat. I suppose repeated exposure to the triathlon pandemic was chiseling away at my wall of resistance. Or, perhaps a part of me knew that to truly understand this triathlon craze from the inside out, I was going to have to walk a mile in their shoes. Or, rather, run, bike, and swim about 13 miles in their shoes. And tonight those girls in pink had done a pretty good job convincing me that this would not only be achievable but also fun. Sure I was still dubious, but I couldn't deny that some kind of triathlon black magic had oozed into the cracks of my protective armor.

That same black magic hexed a lot more women than just me, because that year the MHWTC added 140 brand-new members to the original crew. By the end of the 2011 season, the club had grown to 260 women . . . and I was one of them.

8

INSIDE THE TRIBE

*As we light a path for others, we naturally
light our own way.*

—MARY ANNE RADMACHER

Since that Kick Off Meeting back in 2011, the Mullica Hill Women's Triathlon Club has ballooned into one of the 20-largest USAT-sanctioned triathlon clubs in the country, and *the* largest all-female club. But the MHWTC was certainly not the first of its kind. Like so many cool fads, the sport and its followers started on the West Coast before migrating east. The Women's Tri Club of Chico, California, and Colorado's CWW Triathlon Team broke new ground in the 1990s when they formed two of the first tri-clubs for women in a male-dominated sport.

Since then, more clubs have made the decision to cater exclusively to females, drawing thousands of women into the sport and proving that if you build it, they will come. And they will bring friends. And often, wine.

*Walking with a friend in the dark
is better than walking alone in the light.*

—HELEN KELLER

PIONEERING WILD WOMEN

In 1997, before most of the MHWTC founders were even out of college, a sign-up sheet was being passed around a room in Colorado. The names of about 60 women were written in neat rows down the page. Those women became the pioneering members of one of the country's first all-female triathlon clubs—the Colorado Wild Women Triathlon Team.

The club name evolved after someone scrawled "Team CWW" across the top of that original sign-up sheet. None of the meeting's organizers had given much thought to a club name because they really didn't know if this group would have staying power. At the time, "CWW" didn't stand for "Colorado Wild Women." They were simply the first initials of the last names of three women who spearheaded the meeting. Later, when the club started to take off, they decided to work those letters into something more meaningful. The group had been given the affectionate nickname of "Wild Women" at races, which made "Colorado Wild Women" a perfect fit.

Celeste Callahan was the original "C" of CWW. As a woman growing up in the era before Title IX, she was not encouraged by the sociocultural messages toward women in sports. "There were no sports," Celeste remembers. "I was not to act like a tomboy." She was permitted to play tennis, but even then she was instructed to be ladylike. "When I went one day to play with a boyfriend, my mother told me to make sure I didn't beat him."

It wasn't just sports, either. Celeste remembers feeling like women shouldn't have too many goals outside of being a wife and mother. She was expected to go to college, but the purpose of that was to find a good man to take care of her. "It was inferred that I could not take care of myself," she says.

Celeste *did* find a good man. She started a family and stayed at home to raise her children while her husband worked hard in his career. By the time Celeste entered her 40s, her children were moving toward greater independence, and Celeste found herself searching for something that she could claim as uniquely her own. She turned to running and quickly became addicted. In 1980, she was one of the first women to officially run in the New York Marathon.

After she completed her second marathon in 1982, a running buddy asked if she knew anything about "that thing they're doing in Hawaii." Her friend was referring to the Ironman, but at that point, the name had yet to catch on. After her friend explained what it was, Celeste said, "That's the stupidest thing I have ever heard."

Nevertheless, her interest was piqued when her friend pointed out that there were shorter versions of "that stupid thing they're doing in Hawaii." Together, they committed to giving one of the shorter distances a whirl.

Celeste didn't realize she should wear goggles when swimming laps (after all, she never wore them in the pool as a kid). She and her friend rode bikes with baby seats attached to the back, and when they attended group rides, they would lose the pack after the first block. When she finally bought her first road bike, she bought it right off the floor without a proper fitting. It turned out that it wasn't even the correct size for her height.

Swimming was challenging, and she hated the bike, but running was Celeste's sweet spot. "I was a good runner. . . . I could run 7-minute miles," she says. When she crossed the finish line of the Seafair Triathlon in the summer of 1985, Celeste was hooked for life.

Since then, this grandmother of five has finished 11 marathons, 4 Ironmans, 3 Races Across America, and 1 Race Across the West. A USAT Level II coach and a Level II race director, Celeste was honored as the Grand Masters Duathlete of the Year and was the first recipient of the International Triathlon Union's Women's Committee Award of Excellence in 2013. She has been a long-time leader within USAT, serving on the board of directors in 2004 as the representative for the Rocky Mountain/Pacific Northwest/Midwest Region and then as the general secretary from 2005 through 2010.

When Celeste cofounded the CWW Triathlon Team, it was one of the first triathlon training programs in Colorado. Starting with a core of 40 women, CWW today has a membership of somewhere between 400 and 500 women. It has evolved from an informal group into a nonprofit organization providing professional coaching in all three disciplines. Members of CWW receive instruction from 2004 Olympic bronze medalist triathlete, Susan Williams. There is a coached swim program for both pool and open water, a coached indoor and outdoor cycling group, and a group running program. CWW has helped more than 5,000 women cross the finish line as triathletes.

When Celeste discovered triathlon, a new world of opportunity, friendship, and health opened up to her. Creating CWW was a way to empower thousands of women to experience that, as well. But the true impetus for CWW was even more personal.

On the morning of April 2, 1997, Celeste's best friend Judy was out training for the Race Across America when she was struck and killed by a car. "CWW was started that night and dedicated to her," Celeste says. The multisport community mourned the loss of Judy, who was, at that time, one of the most decorated age groupers in triathlon history. Celeste mourned the loss of her best friend, but because of CWW, Judy's memory and the love of triathlon lives on in the hearts of every woman who steps up to tri.

MORE THAN JUST PRETTY IN PINK

As close as the four founding mothers of the Mullica Hill Women's Tri Club are now, they didn't all know each other in the beginning. They also didn't know very much about triathlon, being newbies themselves. What they did know was that they loved it. And what they did have was chemistry.

Colleen Fossett and Maureen Brigham were neighbors who began doing triathlons together in 2008. Colleen was a lifelong athlete, running cross-country and track throughout high school and college. By her early 30s, she was running half-marathons and then marathons. "I got bored and started doing tris," she says. She and Maureen did a sprint triathlon in Philadelphia with four other friends. "I loved it," says Maureen. "The six of us were on a team. I hadn't felt like that since eighth-grade softball." As Maureen and Colleen continued to train together for various endurance races, they began bouncing around the idea of forming a tri club. "We talked about it for two years," says Maureen. "We'd get really excited about it and then we'd get distracted by life and forget about it."

Meanwhile, in another corner of Mullica Hill, friends Michelle Powell and Lydia DelRosso had just done their first triathlon together and were hooked. Michelle had been a runner all her adult life, but expanded her repertoire when she began working out with Lydia. "She got me on the bike, and I got her to run," Michelle says. "We did a triathlon and I was so excited that I called Colleen, whom I knew because we used to be neighbors. I knew she was into tris." Michelle and Lydia, like Colleen and Maureen, were eager to find a way to pull more women into the sport. Colleen saw triathlon as a powerful tool for empowering women, one of her life's passions. "Triathlon was new and emerging in this area," she says. She wanted to strike while the iron was hot. Lydia was intent on forming some kind of triathlon team to race for a cause. "The idea was we'd all do a triathlon together and raise money for charity," she explains. The four of them wondered whether they could get something off the ground if they combined their efforts and joined forces, which led to that fateful meeting over breakfast in November 2009. That's where the two ideas—charity and empowerment—folded together into one mission.

Though the four founding mothers of MHWTC started out with aspirations of an intimate group, the growth came rapidly. They knew they had something special at that very first Kick Off Meeting. "It felt different, like it was something bigger than us. There was so much excitement." Lydia says. The first year, they surpassed the 100-member mark, which shocked and motivated them.

"Here I was thinking I was an expert in triathlon when I had done, like, two," Colleen laughs. Maureen chuckles when she remembers what rookies they were at the beginning. "I wore my husband's shorts and a bathing suit with a skirt to swim." They might not have had a lot of expertise, but they had a clear vision. They also had the support of more women than they ever imagined. Membership grew to 480 at the close of 2012, making them the largest all-female triathlon club in the mid-Atlantic region at the time. That same year, they were honored with *Competitor* magazine's award for Best Triathlon Club in the Northeast. By 2013, the club had grown to 675 members. "We didn't realize there would be so much interest," Lydia says. "We were figuring things out as we went along that first year. The second year [is] when we got sponsors and tri-suits and the town started to take notice. It took off."

Their bigger, signature events were also launched during the club's sophomore year. "Once we started having organized events, people would come," says Colleen. The evening bike rides attracted around 100 women regularly and the popular, biannual Ride the Farm event drew around 150. The mock triathlons and practice open-water swims pulled in hundreds as well. The annual Fabulous Friday Night 5K started as a manageable, informal little race held in Colleen's neighborhood with an after-party in her backyard. They didn't even have to close the roads for it. Now, it has become so popular that they hold it at a large outdoor venue.

The most well-attended event is the club's signature race, the Queen of the Hill Sprint Triathlon. The founders created a women-only tri that was newbie-friendly, affordable, and local to its core membership. "We thought, we have the support and all the enthusiasm of these women. We wanted to give back to our community," says Michelle, the Queen's race director.

The Queen of the Hill is designed to set everyone up for success. Practice swims in open water and two mock triathlons held the week before the big race help reduce anxiety and provide an opportunity to practice techniques like transitioning. Over 200 women registered for the first Queen of the Hill, which also raised $2,000 for a local nonprofit. In the race's second year, 375 slots sold out almost immediately. Every woman new to triathlon in southern New Jersey wanted a spot in this non-intimidating race, and every seasoned triathlete wanted to return to the neighborhood race where "everybody knows your name."

"There's nothing better to me than the morning of Queen of the Hill," Michelle says. "I see these women at Kick Off and at their first [group] ride, their first open-water swim. . . . That morning, it's like their graduation."

At the close of the 2014 season, the MHWTC had its biggest membership year to date—940 members, clinching the title of the largest all-female triathlon club in America. Although membership was down a little from their record-breaking year, they closed 2016 with over 600 members, which is still pretty remarkable. The youngest club member was 13 and the oldest 72. The average age of a typical tri-clubber: 44.

The club succeeded by stripping away the intimidation factor and welcoming women of all ages, shapes, and sizes. The founders worked hard to get rid of the myth that triathletes are size two, 25-years-old, Type A, lifelong Division I athletes. "I think it's the atmosphere of everyone encouraging each other," Maureen says. "There's more compassion than competition in this group." While the club does have some very competitive athletes, most value the friendships and support more than their finishing times. "It's not the athletics; it's the camaraderie, proving you can do something you didn't think you could," Lydia says.

The healthy size of the club has its pros and cons. Having grown so large, the club has lost some of its intimacy, but it's gained much more. "It was nice when it was so small, but now we can reach more people," Lydia says. The club also had the potential to increase its charitable giving. Colleen agrees. "We have more ability to make an impact in our town." For Colleen, empowerment has always been her primary motivation, and she doesn't want to put a cap on how many lives this club can change. She gets so excited when she sees women out jogging that she rolls down her window while driving by to shout encouraging words. If you ever come to Mullica Hill, go for a jog, and hear a random person shouting out, "You're amazing! Keep at it!" it is not a crazy lady. It's just Colleen. She won't rest until every woman who has ever doubted herself believes.

Colleen remembers the husband of one club member pulling her aside to thank her for giving his wife a new lease on life. He told her that his wife's life, his kids' lives, and their entire family had improved exponentially because of the club. "Knowing you impacted people's lives, when you hear them say their life was improved, that's the reward."

There are seven days in a week and someday
isn't one of them.
—UNKNOWN

If I wanted to do a triathlon, I wasn't going to find a better town, or better support system, than I had right now. If you are one to believe there are no coincidences, then having the perfect tri-club right at my doorstep was more than just happenstance.

Maybe triathlon wasn't such a far-fetched goal after all. Could I actually do this? Or, more importantly, was I being purposefully put in its path?

It was all terribly daunting, but I focused on what Maureen said in her speech to the newbies at the Kick Off Meeting: "It's not a race. I don't call it a race. I say that I'm just going to swim, then bike, and then run."

That's all there was to it. Just swim. Just bike. Just run. If I picked one of those activities and just got started, maybe it would break the ice. I just hoped it didn't break *me*.

AGELESS

"Nobody made me feel old."

THE TELEVISION was on in the background when Linda Garrett heard something that caught her attention. It was a casting call for CNN's *Fit Nation*, a segment that would follow a group of triathlon virgins as they trained together to compete with Sanjay Gupta at the star-studded Nautica Malibu Triathlon. Dr. Gupta, a devoted triathlete himself, was inviting triathlon newbies to submit a video explaining why they wanted to join the team and tackle a triathlon. "That looks like fun," Linda thought to herself. Not the typical response of most 67-year-old grandmothers.

Linda was a great many things—wife, mother, grandmother, semiretired school nurse for children with multiple disabilities—but she was not, nor had ever been, an athlete. Sure, she worked out at a local gym and considered herself a healthy, active baby boomer. But swimming, biking, and running in a triathlon? Any of those three sports alone would challenge a first timer, regardless of age. And yet, something about that call for video submissions felt like her own personal call to action.

Acting on a whim, she propped her cell phone up on her kitchen table, spoke into its camera without any plan or rehearsal, and sent her footage off to the producers at CNN before she could second-guess herself. She didn't think about it much after that, handing it all over to the fates without worrying about what she would do if she was chosen for the team.

To Linda's amazement, she was selected as one of six viewers, out of a pool of hundreds, to train with the CNN 2015 Fit Nation Team. At the age of 67, she was the oldest on the team by 23 years. Actually, she was oldest Fit Nation team member they'd ever had since broadcasting the segment in 2009.

"My first thought was excitement," Linda recalls. "My second thought was, 'What did I get myself into?' I'd been working out at a little gym for five years, but I couldn't swim two laps of a pool [and] I'm not a runner at all."

The team had nine months to train for a "Classic Distance" race: .5-mile ocean swim, 18-mile bike ride, and 4-mile run. A challenging distance even for seasoned triathletes. The other challenge? Their entire journey would be filmed—a documentary of all six team members as they trained up until D-Day . . . or T-Day. Every high and low, every humbling experience, every milestone, all broadcast on national television.

Members of the Fit Nation team came from all over the country, but thanks to social media and several scheduled group-training meetups, they created a strong, supportive, and cohesive group. Linda said every team member received personal attention, expert training advice, and a forum to discuss triathlon-related issues. Workouts were emailed by their coach in Atlanta, and Linda never missed a single one.

Swimming was her biggest nemesis. Not only did she feel physically inca-pable, but swimming was also a source of anxiety. By the time the team met up at Laguna Beach for open-water swim practice, she felt confident in the distance but nervous about the ocean. "I'm one of those people in the beach chair with a book by the water," she says. "At Laguna Beach, the waves scared me. . . . My fear is not being able to breathe." Anxiety got the best of her, and she experienced a significant setback. But Linda was determined, so she found an open-water swim coach and worked to get over those fears.

Like most triathletes, Linda had a sweet spot: "Biking was a joy," she says. She learned a great deal on the 8:30 a.m. Sunday morning rides with the Mullica Hill Women's Tri Club. There, she mastered shifting, road etiquette, and other biking techniques and tips.

Running, however, was the opposite of her sweet spot. Under the best of circumstances, she referred to her running as a "slog," or slow jog. Running became an even greater challenge after she tore her meniscus during training, which required surgery. As if that wasn't enough, she also suffered a bout of shingles. And, did I mention she has asthma? Oh, let's not forget that she's almost 68 years old! Yeah, I think I hear the *Wonder Woman* theme song playing in my head right now.

Linda followed her training programs to the letter and showed tremendous determination and fight. The CNN Fit Nation Team gave her all the emotional tools for success, too. "There is so much support, encouragement, and love wrapped around our team. . . . We were not competing *against* each other," Linda says of her teammates, who are now her friends. "Nobody made me feel old. It means so much to not be judged on the basis of what people think you can and can't do."

September 20 was a warm, clear day in Malibu, and Poseidon graced the racers with calm, clear seas. "I was ready, and I knew I could do it," Linda says. She swam, biked, and "slogged" her way to the finish line of her first triathlon. She came in third in her age group (65–69 years). "Guess I should mention that there were only three of us!" she confesses.

When I asked Linda if she caught the tri-bug after crossing the finish line, she paused to reflect. "I absolutely enjoyed it. It was exhilarating. It was wonderful . . . but I will not run again." Linda says she wants to keep her knees for a long time, and running just isn't going to let her do that. But she hasn't opted out. In fact, she continues to swim regularly and plans to do a 1-mile openwater swim in the near future. She will also bike 55 miles for the Cancer Society's City to Shore bike ride. Last year, she did 32 miles of it with her son and grandson, both of whom are planning to join her again.

"I am not and never have been a natural athlete, but I am actually feeling like I am an athlete," Linda says. "I thought I knew myself, but this journey is like no other and I'm discovering more about my healthier self every day."

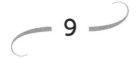

RUN WITH IT

My coach said I run like a girl,
and I said if he ran a little faster, he could too.

—MIA HAMM

After biting the bullet and officially joining the tri-club, I took the first step on my personal fitness journey. I didn't know if it would culminate in a triathlon, but I had to do something to improve my health. My goal was to pick one of the three sports and hope it inspired me to do more. I chose running.

Ah, running. My old nemesis. Given my disdain for the stupid sport, it may seem like an odd choice, but to me, it seemed the lesser of the three evils: least intimidating, least complicated, and least expensive. Sure, I hated it, but running and I had a history, fraught as it may have been with emotional conflict. I ran track and cross-country from age 11 to 15, mostly by default because I sucked at everything else. Though I hadn't run since then, I suppose it felt familiar.

The other reason I chose to start my journey with running was that it wasn't some crazy, difficult thing to execute. No need to learn how to shift gears or change a flat tire. No need to learn the technicalities of a swim stroke. You just *ran*. Finally, it was a minimal financial investment compared to the other two sports. All I had to do was lace up the sneakers I got at Target for $20 circa 1999, pop on an old T-shirt, and go. No huge investment, no sophisticated equipment, no bathing suits in public. How easy is that?

> *Work finally begins when the fear of doing nothing at all*
> *trumps the terror of doing it badly.*
> —ALAIN DE BOTTON

To be precise, I didn't actually start with running. I started with *walking*, because that's how out of shape I was. For two weeks, I peeled myself out of bed at 5:45 a.m. tired, cold, and grumpy, and went on a brisk "power walk." By week three, I ventured out on my first short and breathless run through the flat roads of the development across the street. The route was barely a half-mile, and I slowly jogged that simple loop every other day for one week, walking on the alternate days to work out my tight quadriceps and aching shins. Then, I finally embarked on my first significant run.

Nervously, I ventured onto the hilly streets outside the flat, carless development with my expectations set super low. But when I realized that I ran an entire mile without stopping—something I hadn't thought I could do without collapsing—I felt victorious. I talked about this monumental run for an awkwardly long period of time, ate three times the amount of calories I burned just because I felt badass, and obsessed about my *next* run. Suddenly I was inspired by the idea that maybe I could run further than I thought, sooner than I imagined, and faster than I predicted. Maybe I was stronger than I realized.

As I continued regular runs three times a week, upping my distance by a half mile each Sunday, something strange started happening. I was getting hooked. No one was more amazed by this than I. Next thing I knew, I was reading running articles, printing out a training plan for a 5K, and purchasing better running gear. I learned about wicking and body glide and cushioned running socks. I even got fitted for a pair of real running shoes from a real running store.

When driving past runners, I felt a peculiar urge to jump out of my minivan and join them. I would hear songs on the radio and imagine myself running to them. I reported my dropping times and increasing mileage to my husband in excruciating detail, and God bless him, he pretended to care. I even found myself envious of the sales girl at the running store who had lost multiple toenails while training for a marathon. That seemed so hard-core, and I hoped I would be cool and toenail-less one day. Yes, I was morphing into one of those people who talked about running constantly, boring people with stories that were exciting to no one but me.

Well, not everyone was bored with my stories. Running had become huge in our town since the tri-club throttled up, so I could always find some interested listeners who shared my enthusiasm. But it wasn't just happening in my town. Running was pretty darn huge *everywhere*. Turns out, I had just arrived late to the party.

> *The most effective way to do it, is to do it.*
> —AMELIA EARHART

REASONS TO RUN

Americans love to run. While other sports go in and out of fashion, our love affair with running endures. However, one thing has definitely changed over the decades—the gender composition. When it comes to the widely popular sport of running, females are undoubtedly running the show. There are approximately 42 million runners in the United States, and *over half* are female. In 1990, only 25 percent of footrace participants were female. In 2015, 59 percent of 5K finishers, 61 percent of half-marathon finishers, and 44 percent of marathon finishers were women. More than 17.1 million runners participated in some type of footrace in 2015—roughly 7 million men and *9.7 million women!*

Despite my preconceived notions of the typical "core runner," it is not a 20-something guy with a lanky build and zero body fat who runs marathons every other week. Today's core runner is described as a 39-year-old married woman who runs about 20 miles per week. And the most prevalent age group of runners? Women between the ages of 35 and 49. At the age of 44, I guess I wasn't such an "old" runner, after all.

Debbie K. didn't start running until the age of 50 while training to do her first sprint triathlon. "I fell in love with it," she says. "It has given me life adventures I otherwise would not have had." Krissy B. started running at 35 as a way to find herself again. "I was a stay-at-home mom who was starting to lose her identity. I was so wrapped up in all things 'kids' that I forgot who I was or where I was going. . . . The only way I could get true 'me time' was to go for a run." Marie P. began running at 45. She had never run a step in her entire life. "I started out a walker, but one day I just decided to try running," she says. "Now, I love it and I feel great." Why are so many women taking to running in their 30s, 40s, and 50s? Could it be that our metabolism has slowed and we need a way to burn more calories? Are we more motivated because of our increased maturity? More disciplined? Prompted by the existential angst associated with our inevitable mortality? Trying to carve out time away from work and family to save our sanity? Looking to reinvent ourselves after a period of stagnation? For me, it was all of the above.

Many runners are motivated by setting goals and creating fun new challenges. In fact, approximately 25 percent of people who participate in endurance racing do so for the challenge. Only 10 percent of endurance sports participants surveyed fit the profile of the "hard-core athlete." Most fall into the "average athlete" category, a group motivated by personal fitness goals rather than wins in competition. That's how Jennifer F. describes herself. "I'm not fast by any means, but I just love getting out there," she says. "Running clears my head and makes me happy."

Fitness and weight control are wonderful byproducts of running, and are often a factor in picking up the sport. "I was never a runner and never thought I could run when I was younger because I had asthma," says Sarah F. "After I had my son, I was overweight and having a hard time dieting and losing weight." Then she started running. "I have lost over 40 pounds, improved my overall health, increased my energy level, improved my self-esteem, and inspired friends and family to start running."

Running is one of the oldest aerobic activities on the planet and an excellent cardiovascular workout. A runner's heart beats about 36,000 times *less often* per day than the heart of a non-runner. Fewer beats means less cardiac exertion, which translates to less wear and tear on the heart. Cardio also keeps that heart strong and efficient, allowing the arteries to stay open and elastic and the blood to flow easily. You get the added bonus of burning calories at a decent clip too, about 100 calories per mile (for a 150-pound person). While walking also burns 100 calories per mile, it takes up to twice as long to cover the same distance at that pace. Therefore, when it comes to calories burned, running will give you the same results in less time.

Running also increases your resting metabolism, which means you burn more calories when you're at rest (provided you're not at rest with a bag of cookies in your lap). Furthermore, jogging a total of just 3–6 miles per week has been found to correlate with lower weight and reduced risk of high blood pressure, diabetes, stroke, arthritis, and cholesterol-related health issues.

Running long and hard is an ideal antidepressant, since it's hard to run and feel sorry for yourself at the same time.
—MONTE DAVIS

CHEAPER THAN THERAPY

The benefits of running go beyond the physical. For some, running is a cathartic, healing experience.

"I had never run a day in my life," says Beth G. But the year she turned 40, tragedy struck when her nephew died suddenly. "At first, I dealt with my grief by eating," she says. "I weighed more than I ever did post-kids. . . .

I made excuses. I told myself that it was my metabolism, that I was 40 now, that I just had to live with it." Then came the anxiety attacks and insomnia. At the encouragement of a friend, she joined a gym, and she and a friend walked side by side on the treadmill for 30 minutes regularly. "After two weeks, I found I had the courage to try to run on the treadmill, which is something that I had never tried before."

Beth moved her runs outside, something that caused her anxiety at first, but she overcame it. "I absolutely love waking up early to start my day with a run. I feel so good afterwards, like I can conquer anything!" Beth has done several 5Ks, a 10-mile run, a half-marathon, and five sprint triathlons. Running helped improve her health and served as a much-needed coping mechanism during a dark time. "My life changed," she says. "So, I changed my life."

What is it that makes us feel so good on a run? The release of endorphins, which is often described as a "runner's high," and is a real thing. Endorphins, short for "endogenous morphine," are our body's natural painkiller; a substance resembling morphine produced within our body and released in response to physical pain or discomfort. On a neurochemical level, running also activates the release of serotonin, which is a neurotransmitter implicated in maintaining mood balance.

The other neat thing about running is that if you choose, you can set goals, which resemble personal mile markers. They create celebratory events, dotting the winding path of life's journey. Months after I began running, I too wanted to set a goal for myself—run my first 5K before turning 45—so I signed up for one. This would be my first race since I was 12, a daunting 32-year hiatus.

RACER GIRL

For me, running in a race made everything seem more legit. You got a T-shirt and a medal and felt like a "real runner." I was also attracted to the 5K because it was cheap and convenient, two of my three favorite "C" words when it comes to racing (chocolate is the third, and really should be offered at more finish lines). As a bonus, my friend Theresa was willing to do it with me. Theresa had started running around the same time as I did, and she had been a runner in her youth just like me. Only she had actually been fast, as in she went to the Penn Relays in Philadelphia. I went to the Penn Relays too, but as a spectator cheering on the qualifying girls from my team.

Theresa was very laid-back about the race, but I was ramped up, waking up repeatedly the night before with a nervous excitement completely disproportional to the event. I already knew I could run a 5K; I was doing it regularly on my weekly runs, and my times had been steadily dropping. But this was a race, damn it! My first race in three decades.

We ran it together, and since Theresa's pace was significantly faster than mine, she kept me going at a good clip. I didn't even mind the struggle because she was such good company. I finished with a time that would end up being my personal record (PR) for several years. Most importantly, I beat the 8-year-old kid in front of me. Barely. It didn't really matter since several kids under the age of 12 kicked my butt.

Pain is temporary, but your finishing time
is posted on the Internet forever.
—UNKNOWN

Around this same time, I was talked into doing an 8K with a group of friends. My finishing time was less than impressive due to a minor but bothersome knee injury, but in racing it, I logged the longest distance I had ever run in my entire life—5.4 miles.

Riding on a wave of unbridled enthusiasm at this achievement, I had a momentary lapse of reason and decided to double my race distance by running the Broad Street 10-mile race.

BROADS TAKE TO THE STREET

The Broad Street 10-miler in Philadelphia was the largest 10-mile race in the nation in 2013 and the second-largest 10-miler in the world (the largest is the Dam tot Damloop in Holland). Broad Street is actually the eighth-largest running race (of all types) in America and it was just a hop over the bridge from me. *Runner's World* named it one of the fastest 10-mile courses, likely because the entire course is not only flat but on a slight downgrade.

The Philadelphia Parks and Recreation Department organized and led the first Broad Street 10-Mile Run in 1980. The finish line was crowded with 1,500 finishers in its inaugural year. It grew in popularity along with the boom in endurance running. In 2011, there were 25,244 finishers (11,080 men and 14,164 women). In 2012, the year I planned to race, they were opening up about 40,000 spots. (The following year they went to a lottery system since the demand was greater than the number of bibs.)

Those MHWTC girls in pink were really the ones to blame for my bold decision to run the longest distance I would ever attempt. About 100 women from the club decided to tackle Broad Street, and I got tangled up in all the excitement. Clearly I was suffering from temporary amnesia from my last race in the city—the early rising, the snarled traffic, the parking problems, the bitter cold temperatures, the porta-potty lines, the stomach-turning nerves, all forgotten. Post-race amnesia is a lot like post-childbirth amnesia. The pain and drama fade into one amorphous, general memory, which is eclipsed by the extraordinary happiness at the end.

When registration opened, I took my shot at securing a spot in this coveted race. There was no guarantee; the race had sold out in four days the year before. This year, runners from all over the country overloaded the website, crippling the system and causing pandemonium. The only thing tougher than running in Broad Street was registering for the damn thing. Somehow, after multiple attempts and intense frustration, I did it. The race sold out in five hours, but I had made it in!

The thrill of gaining access to this popular race faded precipitously once I realized that now the training had to start. Training for 10 miles. With little ones at home with me during the day and a husband who worked long hours, I had to do most of my runs at 5:00 a.m. I began my training in late

February, in the freezing cold and dark. After months of running like this two to three mornings a week, plus a long run early on a Sunday morning, it all started wearing on me. Some mornings I would sit on the edge of the bed lacing up my shoes in the pitch dark and try not to cry from utter exhaustion. I felt chronically tired. Constantly hungry and annoyed too, but mostly tired.

As race day approached, the warmer weather helped. As I successfully bumped up my mileage beyond what I had ever done before, the confidence in my capabilities smoothed out lingering nerves. My final long run of 9 miles the week before the race left no doubt in my mind that I could do it, especially since I completed this run during the weekend of my 20th college reunion. I embarked on an impressively hilly run at 6:30 a.m., following two hours of sleep and without a drop of water in my body or breakfast in my belly. Technically hungover too. For the record, I don't recommend doing this.

The Broad Street run was more than I could have ever hoped. I had a really good run. I never felt like I was going to keel over, never got a cramp or had any discomfort, likely because I didn't push myself beyond a nice, relaxed pace. Running, for me, is about enjoyment, so I tend to choose a pleasurable experience over a fast time. It's not as if I can win, so why make myself vomit over it? Just sayin'.

The route begins at Central High School's Athletic Field at Broad and Somerville in Philadelphia, then runs up the entire length of Broad Street, through Center City Philadelphia, goes around City Hall, and finishes up at the Navy Yard in South Philly. Very scenic, and the best part is the vibe from the crowds lining the streets. You can't go more than a quarter of a mile without seeing people cheering and street musicians jamming. I had a smile on my face the entire run, which was sort of goofy because smiling when you're running alone in a crowd of strangers is a little weird.

But even though I had a good race and didn't push myself and was smiling, I'm not going to lie. By mile 6, I definitely felt the lactic acid filling my legs. My feet were going numb and tingly from the incessant pounding. By mile 8, my body's needle was approaching empty. As I burned through my storage of calories (I had neglected to bring any nutrition), I felt myself hitting a wall. But when I started fading, my mind kicked in. It's true what they say—running is 99 percent mental.

Sometimes my mind is my worst enemy, but during this race, I endeavored to make it my best friend and biggest ally. My mind suggested that I think about all the people around me, all of whom had stories to tell. Pondering their motivations, as well as my own, was all the encouragement (and distraction) I needed. With 2 miles to go, I found the new gear I was looking for. My pace quickened, my will steeled, and my joy took flight. I also had to pee. The upside of that was that it probably made me run a little faster. I kept picturing a shiny golden porta-potty waiting for me at the finish line. I'm not kidding.

My goal had been to run Broad Street between a 1:35:00 and a 1:40:00, and I ran a 1:35:58. That time put me in the top 40 percent of 38,068 finishers, which meant that technically I could no longer say that I was in the middle of the pack. Sure, some of my friends ran it much faster and were already enjoying a celebratory beer at the local sports bar before I was even finished. But I have never felt so proud of myself. I was proud of myself for setting a goal, sticking to a training schedule, and running on those cold, dark winter mornings when all I wanted to do was pull the covers over my head and cuddle with my husband. My body felt spent but strong. My soul felt even stronger.

When I arrived home, Anthony was sitting on the back steps of our house waiting for me. He had been receiving text updates about my times courtesy of the computer chip in my race bib and had a huge smile on his face as I walked up the driveway. He was proud of me, and that made me happy. The rest of the day I thought about how I just ran 10 miles, and it also made me happy. And Monday morning when I took my 3-year-old to dance class, I thought, "I ran 10 miles yesterday," and it still made me happy. Never in my wildest dreams would I have ever thought that running 10 miles would make so darn happy.

*That's the thing about running; your greatest runs are rarely
measured by racing success. They are moments in time
when running allows you to see how wonderful your life is.*
—KARA GOUCHER

The first step on my personal fitness journey was complete. Though I still considered myself a novice, I now felt comfortable calling myself a runner. Not a fast one, not a decorated one, not a hard-core, seasoned, ultradistance one. But I was a runner.

Could I possibly be a triathlete too?

For many people, running often leads to other athletic ventures. I suppose that's why running is called a gateway sport. According to a survey conducted by *A Triathlete's Diary Blog*, 65 percent of triathletes started out as runners. So apparently, we start out running and then either get bored, injured, or confident and try other things. Things such as triathlon. So, if the gateway to triathlon was running, I was all set, right?

Well, unfortunately, my gate seemed to be busted.

RUN TO REMEMBER

"The steps to running literally and metaphorically
are shared steps."

LISA HALLETT stood on the shore, moments from starting her very first triathlon. This 33-year-old mother of three was filled with fears and emotion. She was scared of open-water swimming and nervous on the bike. Yet, there she stood ready to take the first step of a 140.6-mile journey. Yes, you read that right. Lisa's very first triathlon was a full Ironman. Go big or go home.

But before she could even begin the race, there was something she had to do. She needed to tell someone, anyone, her reason for racing before she headed out into that water. She needed to speak those words before moving forward. For three years, Lisa had been moving forward with courage and grace after a life-shattering tragedy. With every step forward, she remembered what she had lost . . . whom she had lost. With every step forward, she healed.

Lisa grabbed the closest person to her and told him her story. She told him about John.

❧

On August 25, 2009, Lisa Hallett's dream life turned into a walking nightmare when she received notification that her husband, best friend, and father of her three young children was killed in southern Afghanistan only six weeks after being deployed. Their youngest daughter, only three weeks old, was born right after John's deployment. He had never even held her.

ॐ

Lisa and John met and began dating in college. When he went off to Ranger School, Lisa wanted to give herself a challenge, too. So she signed up to run her first marathon with Team in Training. "I love running. It's part of my soul," she says. "I'd always run as a child, not competitively, but I was always running." That feeling of accomplishment when she finished her first marathon solidified her love of endurance running. More importantly, it became a tool that helped her stay grounded through life's ups and downs.

"Military life is full of challenges," Lisa explains. From managing long-distance relationships to trying to make friends in new towns, there are many twists and turns to navigate. "[Running] builds confidence to take on challenges of everyday life." Whenever they relocated, Lisa would sign up to run a marathon, meeting new people and quickly creating a community for herself

In November 2008 John took company command of an infantry Stryker unit and the following summer was deployed with his brigade to Afghanistan. Three weeks after he left, their third child was born. Lisa was able to speak with him via phone for the first time since he had left. Neither of them knew it would be the last.

A few weeks later, John was delivering medicine to a village suffering from a cholera outbreak when his Stryker was attacked with explosives. Devastated to her core and stuck in limbo waiting for his body to be flown back to the United States and autopsied before she could have the closure of burying him, Lisa turned to the one constant in her life. The one thing that had seen her through many difficult times: running.

Running was a companion, a coping mechanism, a release, and a way to connect with others. She built friendships through running. She could decompress through running. She could remind herself of her inner strength through running. She needed running in her life now, more than ever.

Running, for Lisa, was something that grounded her. "I'm fantastically chaotic," she says. Now, life was chaotic beyond anything she could ever imagine. "My draw to running is to give me that structure." So, two days after receiving the news of John's death, Lisa said, "I've got to run." She was only a few weeks postpartum, technically a little soon to be running, but that was the least of anyone's concerns.

On this slow, short run Lisa finally found the space and time to get in touch with her grief. "I'm in Washington and it rains, like, 300 days a year. But the year [my daughter] is born, it's sunny," recalls Lisa. "The sun is shining, it's glorious . . . and I was *so angry*. I thought, how dare you shine so beautifully when my world is so dark right now! That was the first time I could feel."

In the months that followed, Lisa did everything she could to stay strong for her three children. "They've lost their Dad to war. They can't lose their mother to grief. I had to measure my grief." One of the ways she did this was through running. "I got really into this endurance racing. . . . The distance was what I needed to escape the chaos of my life."

But she wasn't running away from her grief; she was running straight into the heart of it. "Running was my lifeline," she says. The more miles she ran, the more layers she could shed and the more deeply she could process the depth of her sorrow and work her way back up to the surface. It gave her that time to feel and to heal. The first few miles she ran, Lisa's mind busied itself with practical things as she extracted herself from the hamster wheel of all she had to do that day. By mile 4, she started to separate herself from the world around her and process her emotions in the quiet of her mind. Then, if she ran long enough, she would hit the wall and dig deep to get through. Finding that inner fortitude in each long, hard run reminded her of her inner strength. "It's that unfiltered breath. That weight was gone." The greatest part of all? On every run, she remembered John.

It wasn't long before Lisa had an epiphany. What if she paired the power of a good, long, healing run with a greater purpose? "I knew what running did for me. I knew what a powerful coping strategy it was," Lisa says. She was surrounded by a community of women who also understood the healing power of running, the strength it gave, and the bonds it created. Before she knew it, the concept for *wear blue: run to remember* was born.

In February 2010, Lisa and fellow military wife and friend Erin O'Connor cofounded *wear blue: run to remember*. This national running community honors the service and sacrifice of the US military, bridges the gap between the military and civilian communities, and creates a living memorial to the fallen. Organized weekly runs are held in four large, active chapters. In addition, dozens of informal running groups (that Lisa refers to as "meetups") are held around the country. Each of the four chapters feed into a popular race, such as the Rock 'n' Roll Marathon Series, the Army Ten-Miler, or the Marine Corps Marathon. At those races, *wear blue: run to remember* sets up a tribute mile, lining both sides of the course with pictures of fallen heroes and a row of flags held by their loved ones. "It's a life-affirming memorial," Lisa says, and it's considered the most powerful and touching mile of these races.

Before every *wear blue* run, a Circle of Remembrance is held where runners stand quietly in a circle and call out the name of the person they lost. Every step they take on that run evokes their loved one's memory so that person lives on in the present. "They become a part of the power that makes today's steps more purposeful," Lisa explains.

Lisa completed several more marathons, a double marathon, and five ultramarathons. But when she developed a nagging overuse injury, she was forced to take a break from her beloved sport. She wasn't down for the count, though. "I needed to cross-train so I could do something physical," Lisa says. Her friend Elizabeth was a triathlete and suggested biking. After they biked together for a while, Elizabeth suggested trying an Ironman. Lisa just laughed. "Are you kidding me? One, I could die and two, I'm a runner," she told her friend. Lisa couldn't even put her face in the lake, let alone swim over 2 miles in it. She was also a nervous cyclist. But then, something convinced her. It wasn't Elizabeth. It wasn't competitiveness. It was the date of the race.

The Ironman Canada in Whistler was being held on August 25, 2012. That date marked the three-year anniversary of John's death. "I signed up. I never did a triathlon in my life," she says.

No triathlon experience? Not a swimmer? Afraid of open waters and cycling? Trying to train while working and raising three small children alone? Minor details. She hired a great coach and started training, and on race day she felt physically ready.

"I stood at the starting line, terrified," Lisa remembers. Once the swim started, true panic took hold. But Lisa had survived tough things before, and she tapped into the power of her mind. "With each stroke, I'm saying the name of someone who loves me and wants me to succeed. Each of these people, I'm deriving so much strength from them." Buoyed by this strength, she began to truly enjoy herself. "I'm shockingly disappointed when the swim comes to an end," she laughs. She made it through the bike ride, and when she got to the run, she was finally in her comfort zone.

Lisa Hallett crossed the finish line well under the 17-hour cut off. "My very first Ironman was magical," she says. So magical that in June 2013 she did a second one at Coeur d'Alene. There, her story caught the attention of David Deschenes, executive director of the Ironman Foundation. Before she knew it, she was receiving an invitation to compete in the 2014 Ironman Kona as a special interest athlete.

"It was amazing exposure to be a 'back of the pack' athlete competing at the Super Bowl of triathlon. Where else can your everyday athlete compete in the same race with the elites? It's inspiring." But Lisa admits that Kona was a little more nerve-wracking than her previous Ironman races. It was her first ocean swim, which scared her. "I showed up to Kona and I didn't know what I was doing," she laughs. "I was a train wreck!" As a featured athlete, she had cameras filming her for national television, which added pressure. While Lisa feels embarrassed about having her helmet too high—what she calls a "rookie mistake"—it was her heartfelt humanness and quiet courage that endeared her to millions of viewers. Lisa Hallett's story and her organization, *wear blue: run to remember*, was featured on NBC. Viewers connected with her, and they adored her.

Wear blue: run to remember has grown in scope and reach since 2010. There are currently 15,000 runners and 50 organized, active running communities meeting on a regular basis. The three anchor chapters in DuPont, Washington; Fort Bragg, North Carolina; and Springfield, Virginia, hold group runs once a week. There are also the meetup communities, fingers of the major chapters, that hold runs on a more informal basis.

"I [don't] want to be part of a widow's group. I identify myself as a military spouse," Lisa says. As such, she feels a deep sense of commitment to aiding that community. "I need to see our military families move forward. . . . The steps to running literally and metaphorically are shared steps."

Lisa doesn't run to forget. She runs to always remember. She runs to remember John and the many men and women who gave the ultimate sacrifice for us, for our country, for our freedom. She encourages others to do the same. "Make your steps purposeful," she says. "Create a sea of blue to show people their loved ones are not forgotten."

10

TRI GIRLS AREN'T CHEAP DATES

I have money to last me the rest of my life,
unless I buy something.

—JACKIE MASON

Running was supposed to lead me down the yellow brick road to my first triathlon. It would condition my body, improve my cardiovascular ability, and, most importantly, build my confidence. I convinced myself that I was training for one leg of the triathlon and eventually I'd add the other disciplines. Then I'd do the MHWTC's Queen of the Hill triathlon once—and only once—not for bragging rights, or bucket lists, or fitting in, or some great sense of inner satisfaction. I would do it simply to understand why women became so hooked. That was the deal I made with myself. I would do it for the book. I was sacrificing myself in the interest of research. That was the plan.

The running part was working out great, and the writing was going well. The problem was that after 18 months of training for this triathlon's final leg, I still hadn't touched a pool or a bike. I didn't have the time. I didn't own a bike. I couldn't justify spending a thousand bucks to buy a bike. I didn't know how to swim properly. I felt self-conscious in a bathing suit.

I felt stupid around people who knew what they were doing. I needed to be in better physical shape. My kids were still little. Two of the four were not yet in school all day. My husband worked 70-hour weeks. I had little to no help with child care. The list of excuses went on and on.

Add to that list the unique drama that comes with having a special needs child. The daily care and supervision needs of my eldest daughter were high. Unfortunately, at this time her seizures were spiraling out of control, and she had started wearing a scoliosis brace 18 hours a day. In addition, my 4-year-old was diagnosed with a speech disorder, so I was carting her to private speech therapy twice a week. I was also doing freelance writing and consulting, so I'd often be under the gun with deadlines. I was bogged down and overwhelmed enough and didn't need to add more anxiety-provoking things to the mix.

But why was I focusing on excuses and rationalizations while others focused on solutions and inspiration? Anyone can come up with 101 realistic reasons for avoiding triathlon training. That's easy. But I knew that other women were facing similar trials and tribulations, many even more challenging than mine. Yet, they still found a way to train and race, while I continued to justify my avoidance. They were unwittingly foiling me.

I had to face the fact that my triathlon excuses were a flimsy curtain behind which stood the truth. I needed to figure it out, break free from what was *really* holding me back, and move beyond it. If I could clear out some space for a little self-examination and isolate my fears and doubts, I knew I could conquer them.

It wasn't rocket science to sort my pile of excuses into three general categories: money, guilt, and fear. Actually, the expense of doing triathlon bled into all three categories.

> *You can quit and no one will really care . . .*
> *but you will always know.*
> —JOHN COLLINS

Triathlons are not for the faint of heart nor the miserly of wallet. My first challenge was to avoid going into severe sticker shock at the number of dollar signs attached to this sport. Why the problem with spending money? In a word, I'm a cheapskate. Put it this way: I could be a billionaire, and I'd still whine about paying $12.00 for a pair of running socks. I think outlets are too expensive. I made my own wedding veil because I couldn't believe what they were charging at the bridal shops. I seldom buy anything without a red markdown tag. While others brag about how much they spent at Saks, I can't shut up about how much I've saved at Sears.

Part of this thriftiness comes from being broke during most of my adult life. At first, it was part of the adventure of young adulthood, but then it started getting old. When Carlie was born, her dad and I were fresh out of college with barely two nickels to our name. Creative use of milk crates as bookcases, bargain basement furniture, hand-me-downs, and yard sale finds helped us decorate our tiny rentals.

When we divorced and I became a single working mom, it really sucked. It was a hand-to-mouth, paycheck-to-paycheck situation that caused a significant amount of stress. You know, like eating a can of beans for dinner, sleeping on a mattress on the floor, selling your crap at the pawnshop for rent money, and other fun stuff like that. I know it probably built character, but it also left a deep impression.

After Anthony and I married, we didn't skyrocket to financial security overnight, but rather worked our way up the ladder slowly, rung by rung. We went from two 30-something recent doctoral graduates, with $200,000 in collective student loan debt, to a very comfortable place in life. At first, we did this by having five jobs between us and saving aggressively. When our third daughter was born, we relocated to southern New Jersey and found ourselves financially secure enough for me to leave the workforce and become a stay-at-home mom. That right there? *That* was the moment. I trace my spending guilt to that moment when I stopped contributing monetarily to the household.

This frugality was certainly going to be challenged in the face of tri-athlon, but I felt confident that it was something I could reconcile. Hey, if I could find my daughter a sweet Barbie dollhouse marked down from $125.00 to $38.00, I knew I could find a way to tri on the cheap.

*Think of yourself as an athlete. I guarantee you it will
change the way you walk, the way you work, and the decisions
you make about leadership, teamwork, and success.*
—MARIAH BURTON NELSON

FEE FOR ADMISSION

Triathlon has a reputation of being a sport most people can't afford. The financial investment of triathlon, even at the recreational level, keeps it a sport for those with discretionary income. The average annual house-hold income of a typical triathlete ranges from $126,000 to $174,000. Make it an Ironman, and the average household income jumps to around $247,000, as reported by the World Triathlon Corporation's 2015 survey. Of course, over time these numbers will change but one thing remains true. As a whole, triathletes are typically "highly professional and advanced socioeconomically."

The estimated investment of an average recreational triathlete ranges from $1,500 per year up to $4,800. Why so pricey? Roll three sports up in one, and you've tripled the cost right out of the gate. I have the same expe-rience signing my three kids up for soccer or buying water park tickets. Youth soccer and water parks have nothing on triathlon, though.

MAKING AN INVESTMENT

Nicole, author of the blog *Fitness Fatale*, documented in detail both the start-up and ongoing costs of her new triathlon hobby. As a newbie train-ing for her first sprint triathlon she borrowed a bike and purchased only the bare essentials, scoring at sales and using gift cards along the way.

As a fellow beginner triathlete, I identified with her frugality and tracked her progress, figuring her total expenditures would be a good barometer for me.

Nicole estimated her related equipment and gear to be about $1,000 (which excluded an eventual bike purchase). She spent another $1,300 on race registrations and her USAT membership. Now we're at $2,300—not an unreasonable investment in a hobby or recreational activity.

Of course, her story didn't end there because, as you might expect, Nicole became hooked on triathlon. Upon taking the sport more seriously, she invested in a higher-quality road bike, which retailed for $2,800 (though she got it for just under $2,000). And then there was the bike fitting, an upgraded saddle, a cassette, and a chain, which increased the cost of that $2,000 bike to $2,450. After a few more odds and ends, high-quality sunglasses, cycling jerseys, and gloves, her biking expenses totaled $2,800. Add that $2,800 to the original $2,300 and her total cost hovered around five grand. A decent chunk of money, but people spend more on a family trip to Disney or a new pair of boobs.

Ah, but then Nicole took the leap into training for an Ironman, and the cost of her hobby increased exponentially. There was the race fee, hotel and airfare, bike transportation, apparel, and a Garmin watch, all of which had large price tags. She estimated the cost of becoming an Ironman at around $4,500, making her *total* investment in triathlon $9,623 in a single year. That is a few new pairs of boobs.

Of course, this is just one woman who decided to do an Ironman-distance race. Not every triathlete will go to that extreme. Nevertheless, you can imagine how those dollar signs rattled someone like me. I reminded myself that I was not tackling an Ironman distance, just one local, reasonably priced sprint tri, which involved no travel and no pressure for super-high-tech gear. All I needed were the basic necessities. The brass tacks. The bare-bones. I just needed to figure out what the basics were and create an itemized breakdown. Then, I could choose what made sense for me and my budget.

CHA-CHING
The Bike

The biggest upfront expense in triathlon is, hands down, the bike. If you already have one, inherit one, or score one at a sweet deal, you are fortunate indeed. Even then, you will need to invest in a proper bike fitting, and likely a few modifications, so that "free bike" isn't really totally free. And I warn you, if you start loving the sport and want to do more than one, I guarantee that at some point you will want to upgrade.

What's especially enticing about the bike is that it's an area in triathlon where you can buy some speed. I don't mean this in a bad way. Cycling involves strength and technique, supplied by the human being who trains smart and works hard. However, all the muscle and training in the world can't change one important factor when it comes to your bike speed. That is wind resistance. The lighter and more aerodynamic the bike, the more you can slice through that wind and minimize drag, and the faster you will go. Period. That can be obtained with a higher-tech (higher-priced) bicycle. Those willing and able to invest in that type of speed machine will shave minutes off their time immediately.

A road bike can cost anywhere from $600 to $13,000. A nice bike for a recreational triathlete will probably fall somewhere between $899 and $1,300. But that's not really the final price.

There are all sorts of upgrades and tweaks to "trick out" your new baby. Some things associated with cycling are mandatory, like a helmet. While a proper bike fitting and regular tune-ups are not mandatory, if you want to avoid injury and keep your bike in tiptop shape, they are generally considered nonnegotiable. Other common upgrades include changing to a more comfortable saddle (bike seat), switching out your pedals, or adding aerobars to achieve that perfect tuck position. These small but important things can start adding up in that expenditure column by the hundreds. Let's not forget that you need a pump to regularly inflate your tires and a fix-a-flat kit just in case. Also, you'll have to get your bike from point A to point B, so you'll need a bike rack on your car, an expense that varies depending upon the number of bikes it holds and whether it's a roof rack or requires you to get a hitch for your car. Just like a newborn infant, your bike will have lots more paraphernalia than you imagined and not come with a manual, so you will benefit from a community of seasoned cyclists who have lots to share.

The Swim

The key thing with swimming is, of course, having a place to swim. Typically, this does not come free. Membership in a gym or community pool is your first investment. Need lessons or coaching? Plan to invest a decent amount of green. Depending on the types of races you select, and the climate where you live, you might decide to purchase a wetsuit. Of course, you need good goggles (not the cheap ones from the dollar store), a swim cap, and a bathing suit that's comfortable for swimming laps (i.e., probably not a skirted tankini or a sexy string bikini). You also might want to pick up training fins, a kickboard, and pull buoys. Overall, swimming costs are considerably lower than cycling costs but will certainly be another investment of several hundred dollars to more than a thousand dollars a year, depending upon your need and desire for coaching or clinics, and your access to a pool.

The Run

Running is the least expensive of the three sports, which was the main reason I started with it, and loved it best. A decent pair of running shoes will cost around $100. That, and a sports bra, is about all that's required. Simplicity at its finest.

Looking the Part

Of course you need *clothes* to wear while you're running, swimming, and biking. You can find inexpensive fitness apparel if you're not one for brand names. And you can certainly get away with owning just a small handful of absolute necessities. What are they? For running, tops made of comfortable and breathable fabrics with wicking are best. It's good to own a few pieces for different weather conditions, such as an assortment of running shorts, capris, and full-length pants, plus a few pairs of decent running socks (believe me, socks make a bigger difference than you think). You could make do with only a few items, but that's a lot of laundry to keep on top of. And anyway, limiting the fitness wardrobe takes some of the fun out of it. This stuff is cute.

If your climate includes four seasons and you plan to run in all of them, then ear warmers, running gloves, and knit hats are a good idea. Sunglasses are a staple because warm or cold, the sun can be bright. They don't have to be $500 designer shades, but they do have to be sport sunglasses (not those big movie-star Chanel knockoffs that make you look great driving around in your minivan but like a stone cold loser trying to run 5 miles). I got mine at Target for a nominal price, but the really nice ones cost more than my wedding band.

And of course, we can't forget the most important piece of apparel of all—a good running bra. Or three, unless you want to root through a stinky pile of laundry every time you head out for a run.

Unfortunately, you can't wear the same stuff you run in when riding the bike. Not only will you look like a complete Wilma, but certain fragile girl parts will suffer the consequences. At least one good, well-padded pair of bicycling shorts is imperative. You may be able to get by on a single pair. But if you fall in love with cycling, you will probably have more bike shorts than you do jeans.

Cycling apparel is not only about looking the part but also about avoiding drag and maintaining safety. For instance, tight-fitting cycling pants keep loose clothing from getting caught in your bike chain. Since real cycling apparel is mainly sold at specialty shops, it's a little harder to find a killer deal.

That's your triathlon training attire, but probably not what you'll wear on race day. Most women invest in a tri-suit. A tri-suit, or "kit," is a one- or two-piece outfit made of a thin, breathable, quick-drying material that you can swim, bike, and run in without worrying about major wardrobe changes. (Yes, you wear your sports bra underneath. No, you don't wear panties.) The kit is as light and fitted as a bathing suit, so it's easy to swim in, the shorts are padded enough to add comfort on the bike, but not too padded for the run, and everything is tightly fitted and dries quickly after the swim.

Tri-suits are not mandatory, but they make life easier and are worth the investment. Some clubs include a team kit with the membership fees. Others, like the MHWTC, keep their membership fees low and offer their pink-and-black team kit at a good price point as an optional purchase. My two-piece tri-suit was about $100. You will definitely find them for higher prices than that, but probably not much lower.

CASHING IN ON THE EXPERIENCE

The cost of earning that finisher's medal goes beyond the blood, sweat, and tears. Race registration alone can cost hundreds, or even thousands, each year. Registration fees vary, depending upon the distance, popularity, and prestige of a race. For instance, a sprint triathlon may cost as little as $50 as or much as $140. Olympic or international distances average about $200 and half-Ironmans, more than $300. Full Ironman-branded races range from $650 to $800. The 2016 Ironman World Championship fee was $890. That is correct, you are *paying* them for your pain and suffering. Non-Ironman-branded long-course triathlons are a little more economical, ranging between $400 and $500.

In addition, everyone who participates in a USAT-sanctioned event must be a USAT member. If you race more than once a year, it's worth it to pay the USAT's annual membership, which is a little less than $50. Or, you can opt to tack on an additional $12 for a single-day license when you register for your race.

Just as we pay a premium for the label on a pair of jeans or a handbag, the more recognizable and prestigious races charge higher ticket prices for admission. The Escape from Alcatraz triathlon held in San Francisco is a perfect example of the correlation between event popularity and price.

This highly coveted race increased its registration fees by $300 in 2016, and it still sold out immediately. Now, to swim from a ferry positioned near Alcatraz Island and across the San Francisco Bay to Marina Green Beach, you will pay $750. Compare this to the average registration fee for running races—$25 for a 5K; $50 for a 10K or half-marathon; $80 for those unique mud, color, and zombie runs; and around $100 for most marathons. But even with footraces, the more prestigious the race, the more you pay. The New York City Marathon will cost you more than $250 and the Walt Disney Princess Half, around $160. Runners would argue that the swag and the unique experience these races offer are more than worth it. I suppose the same holds true for the pricier triathlons.

Of course, registration costs do not include related travel and overnight accommodations. When traveling by air, you're paying to fly both you and your bike, which you must transport in a bike suitcase, another investment of a few hundred dollars. Or, you can rent a bike when you get there. The average triathlete will spend approximately $5,000 per year on triathlon-related travel.

Other Miscellaneous Crap You Realize You Can't Live Without

Naturally, as you fall in love with running, swimming, cycling, or all three, there will be other insidious, miscellaneous items that you want/need. The itemized cost of each won't be much, but it can all add up under your radar: water bottles, visors, race belts, Bondi bands, cell phone arm straps, arm warmers, training books, gels, anti-chafing products, energy drinks and training nutrition, a bag for all your paraphernalia, and various car magnets that let other motorists know how many miles you conquered. Then there are the fancy, expensive gadgets you might start coveting, like a Garmin watch to keep track of your pace, laps, splits, and other things that sound really fancy. Or, you may find yourself in dire need of a bike trainer, a contraption costing a few hundred bucks that turns your road bike into a stationary bike. That way, you can pedal like a maniac all winter long while binge-watching *Downton Abbey*.

Want to join a triathlon club? Membership fees average around $50, though some are over $100 a year particularly if professional coaching is included. Or you can plunk down several hundred dollars and register for a triathlon training camp. Want to improve those race times with a coach? Individual or small-group coaching represents both an emotional and monetary commitment. Prices will vary depending on the type of coaching, the coach's expertise, and your geographic location, but it's safe to say that coaching will cost you at least $1,000 for a period of a few months.

Most of your major triathlon investments are part of your start-up costs, something that accompanies any new endeavor, from a business to a hobby. Ongoing expenses, like race registration fees, associated travel and lodging expenses, bike maintenance, coaching or lessons, and any upgrades or wish-list items you didn't get during your initial purchases will likely be spread out over time and subject to your own discretion.

Checks and Balances

Although triathletes tend to be white-collar professionals with discretionary income, in the sport's defense, it is far from blue-blooded, and you don't have to be a millionaire to partake. Furthermore, it is certainly not the most expensive pastime or hobby out there. The title of the world's most expensive recreational activities belong to sailing, Formula One racing, equestrian sports (particularly dressage), mountain climbing, polo, skydiving, pentathlon, bobsledding, hot air balloon racing, ski jumping, speedboat racing, and wingsuit flying. So, if someone gives you a hard time about the high price of triathlon, just tell them, *Hey, back off. At least I'm not wingsuiting!*

Now, I've tallied a pretty exhaustive list of triathlon expenditures that, on paper, seems a little overwhelming. But, honestly, triathlon doesn't have to break the bank. You are going to drop some cash—I can't sugarcoat that—but it's like buying a car. Are you going to be getting a brand-new, fully loaded Mercedes Benz, or a certified, pre-owned Camry? Both options will meet your needs, but one is more luxury and the other more practical.

Whatever direction you take, it's an investment in your health and that is definitely priceless.

For everything you have missed, you have gained something else, and for everything you gain, you lose something else.
—RALPH WALDO EMERSON

I tried to manage my own spending anxieties by reminding myself I was doing only one local sprint triathlon. I was negating a huge expense by borrowing a bike, and I didn't care that it was a hybrid and didn't fit me right because I wasn't planning on breaking the sound barrier; I was just trying to finish. I was determined to get by on the least amount of paraphernalia possible: tri-suit, club dues, helmet, race fee, and a few pieces of athletic apparel from the clearance rack. I figured it would probably cost less than I spent on wine in a year. I was ready to crack open my wallet with minimal guilt. Then, I almost hyperventilated after spending $100 on four triathlon-related items at a sporting goods store. But when a friend laughed, saying she spent more than that on her helmet alone, I felt a little better.

Still, I was going to leave the tags on everything just in case my chicken became bigger than my brave.

ON FIRE

"You have to fight for yourself."

ON THE MORNING of April 18, 2013, Erin Briggs knew something wasn't right. "I told my husband I did not feel well, but opted to go to work anyway. Once I arrived, I knew I had to leave." For weeks, Erin had felt increasingly irritable and intense. She had also found herself becoming oddly obsessed with the Boston Marathon bombing, disproportional to the empathetic reactions of the general public. She started feeling convinced she was being followed. "By Thursday, I had hallucinations and severe paranoia," she says.

She called her husband and her sister when she left work on April 18; both of them met her at the house, seriously concerned. "By the time I arrived home I was confused and disoriented," she says.

Erin was taken straight to the emergency room, where doctors suspected a stroke. It wasn't. Despite numerous tests, they were unable to determine what was causing her symptoms. Meanwhile, her mental status was quickly deteriorating. "I only remember the first day," she says. "I was acting out. They had to put restraints on me." That's the last day she remembers with clarity. "I have a file as thick as the Bible," she says. This file, along with information told to her by her loved ones, is all she has to go on. After that first day, there is just a black hole of memory loss.

Erin was hospitalized while doctors tried to understand what was going on. "I went through hundreds of tests. The EEGs were abnormal, but the doctors still did not have a diagnosis," she says. "I was catatonic at times and getting progressively worse. I didn't eat. I lost a lot of weight." They found a lesion on her brain. She was having seizures. One doctor diagnosed her with post-traumatic stress disorder. Another diagnosed her with bipolar disorder and started her on psychotropic medication. Her husband knew this was not psychiatric in nature, but no one had any other explanations.

The reality was that Erin was gravely ill with a disease that was attacking her brain, but no one could identify what it was or how to treat it. Her condition remained a mystery until her husband came across the book *Brain on Fire*, a *New York Times* bestseller written by Susannah Cahalan. He watched video excerpts of Susannah talking about what seemed to be her descent into madness but was really a rare type of encephalitis. The similarities between Susannah and Erin were indisputable.

After 18 days of hospitalization, they finally got the answers they were waiting for when a blood sample sent to the Mayo Clinic in Minnesota came back with a diagnosis. "I had a rare autoimmune disease called Anti-NMDA receptor encephalitis," Erin says.

Under normal circumstances, the body produces antibodies to fight against things like viruses or tumors. These antibodies will not attack the host (our own bodies). However, in an autoimmune disease, antibodies are created that *do* attack the host. Anti-NMDA receptor encephalitis occurs when antibodies produced by the body's immune system attack NMDA receptors in the brain. NMDA receptors are proteins that control the electrical impulses of the brain and aid in things like memory, judgment, and human interaction as well as autonomic activities such as breathing and swallowing.

The first symptoms of anti-NMDA receptor encephalitis are flu-like symptoms. Then, it progresses into short-term memory loss, sleep disorders, speech dysfunction, confusion, hallucinations, delusions, and seizures. Vision and hearing may also become impaired. Movement disorders, such as full body spasms, often become so violent and uncontrollable that the individual needs to be restrained. Sometimes catatonia, an unresponsive vegetative state, occurs. The person may slip into a coma and require assistance for breathing. The heart can become severely compromised, which contributes to the mortality rate of the disease.

Because many patients with this condition also have ovarian tumors, they removed Erin's ovaries as a precaution. She began a treatment of steroids and plasmapheresis. "Unfortunately, I continued to decline," she says. Her husband, her champion and tireless advocate, tracked down the doctor who first discovered this disease, and he recommended an alternative course of treatment. She began chemotherapy and immediately showed signs of improvement.

"Eight weeks after I was admitted, I left the hospital and went to an inpatient rehab facility," Erin says. Wheelchair-bound, atrophied, and struggling to communicate, Erin had to relearn how to write, read, walk, talk, and take care of herself again. "I was determined," she says. "I worked hard in rehab. I got stronger and after five weeks was able to come home to my family."

She continued outpatient physical therapy, speech therapy, and occupational therapy for another two months, along with more chemotherapy. Recovery from anti-NMDA receptor encephalitis is generally slow, taking months to years, and is marked by many ups and downs and sometimes even a reemergence of symptoms. Some never recover completely. But Erin had a goal to work toward. "While I was recovering, I decided that I would join the tri-club and complete a triathlon."

Erin was not a triathlete. She had started running in her 30s and participated in some local races. Although she had many friends in the Mullica Hill Women's Tri Club and followed the club on Facebook, she felt too intimidated by the sport and never joined.

After going through hell and back, her perspective shifted: "It gave me that courage." But she had been in a hospital bed for weeks. "I lost a lot of muscle," Erin says. "I was also terrified of the swimming."

In February, Erin and a group of friends attended the MHWTC Kick Off Meeting, and she left feeling inspired. Her friends, eager to support her goal, worked with her tirelessly in the pool and on the bike.

On June 28, 2014, Erin was as ready as she could be for the Queen of the Hill. Her brain had been on fire. Her body had been starved and ravaged by steroids and chemotherapy. Her ovaries had been removed, and she had to relearn how to walk and talk and care for herself. But she had survived an ordeal that could have killed her. She could certainly survive a triathlon.

At the beginning of the race, Erin struggled. "I panicked halfway through the swim. I almost gave up. But with the help of an amazing swim angel, I kept going. It was not easy and that last mile was very emotional for me as I recalled all that I had been through over the past year." Nevertheless, after 1 hour and 47 minutes, Erin crossed the finish line. A good friend, who had finished before her, ran back on the racecourse to meet Erin and run with her down the homestretch. She will never forget that moment, a declaration of her own strength coupled with the power of true friendship. "It's one of my greatest accomplishments physically and mentally. I had never really done anything like that in my life!"

In doing a triathlon, Erin was sending a message of strength not only to herself but also to her two daughters, ages 13 and 16, who endured the dark and uncertain time of their mother's serious illness and long recovery. "You have to fight for yourself," Erin says. "My kids needed to see that."

"It is a fatal condition," explains Erin, knowing she was one of the lucky ones. Relapse is a reality, occurring in up to 25 percent of those diagnosed. Erin continues to struggle with side effects of both her illness and the aggressive treatment. Fatigue is an unfortunate side effect, as is an accelerated heart rate. But Erin chooses to focus on the amazing future ahead of her and the strength she gained from all she endured.

"Nobody thought I'd be able to do [a triathlon] nine months out of rehab," she says. "I'm still not 100 percent, and I'm not sure I will ever be, but I do know that completing the triathlon was a huge step in my recovery."

11

SWIM, BIKE, RUN . . . DIVORCE?

If you're in a relationship,
you're not training hard enough.

—UNKNOWN

Although I knew my husband was immensely supportive of my triathlon adventure, I still felt guilty about the amount of time, money, and emotional resources I would need to devote to this endeavor. The media were not making me feel any better. Psychologist and triathlete Dr. Pete Simon coined the phrase "Divorce by Triathlon" in a blog post that kickstarted a larger conversation. Since then, several articles have been written about the stress and strain triathlon can cause in a relationship, including a much-circulated *Wall Street Journal* article entitled, "A Workout Ate My Marriage." Triathlon-related issues, once debated between couples privately, were now sweating it out in the spotlight.

Research on triathletes and their relationships is concerning, and rather debasing. Triathletes have been described in the literature as selfish and self-centered, with "compromised social lives" due to the intensive time demands of training. Ouch.

I wasn't a triathlete yet, but this wasn't talking me into it.

I wasn't worried my husband would leave me because I was doing a triathlon, or that it would be a point of contention. In truth, he seemed quite happy I was doing it. Much happier about it than I, in fact. But still, I knew my training would eat away at the limited free time I had with him, and impact the amount of time and attention I gave to the kids and the household. Everyone's life would alter a little because of my personal endeavors. I definitely struggled with the mere *thought* of it all. How would I actually do this without feeling like a horrible wife and mother?

I knew that if I were to proceed with the training regimen necessary for a triathlon, I had to come to terms with all this guilt.

> *It's not selfish to love yourself, take care of yourself,*
> *and to make your happiness a priority. It's necessary.*
> —MANDY HALE

According to data from the USAT, approximately 25 percent of members are single, widowed, or divorced. That means the other 75 percent are married or in a committed relationship. What that *also* means is that 75 percent of triathletes need to balance the person they love with the sport they love. In committed relationships, with or without children, domestic responsibilities will shift, and time spent together is sacrificed when triathlon enters the picture. But, if you think about it, that can occur in any situation. Relationships are full of negotiation and compromise, and triathlon is just one of a zillion things that can either rip couples apart or draw them closer together.

A TALE OF TWO TRIATHLONS

"When asked how I can do [triathlons] . . . my reasons always start with Greg," says Pamela P., a 39-year-old wife, mother, teacher, and Ironman. Her husband, Greg, is her biggest fan, and she gives him full credit for making her triathlon dreams a reality. "He is not an athlete himself, but I think his support and the work he does with our family to keep the dream alive elevates him to an entirely different level," she says. "He even makes sure the kids are at just about every race. Yes, he's that good. I would shout it from the rooftops if I could!"

When Heather M. fell in love with triathlon, her confidence skyrocketed, and her social circle expanded. But her husband wasn't feeling the triathlon love. "He started to get so angry," she says. "He felt like I was addicted to exercise and triathlon." Heather admits that triathlon training gave her an outlet, an escape from a marriage that she describes as deeply troubled, long before triathlon entered the picture. "I felt if I could find a way to be happy—if I could pour myself into triathlon—then I could survive," she says. Heather remembers one race when she crossed the finish line expecting to see him there waiting with the kids, as he'd promised. They were nowhere to be found. He never came. "I started to cry. I thought, *You don't even show up for me.*" They have since divorced.

Dr. Benjamin Caldwell, a Los Angeles–based licensed marriage and family therapist and author of *Saving Psychotherapy: How Therapy Can Bring the Talking Cure Back from the Brink,* has worked with many couples involved in triathlon. "It's not at all unusual for couples to struggle with this," Dr. Caldwell says. He himself is a six-time Ironman finisher with several half-Ironman finishes and more than 40 marathons on his race card. So when it comes to helping couples negotiate triathlon in their relationship, Dr. Caldwell has the unique experience of seeing it from both a professional and personal perspective. "I have firsthand experience in negotiating the difficult balance between family, work, and sport," he says. "I haven't always been successful at it, but I've learned a lot along the way."

Dr. Caldwell understands how a new triathlon hobby can feel like the third wheel on a date, the uninvited houseguest who just crashed your pad and ate all the food in the fridge, or even like a clandestine romance. This is especially true when only one person is obsessed with this new and time-consuming hobby. When researchers Matthew Lamont, Millicent Kennelly, and Erica Wilson investigated the impact of triathlon on relationships, they found varying degrees of strain. However, the couples reporting the most strain were those in which only one person was involved in the sport.

"Any time one partner in a relationship takes up a new activity, it can create problems. But triathlon poses a uniquely threatening combination of factors for a lot of relationships. It's expensive, which can breed resentment, [and] it is time-consuming, especially at longer distances, limiting the time that the triathlete may have for other responsibilities," Dr. Caldwell explains. If the triathlete is more solitary, his or her partner may feel shut out and inept at knowing how to offer support. If the triathlete becomes enmeshed with a group or club, the partner may perceive these new relationships as a threat. "There are a lot of potential pitfalls to navigate," Caldwell says, "and there are understandable reasons why the partner of a triathlete might struggle with resentment or insecurity."

Meredith Atwood, the woman behind the popular blog *Swim Bike Mom* and author of the book *Triathlon for the Every Woman*, remembers how the comfortable dynamic in her marriage shifted off its axis when she fell hard for triathlon.

She was a busy attorney and mother of 1- and 2-year-olds when she discovered triathlon in 2010. "[My husband and I] had let ourselves go in college. . . . We spent our time drinking beer and eating unhealthy food and being miserable. We just didn't know we were miserable!" she says. Once she became a triathlete, things changed. She changed. "We find a sport, and through the sport, find out a lot about ourselves," she explains. "If you have someone who is evolving, and the other person is not—they're still sitting on the couch drinking beer and eating ice cream just like before—it can cause a rift."

Since Meredith and her husband were both busy, full-time professionals and their children were so young, exhaustion levels were high. Even at the beginning, when she was only doing 5Ks, the negotiation for child-free time had to be addressed. "I'd come home and there was this 'air' in the house," Meredith says. She could tell that her newfound hobby was causing some tension. Instead of getting angry or upset, Meredith came up with a solution. "I signed him up for a race," she laughs. "I said, 'We're going to do it together, and train together.'" So, they did. She wanted to keep doing the things that she loved, but she also loved her husband and wasn't willing to sacrifice one for the other. Getting her husband, and eventually her children, involved seemed like a no-brainer. Because he was naturally athletic, he really only needed that initial push before he was right there in the mix. Now, he is a seasoned triathlete and half-Ironman competitor, and has earned the affectionate nickname of "The Expert" on her blog.

IRONCLAD ROMANCE

"A secret to a happy marriage is to either share a hobby with your spouse or at least not have your hobby impact your time with your spouse," says Traci H. "At first [my husband and I] shared nothing in common. His only hobby was golf, and my only hobby was shopping. We weren't doing a whole lot together." In addition, before Traci started triathlon, she struggled with social anxiety and diminished confidence. "It was difficult for me in social situations. I used to avoid parties because I was anxious. I relied on [my husband] too much. He was my social crutch." After the birth of her two children, Traci experienced a 30-pound weight gain, which lowered her confidence in her body. When she began training for triathlon, Traci shed nearly all the weight and, as a result, experienced a tremendous increase in body confidence. Joining the tri-club helped her to be more social, and soon she felt relaxed at parties and in groups and had a slew of close friends. Traci's confidence and independence not only benefited her but had a positive impact on the intimacy and strength of her marriage.

In some relationships, however, when one person changes, the other may start to feel insecure or threatened by it. When Dr. Caldwell works with couples trying to navigate the training demands of triathlon, he stresses the importance of each individual understanding the other's feelings. He admits it can be difficult because we tend to surround ourselves with people who amplify our complaints instead of challenge our opinions, creating what he refers to as "an echo chamber." This can often be seen when enthusiastic triathletes surround themselves with other enthusiastic triathletes all struggling with the same relationship frustrations. It also occurs when non-triathletes vent to other non-triathletes who don't "get" the whole passion thing.

Although the triathlete's reasons for engaging in this sport are valid, the partner's feelings about it are also valid. If both perspectives can be communicated in a safe environment, each person can work toward understanding the other.

Barbara F. and her husband, both triathletes, developed a system early on to balance their workouts while still being there for their two young kids as well as for each other. "My husband was also a priority, so I did my best to have a home-cooked dinner for him and my kids whenever possible. Our early wake-ups did shorten our evenings together, but we worked on spending at least a few hours together each weekday evening and the majority of each weekend. Even if we were doing mundane tasks, we did them together," she says.

Pamela P. endeavors to never take her husband's support for granted. "I say 'thank you' a lot. I often get him treats or gifts along the way." Finding this balance requires work, on both sides, but she says the reward is well worth the mutual sacrifice. Because she values all he does to make her dreams come true, she feels it's important to stay responsive when he has a need or request. "If he asked, although he never has, I would skip a workout."

Traci H. is also fortunate in that her husband has always supported her triathlon pursuits. Part of that has to do with how happy it makes her and the benefits he reaps from her increased happiness and confidence. But part of it has to do with Traci making sure she doesn't get so immersed in triathlon and volunteering and socializing with the club that he feels neglected or undervalued. "I try to respect my time with him," she says. She learned how to play golf, her husband's favorite hobby, so they had something to share. He bought a road bike and started to ride a little. In addition, she recognizes that triathlon has an impact not only on her time but also on their bank account. As the saying goes, the things couples fight most about are time and money. What does triathlon tax the most of? Time and money. "It's expensive," Traci admits, "so I try to be cognizant of that. For instance, because I'm doing a 70.3 this year, I'm not doing a lot of the other little races I usually would do."

Unfortunately, other relationships don't adjust as smoothly. Or at all. "My relationship is strained because of triathlon," Janet admits. "I want to do my first Ironman next year but [my husband] says he will divorce me." Laurie P.'s marriage recently did end in divorce, and triathlon was to blame, at least from his perspective. "My ex claimed that my career and triathlon training were both selfish," she says. "He wrote in [the] court papers that I valued work and exercise more than our children."

Dr. Caldwell believes that when relationships suffer or succeed, it's not about triathlon per se, but rather about the overall emotional climate. "Can you trust that, through the changes that triathlon brings, your partner will continue to know you, accept you, love you, and comfort you in times of need? Can your partner trust those things in you?" If the answer is yes, on both sides, he says couples can adapt to the changes in the relationship and in each other. "If the answer is no, don't worry that the relationship is doomed, or that your venture into triathlon is," he says. In fact, many times a new challenge to a relationship will actually foster the kind of climate Dr. Caldwell describes. "These aren't easy problems," he says, "but they are workable ones."

DIVORCE BY TRIATHLON?

For some, triathlon becomes a serious source of tension and resentment. Heather M. says if you ask her husband why their marriage ended, he would point at least one finger at triathlon. But she contends that triathlon didn't cause any problems that weren't already there. "Rarely is it triathlon itself that's the problem," Dr. Caldwell explains. Rather, it's a symptom. It's what triathlon represents, a perceived threat to the relationship. That was Dr. Pete Simon's point in his Divorce by Triathlon post where he likened "Divorce by Triathlon" to "Suicide by Cop." Couples in relational strife might throw themselves into triathlon as an escape, or even subconsciously use it as a convenient way out. Triathlon becomes the scapegoat.

For Heather M., triathlon was neither a scapegoat nor a destructive force. For her, it was a saving grace. "Mentally, I got stronger and felt better about myself. Triathlon is what got me strong enough to change my life," she says. "Nobody wants a divorce, but [triathlon] made me stronger, mentally. I thought, I can be strong and I can end my marriage."

Sometimes triathlon can be a wrecking ball shattering a relationship, and other times it can be a tube of superglue binding it tight. The same can be said for lots of things: facing a health crisis, parenting a child with special needs, becoming an adult caregiver to an aging parent, dealing with financial stress, moving, changing jobs, losing a job . . . anything that throws a monkey wrench into your life plan and shakes up the relational status quo. Strong relationships weather these storms, while fragile relationships are lost at sea.

"If your marriage breaks up over a sport, it was going to break up anyway," says Meredith Atwood frankly. "It's indicative of a bigger problem."

CHASING IRON: A FAMILY AFFAIR

Once Meredith and her husband became triathletes and negotiated their respective times to train, they got into a new groove. That is, until she decided to tackle the Ironman. And then three more. "[Ironman is] a whole different ball game, especially your first. You freak out constantly, and take that out on your family without meaning to, because you're scared," she says. While she holds her Ironman achievements near and dear, life experience and time have given her the space to reflect. "We do have to step back and see the impact we make," she says.

The person training for the Ironman is sacrificing a lot for their dreams, but they aren't the only ones. "There's a tremendous sacrifice of the other person," Meredith says. She understands the level of that mutual sacrifice because she has lived it. "My first Ironman almost undid our family," she confesses. "I came in from a long run one day, and [my husband] had actually packed his stuff." Yeah, it got that real.

However, today, Meredith's marriage is stronger because they weathered those storms successfully. She currently coaches about a dozen women, and when they come to her ready to tackle a longer-course triathlon, she makes certain their preparation goes beyond the physical. She says they also need to be fully prepared for the disruption that training causes the family unit and the pressure and burden experienced by everyone involved, not just the athlete. "I've lived through it, through training and working full-time—it's stressful," she says. "If someone wanted my opinion, I might advise against it. If I have an athlete who says their marriage is in ruins, I would tell them *not* to do an Ironman." But, despite her own learning curve, she can attest to the fact that it can be done with marriage intact.

Dr. Caldwell says that the initial tension over triathlon usually results from lack of communication and a detailed plan. "[The couple] didn't communicate well enough about the transition into triathlon to adapt to it very well," he explains. Meredith definitely understands how essential a detailed plan and schedule are to keep the household, and marriage, running smoothly.

"A decision to go long course requires a family meeting. You need to sit down with your spouse or significant other and ask certain questions," she says. For example, whose job is it to keep up with the laundry? Go food shopping? Cook? Clean? Take the kids out on Saturday afternoon? When both mom *and* dad are triathletes, who is going to take the kids roller-skating and who gets to disappear on a 60-mile bike ride? These questions can turn into heated arguments if ground rules haven't been established in advance.

Even after all that is ironed out, don't be surprised if it needs to be revisited on occasion. Things change. Circumstances change. "If you start to have a spouse or significant other get resentful . . . you need to have a family powwow," Meredith emphasizes. Trying to train for these longer races with the stress of constant arguing and lack of support just takes too much of an emotional toll.

"I realize now that I was selfish in a lot of ways. You don't mean to be a selfish person about it, but it can happen," she continues. "I have a lot of regrets, but it was a growth opportunity for our marriage. It was tough, [but] I do think it was worth it, because we survived it."

Even for those sticking with shorter triathlons, the packed race schedules, expensive equipment, long training runs or rides eating into the weekend, and 7:30 p.m. bedtimes can be annoying to a partner. Sometimes the triathlete is supposed to be spending time with loved ones but isn't entirely present (i.e., distracted with downloading a workout, researching a bike trainer, or falling asleep in the middle of a conversation), which further irritates the situation.

"Training can become obsessive and very self-centered," says Maureen B. She believes strongly in the importance of maintaining balance. As a woman gets more intense with her training, either with longer courses or with improving her short-course times, she may find that other priorities start to slip. "Something always has to give. You can't train like that and have a clean house and dinner on the table and be everywhere for everyone," Maureen admits. How does she know when the balance is starting to topple? "If you're yelling at your kids because you couldn't get your run in? You know it's going too far."

But Traci H. has a different philosophy on the perceived "selfishness" of the sport. "I guess there's potential for [selfishness], if you don't give consideration to anything or anyone else," she says. "But I could never label triathlon as selfish, because that means it's only benefiting you. There is a collateral benefit to others when you're doing something that makes you feel great. Gaining confidence helps in all other areas of your life, which also positively affects your relationships."

We all have dreams. But in order to make dreams come into reality, it takes an awful lot of determination, dedication, self-discipline, and effort.
—JESSE OWENS

ENTER CHILDREN, STAGE LEFT. AND RIGHT.
AND HANGING FROM THE CHANDELIERS

When a committed relationship involves children, there is a whole other set of issues to negotiate. But even though Lamont, Kennelly, and Wilson found that some athletes reported concern that triathlon was negatively impacting time with their children, others reported triathlon as having a positive effect.

Approximately 44 percent of USAT members have young children living at home, so the demands of triathlon and parenthood are in a tug of war for many. Meredith's advice is simple and pointed: "When you have young kids, you have to chill out."

Beyond the basic questions of who's going to watch the kids for two hours, there's the added guilt of missing time with the kids. "The guilt was definitely there, especially at the beginning," says Jennifer H., a clinical psychologist, divorced mother, and triathlete. Yet, motherhood is also a huge reason women start doing triathlons in the first place. Jennifer knew that taking an hour to run or train was important not just personally, but because of the message it was sending her four children. "There's a bigger modeling component," she says.

Bridget S. vowed when she was pregnant that she would not be an overweight, unhealthy mom. She had gained 30 pounds after she married, before getting pregnant, and was determined to lose the weight and be a role model of health and physical fitness for her kids. She made good on that promise, transforming her body and becoming super fit through triathlon. Today, she feels amazing inside and out. "I have never been this thin and fit in my whole life," she says. But, more than her physical appearance, her age group wins, and her finisher's medals, Bridget is most proud of keeping that silent commitment she made to her children years ago. Her son did his first kids' tri at the age of 7. Her younger daughter is on the swim team and eager to do her first kids' triathlon. Grown daughters can inspire their own mothers, too. Bridget's transformation through triathlon inspired her own mom to start cycling for exercise at the age of 62.

When it comes to modeling fitness, actions really do speak louder than words. A paper published in the April 2014 issue of *Pediatrics* found a correlation between a mother's activity and the activity of her young children. Mothers who were less physically active had more sedentary children, and we all know that lack of exercise in childhood is associated with increased risk for a variety of chronic health conditions in adulthood, including diabetes, heart disease, and even mental health issues.

So, active moms leading active lifestyles have a direct impact on their children's activity levels and overall health outcomes. That is a really good thing. The bad thing, however, is that maternal physical activity has significantly declined over the past 45 years in the United States. An article published in the Mayo Clinic Proceedings reported that women exercise *less* once they become mothers. That is not so great for moms, and according to the research, it doesn't benefit the little eyes watching them either.

"As a woman, we put everything on hold. It takes a strong woman to say, 'I'm going to take care of myself too,'" Meredith says, highlighting the airplane analogy about putting your oxygen mask on first before helping a child put on theirs. "I think triathlon and the running movement have allowed women to say, 'I can take a break.' We go out on a bike ride and we come back as better parents." She also encourages women to make physical fitness a family affair. "If you're starting out in the sport, I think making it a family mission to get involved is key." Both her children did their first triathlons last year.

"I have always been active and found that I am a better wife and parent if I give myself time to exercise," says Barbara F. But she valued her time with her kids also and didn't want to disrupt their routine or overburden her husband with child care responsibilities. So she got creative with her workouts. "I would awaken at 4:30 a.m. so I could work out in our basement, shower, and then help my kids get ready for school," she says. She found ways to incorporate training into her day without taking time away from the family. She coached her son's soccer team and would join them on their team training runs. She'd forgo the sideline socializing at her daughter's softball practice and instead squeeze in a run. When her kids were on the swim team, she would grab an open lane during their practice and swim her laps. She found a way to be present for her children while also training. The key was finding the right balance.

But balance is a verb. It will look different to different people in different families. It seems that the most important part of the whole "balancing act" is the ability to be honest with yourself, listen to your family's feelings, and constantly step back, reevaluate, and be flexible. Because life itself is in a constant state of flux. What worked 10 months, 10 weeks, or even 10 minutes ago might not work now. It's the flexibility to adapt, the insight we have into ourselves, and the willingness to see multiple perspectives that contribute to success, not relentlessly trying to convince your significant other to always see your point of view.

> *The bottom line answer is that exercise can be both a selfish and an unselfish act. The motive behind it is what matters.*
> —ERIC C. STEVENS

Dr. Caldwell's significant other is not a triathlete, but she has always been understanding and supportive of his involvement in the sport he loves. However, things have changed now that they've had their first baby—renegotiations, redistribution of resources, rewriting the proverbial "rule book." "She has learned to love race day because we try to make it a fun and inspiring family event," he says. "I go a little faster on my training run because I know she and our daughter are waiting for me at home, and I go a little faster on race day knowing that they'll be around the next corner to cheer me on."

As with anything else, weaving triathlon successfully into life, love, and family requires communication, insight, empathy, and negotiation as well as give and take. As *rUnladylike* blogger and marathon coach Jessica wrote in one of her insightful posts: "If training for long-distance triathlons is going to destroy relationships with the people you love and care about most in the world, it is probably time to reassess your goals. Because at the end of the day, [it] isn't going to be worthwhile if no one is waiting for you at the finish line."

BACK IN ACTION

"I feel like I shouldn't be able to do what I'm doing. . . ."

WHEN I WAS 9 years old, I was diagnosed with scoliosis and spondylolisthesis," says Tara Emrick. Suffering from chronic pain since the age of 6 and a progressively worsening spinal curve, she was put in a back brace. However, her curve continued to rapidly progress, going from 32 degrees to 64 degrees. At that point, a Harrington rod surgery was recommended.

She had the surgery at the age of 12. The procedure was major and the recovery tough. She was stuck in her house the entire summer, wearing a back brace 24 hours a day, watching the world go by outside her window.

Though the surgery corrected her curve significantly, a pain-free life did not follow. Tara required a second, corrective surgery at the age of 16 to remove some of the hardware from the previous surgery. "The pain continued in my low back and was just part of my life," she says.

In addition to her scoliosis and spondylolisthesis, Tara developed degenerative disc disease in three levels of her back and arthritis in her cervical spine. Pain and weakness in her left leg made it difficult to walk, and eventually she became so disabled that she had to end her nursing career and find a desk job until her back slowly recovered and the leg weakness improved. She relied on pain medications, time, and luck.

Four years ago, Tara's pain returned along with the leg weakness. She tried injections and consulted with specialists. At the time, both of her children were on the swim team. This planted the seed that perhaps swimming would be good exercise for her. She took lessons and began swimming regularly at the YMCA. It seemed to help. "The pain wasn't constant anymore," she says.

"When I turned 40, a friend of mine talked me into doing a one-mile open-water swim in the bay." It was the September Splash at Wildwood Crest. "I knew I was in last when the kayaker was next to me," she jokes. She did indeed come in last, which had much to do with the intermittent episodes of panic that caused her to stop and regroup every so often.

Around this same time, Tara saw a friend's Facebook post about the Mullica Hill Women's Triathlon Club. She wasn't particularly interested in triathlon, but she joined the club for friendship and fitness. "I wanted to get more open-water swim training," she explains. She could even picture herself participating in a triathlon on a relay team one day, but only as the swimmer. Never the biker or runner.

But the tri-club worked its magic, and the next thing Tara knew, she was going on group bike rides with the club. She "accidentally" started running, as she describes it, while walking her new puppy. The pup wanted to go faster than Tara could walk, so she began doing a walk-jog and then gradually running. To her amazement, Tara realized she was capable of doing all three sports that comprised a triathlon, so she decided to go for it.

Tara completed her first triathlon, a local sprint distance race, in June 2014. "I just wanted to finish," she says. "When I crossed the finish line, I couldn't believe it." In 2015, she did the Queen of the Hill.

Remarkably, Tara says she doesn't feel pain while running, biking, or swimming. "I get more pain when I'm standing waiting for the race to start. Standing [is] the worst. I'm in tears." Her pain, however, is not her greatest challenge. "The greatest challenge for me is my body image issues with having a rib hump on the right side of my back," she confesses. "I become self-conscious when I have someone riding or running behind me. It challenges me to try to stay positive and not get down and ruin my race because of it."

Tara has done eight sprint triathlons, one international distance, and a half-Ironman. From a little girl who spent her summer recovering from major spinal surgery to a triathlete who no longer lives a life crippled with pain, Tara is amazed at what she has accomplished because of triathlon. "It's a whole different life. It's not what I ever pictured. I'm active. I'm an athlete."

When you ask Tara what she's most proud of, she doesn't recite her fastest times, her longest race, her ability to inspire others, or her persistence in over-coming adversity. "My greatest accomplishment is getting my kids interested in triathlons and running," she says.

Tara's daughter has also been diagnosed with the same rapidly progressive scoliosis. "We were driving [to a race] and my 11-year-old daughter looked at me and said, 'I'm so proud of you Mom. I want to be just like you and do triath-lons and my kids will do triathlons and it will all be because of you.'"

12

TRIATHAPHOBIA

A ship in the harbor is safe.
But that's not what ships are built for.

—ANONYMOUS

Once I jumped off a cliff in Barbados. I was married to someone else when I did, in what seems like a lifetime ago.

My ex-husband and I tied the knot at City Hall in our early 20s. Getting hitched seemed like the right thing to do after finding ourselves unexpectedly pregnant. We faced the typical challenges of a newlywed couple when marriage and parenthood enter your lives simultaneously, without plan or intent. He, a bartender, and I, a graduate student working a low-paying job in the social services field, found ourselves navigating a whole new world with limited finances and lots of stress. When our daughter, Carlie, began having seizures shortly after birth and developmental delays during those first few years, even more stress was added to this big life adjustment.

The year before we separated, and eventually divorced, we left a 5-year-old Carlie in the capable hands of her loving grandparents and took a long-awaited vacation with another couple—a week-long budget excursion to a humble surfer hotel on the gorgeous island of Barbados. The guys could surf, the girls could lie by the ocean and sip fancy rum drinks with umbrellas, and he and I could make one last-ditch effort to resuscitate a marriage that was in serious defib.

While lounging on the beach one day, our friend Chad noticed a young couple jumping off the ledge of a rocky cliff into the ocean. "Dude, let's go do that!" he shouted, springing up from the sand. His girlfriend, who was more adventurous than I, seemed interested as well. As usual, I didn't even entertain the idea but followed them there.

The four of us lined up on the narrow ledge and watched Chad leap first. He went, unflinchingly. To my surprise, his girlfriend backed out. Suddenly, a strange force overtook me. "I want to do it," I said, scarcely recognizing my voice. I sounded sure and steady, and that wasn't me.

If I had taken a nanosecond to remind myself that I was scared of swimming in the ocean, I would have never considered it. All my fears were suddenly replaced with a want—no, a need—to do this. I stood staring down at the roiling sea, toes curled over the rocky ledge. I wanted to jump so badly, but my body stayed cemented to the ground, as if invisible hands were pinning me in place by the shoulders.

I stood there for several minutes, desperate to jump but unable. Then, I heard my husband's voice saying, "Leesh, don't. C'mon. Let's go." I think I remember a chuckle and head shake in there. He extended his hand to me for effect. Sure, he could have been trying to give me an "out." Yet at the time I sensed a condescending edge to it, as if he knew all along I'd never be able to do it. It could very well have all been in my head—five years of pent-up issues between us clouding my perception.

I looked at him and his outstretched palm, reaching to escort me off the ledge and back into my weakling, unsure little bubble. There were lots of things tied up in that moment on the cliff. Jumping represented something bigger: The courage to hurl myself into the unknown, to be lost at sea for a while, and to swim myself back to shore for a new beginning. Part of me didn't think I had it in me, but this other part of me, bolder and stronger, believed I did. That's the part of me that leapt.

Jumping from that cliff was the first impulsive, adrenaline-rush, "extreme," out-of-my-comfort-zone thing I had ever done. Don't get me wrong; I've done dumb stuff, silly stuff, things I didn't think through very well, such as splurging on an overpriced impulse buy, doing a dorky dance in public, having one more beer when I should have packed it in for the night, or driving in a snowstorm when common sense told me to stay off the roads. I could be an idiot, but I wasn't parasailing. I was more of a "feet on the ground, play it safe" person and growing more so every day. Boring, you might ask? I prefer "sensible."

I suppose that's why taking that leap off the cliff all those years ago has stayed with me as a touchstone of strength. It felt like I was setting myself free with one symbolic act of fearlessness. That act set the wheels in motion for some major changes in my life. Neither the literal leap nor the successive leaps of faith required of me over the next several years would have been possible without the courage to face that one initial fear blocking my path. I'm not just talking about the fear of jumping into the ocean, but that did seem to break the ice. I'm talking about my fears of being alone, being a single mom, making my own rent, struggling to pay the bills, and discovering who I really was for the first time in my adult life. My fear of failing at it all, my fear of succeeding beyond what I felt I deserved.

I was starting to wonder if triathlon, for some, was like that cliff was for me. A way to get unstuck, find the power to change, and uncover who you are meant to be in the life you were truly meant to live.

Stand up to your obstacles and do something about them. You will find that they haven't half the strength you think they have.
—NORMAN VINCENT PEALE

IT'S ALL IN YOUR HEAD

Triathlon is undoubtedly a physical sport. You need to condition your muscles, build your endurance, perfect your technique. Yet, that physical part is a cakewalk compared to the mental part. One study found that 80 percent of triathlete performance has to do with psychological factors, suggesting that the mental state of mind trumps the physiological state of the body. Unfortunately, managing the mental part isn't always as easy as it might sound on paper. A large part of that has to do with the crippling effects of our fear.

Fear played the most significant role in my own avoidance of triathlon. The more I talked to people, the more I learned I wasn't the only one. Usually, there is some aspect of triathlon that causes apprehension, doubt, concern, mild worry, moderate anxiety, or flat-out terror.

Of course there are always those adrenaline-junkie, fearless types, who seem to saunter into triathlon without a care in the world, jumping in a shark-filled ocean with a whoop of joy and casually careening over the finish line as if it were all fun and games. My friend had an ocean swim in her first triathlon. She waltzed into the surf without a care in the world and thought the whole thing was great fun. Yeah, not me.

Fears can take many shapes. There are the obvious ones like swimming in open water and crashing on the bike. But you would be surprised at how many fears are abstract. The fear of failing, of coming in last, or of being the heaviest, oldest, least-in-shape person out there. Then there is the fear that is common to women in both triathlons and childbirth—the fear of needing to poop midway through all the action. (From what I hear, that struggle is real.)

When fear pops up, it's generally a sign of our edge. . . .
Fear calls our attention to an area of our lives we need to
work on. It's really one of our best teachers.
—LAUREN BROOKS

Ironically, the things that initially talk us out of triathlon become the very reason triathlon is so transformative. You may be a fish in the water but hate running. You may be an avid runner but petrified to swim. Or, you may be like a friend of mine who had only ever ridden a unicycle and felt entirely uncomfortable on two wheels (true story). Even those phenomenal triathletes who excel at all three sports will still admit that one of the three events is their weakness. Thus, the challenge.

AQUAPHOBIA

When it comes to triathlon fears, swimming tops the list. Most of these fears result from a general discomfort and inexperience with open water. Some of that fear is legitimate. The swim leg of a triathlon race carries the most fatality risk, statistically speaking. There have been 109 reported deaths during USAT-sanctioned triathlon events between 1985 and 2015, and 71 percent of fatalities occurred during the open-water swim. According to Dr. Larry Creswell, a cardiologist, heart surgeon, and leader of the USAT medical review panel on triathlon-related fatalities, there is some evidence of a pattern. Middle-aged men appear to be at most risk. "The risk of dying in a triathlon is three times greater in men than in women . . . and the people who have died in a triathlon are an average of 12 years older than participants as a whole," he explains. In addition, more than half of those who have died, other than in a crash, had an unsuspected heart condition. His blog, *The Athlete's Heart*, discusses this in more detail.

That said, the mortality rate in triathlon is far from staggering at about 1 per 70,000 participants. To put that into some context, triathlon is less risky than base jumping (1 in 60), mountain climbing (1 in 15,700), hang gliding (1 in 560), football (1 in 50,000), motorbike racing (1 in 1,000), canoeing (1 in 10,000), and scuba diving (1 in 34,000).

Still, sometimes it isn't about statistics or stories. Sometimes swim fears are rooted in scary early experiences in the water. The inspiring thing is to see how these deep-seated fears can be faced and worked through thanks to triathlon.

"I almost drowned when I was 10 while canoeing with my family," says Tamie B. After joining the tri-club, she taught herself breaststroke and went to her first practice swim in open water. "I looked around at all of the experienced swimmers and lifeguards and knew that I would be safe." Afterward, she began taking lessons to learn freestyle. She says, "Taking lessons has helped, and a lot of self-talk reminding myself that I am safe." She is planning to do an Olympic-distance Aquabike and the Escape to Lewes 1-mile swim in the near future.

Gwen was an avid swimmer until the age of 14, when her brother drowned. When she became a mother, she committed herself to getting over her fear of the water. "The first time in the water was the hardest. I puked in the bathroom before suiting up." She barely made it around the open-water swim practice course. "I got out of the water and ran for the bathroom and vomited again." When she crossed the finish line of her first triathlon, Gwen burst into tears of happiness and pride at beating down her nemesis. Since then, she has completed multiple triathlons, including 70.3 distances. And while she admits that she still pukes before races, it isn't stopping her.

Rose Marie nearly drowned on a family vacation when she was 12 years old. As a result, she did not swim for many years, but at the age of 54, she decided to take swim lessons. Three months later, she finished her first triathlon. "I panicked on the swim. I did backstroke and wound up in the weeds. I discovered I could walk the lake and so I faked the swim. But I cried when the race was over because I 'cheated,'" she says. Eager to prove something to herself, she did another triathlon the following month. "I panicked again but did the whole swim as backstroke. " Rose Marie continues to race, and has even done an Ironman distance and a 5K open-water swim. "It's never too late to learn. Beating back a demon fear is the most empowering feeling ever!"

For many people, there are no associated childhood traumas, no discernible reasons for panicking in the water. And yet they do. Some feel confident and comfortable while swimming laps in the pool, and then are shocked when fear grips them on race day. The chaos of other swimmers splashing nearby, the cold temperatures, their inexperience with open water, and increased adrenaline can all inject an unexpected and intense bolt of fear.

That was the case for Bridget S. Although she had lifeguarded as a teenager, Bridget felt uncomfortable in the open water as an adult. "When I did my first [triathlon], I was horrible," she says. The swim almost made her quit the race entirely. With the support of another newbie, she finished the swim on her back. "The first year I came in close to last for my age group," she laughs. Today she stands on the podium as an age-group winner because her bike and run are so fast. She still panics every time she gets in the water but has learned to manage it by rolling onto her back periodically and focusing on getting from one buoy to the next. "I like to beat my time," she says, "but I am happy if I manage my panic in the swim."

Amanda W. had never experienced a major anxiety attack in her life until she got into the lake for her first open-water swim. "I was thinking, *This is how I'm going to die.* The cold, the dark, and the solitude [were] so scary and overwhelming to me. I kept talking to myself, saying 'Calm down; you can see land; it's okay!'" Her sister-in-law was also swimming the lake that day and saw Amanda's panic. "She was my savior at that point and we swam together the rest of the way. I can get in the lake now with no problem, however, the fear of that moment has never left me."

> *What would life be if we had no courage to attempt anything?*
> —VINCENT VAN GOGH

CYCLOPHOBIA

Biking also makes people nervous. A 2014 survey commissioned by People for Bikes found that 54 percent of women are afraid of getting hit while riding. And although many racecourses are closed to traffic, avoiding roads while training is virtually impossible. For some, riding in groups creates anxiety. Even clip-in pedals can be a concern for newer riders who worry they won't be able to get their foot unclipped before tipping over.

For Mary D., her fears stem from a childhood bike crash. "When I was 10 years old, I fell off my bike and hit my head on the street gutter," she says.

The incident resulted in a concussion. "Every time I get on my bike I relive that moment and challenge myself to conquer my fear. Haven't fallen since."

For Amanda M., working as a critical care nurse exposed her to a lot of trauma. "My life at one point revolved around declaring people brain dead and seeing families suffer. I had a patient in [his] 30s. His life ended on a bike," she remembers. "It was really hard for me to get on a bike for my first group ride." Thanks to the support of two tri-club members who never left her side, she made it through. "Every time I get on the bike, I secretly wonder if it will be my last day," she admits. "It still scares me to death, but I do it more willingly now."

Diane I. was new to triathlon and getting comfortable training in all three disciplines when she learned her mentor had been hit by a car while cycling. Although her mentor was not seriously harmed, the incident shook Diane. "Every time I go out on my bike I am worried that I'm going to get run over by a car. But I do it anyway, and each and every time, I know I am conquering my fears."

Breigh races competitively on a cycling team and was the New Jersey Category 4 State Champion in 2015. Yet even she is not without fear. "I'm petrified to race," she confesses. "I don't know how I get on the line sometimes." So why does she do it? The answer is simple. "Because I can win, or help a teammate win," she says, shrugging. That's enough to convince her to press forward.

> *You miss 100 percent of the shots you don't take.*
> —WAYNE GRETZKY

Cycling spawns some lesser anxieties as well. Bike mechanics and maintenance, such as checking tire pressure, adjusting cable tension for brake tuning, cleaning and lubricating a chain, popping a chain back on, or fixing a flat, can be intimidating.

"The bicycle can be a little challenging because you need that mechanical skill. There's an intimidation factor," says Sarai Snyder of *Girl Bike Love*, an online community for women cyclists. For some, these anxieties can become barriers to riding. However, Snyder believes this is the very reason it empowers. "Once you master these skills, there is a tremendous sense of empowerment," she says. "Women are less risk-averse when they understand the reward [and] the joy."

FEAR OF DFL

DFL is athlete code for "Dead F'ing Last." When I was a kid, I didn't know the lingo, but I knew how it made me feel. Coming in last was connected with a visceral sort of dread. When I ran cross-country and track, I was never good enough to win anything. But that didn't mean I didn't have a goal. That goal was to avoid last place at all costs and maintain some shred of dignity, as if the last person over the finish line would have rotten tomatoes thrown at her or something. I did come in last place in a track meet once, in front of bleachers full of people. I remember the physical weight of shame inside my body and the immense embarrassment at the horror of it all. I couldn't look anyone in the eye, and I snapped at my family on the ride home. I'm sure those types of things build character, but as a self-conscious, insecure preteen, I felt more torn down than built up.

I'm a big girl now (at least in theory), and although I still have a lingering fear of looking stupid or slow, I am generally less self-conscious about almost everything at this point in my life. In fact, today when I watch those last-place athletes fight their way to the finish without quitting, I'm deeply inspired. Those last placers get cheers that are as loud, if not louder, than those coming in first. The heart, soul, and humility it takes to finish something you know you're not necessarily good at makes coming in last not only completely irrelevant, but flat-out heroic.

Blogger and triathlete Amy Moritz wrote a post on her blog, *The Accidental Athlete*, titled "Dead Last: The Power of Showing Up." Part soul-searching, part philosophy, part pep talk, Amy breathes truth and insight into an anonymous quote circulating in social media, which reads: "DFL trumps DNF trumps DNS."

I'll decode this for the layperson: "Dead F'ing Last beats Did Not Finish, which is far better than Did Not Start." A few lines she wrote spoke directly to me: "Finishing last, or first or in the middle, doesn't define you. Other people's opinions do not define you. . . . Outcomes only define you if that's how you choose to define yourself."

I knew that if I did this triathlon, my finishing time would be posted on the Internet for all to scrutinize. Though I felt my old fears fluttering up in my stomach, I reassured myself with the thought that, honestly, did people have nothing better to do than look up Alicia DiFabio's race time? Did anyone really care? Anyway, I was starting to see the truth in the idea that if you put in the work, show up, and get 'er done, you're a winner. That might sound like some canned pep talk I give my kids, but I was starting to really believe it myself.

OUR BEST TEACHER

I was living a safe, uncomplicated life with minimal risk exposure. I liked it that way and was not feeling compelled to dramatically change. This prudence has kept me away from drugs and cigarettes and keeps me wearing a seatbelt and staying on top of my health. It's prevented me from engaging in the type of recklessness that buys six seconds of YouTube fame and a bunch of broken bones. While some might find my careful, suburban, soccer mom life humdrum, I appreciate my conservative nature. That is, with one small caveat. My definition of "risky" has expanded as I've gotten older and become a parent. All of a sudden, I noticed how many things I avoided—amusement park rides, ice skating, sledding, plane rides, going off the diving board, going down a water slide, flipping on a trampoline, or just trying something new, like triathlon.

"[It's] easy to confuse fear with actual danger. We mistakenly assign real risk to our internal fears of failure, embarrassment, ridicule or any number of things that make us uncomfortable," writes Lauren Brooks on the blog *Breaking Muscle*. Watching the women of the tri-club face their fears again and again made me realize how small I'd been living.

Diane I. experienced many insecurities before being brave enough to even consider doing a triathlon. "I was suffering from depression and severe social anxiety for years. I didn't want to be on any kind of pill and desperately wanted to improve my quality of life," she says. "I was terribly overweight, out of shape, and didn't feel I was worthy enough to enter a gym." She read a story about the Mullica Hill Women's Tri Club in a local magazine and, after much internal debate, mustered up the courage to join. "I had tremendous anxiety about wearing my tri-suit, and then about having either a panic attack or hyperventilating while in the water, though I knew I could swim well." Nonetheless, she decided now was the time to conquer her fears. "I just didn't care anymore about what I looked like to others."

She bought a pre-owned tri-suit to save money. "I couldn't zip it up. So I waited six weeks before putting it on again. Although I had only lost a small amount of weight, if I sucked it in, I could finally pull up the zipper and pray it wouldn't snap and break."

She went out on a 10-mile group ride one night, despite her self-consciousness. "When I showed up with my old bike and basket, I was afraid the ladies might make fun behind my back and shun me," she confesses. "But it was all I had, all I could afford. I just did the best I could." And although she says she couldn't keep up with the pack the first go-round, she went back. This she attributes to the group's encouragement and what she calls her complete lack of pride. "My goal was to improve my quality of life and be there for my boys, actively."

Swimming was another challenge for Diane. She remembers when eight laps in a pool felt like forever. "Now I swim 1.2 miles at a time and it's effortless," she says. The club members she was afraid would judge her turned out to be wonderful friends and a huge support system as she worked toward her goals. "The club, their energy, and their love told me I could do it."

Diane could have stayed in her cocoon, but there was a part of her who fought to change the plot of her story, fought for the life she wanted and deserved. When she bulldozed through all those insecurities, anxieties, and depression, she exhumed her true self and found the life she was meant to live. For her, triathlon was the vehicle for that transformation to occur.

As for me, I didn't feel that I necessarily needed a major transformation. But I did know that finding the edge of my comfortable little world and squashing silly lingering fears that kept my life small would help me grow. At minimum, I needed just a little adventure.

Life shrinks or expands in proportion to one's courage.
—ANAÏS NIN

On April 1 at 7:55 a.m., I sat in front of my computer with a hot cup of coffee, my credit card, and the MHWTC website open to the registration link for Queen of the Hill. (And no, it wasn't lost on me that this was April Fool's Day.) If I didn't commit to this race, I would never give myself the push I needed to start training. Like jumping off that cliff in Barbados, I stopped overthinking, centered myself, and took a leap of faith. According to Martin Luther King Jr., if I leapt, the staircase would appear.

By 8:05 a.m., I stood on that first step as a fully registered participant in my first triathlon. Time to start the climb.

GOING THE DISTANCE

"Triathlons are like a second chance at life."

NEARLY 19 HOURS had passed since the 2013 Ironman Arizona had begun. It was 1:30 a.m., and there was little evidence that a race had even been held that day. No aid stations along the once-closed roads, no lights, no race officials or water, no cheering spectators, and no finishers medals. Per Ironman rules, those who couldn't finish the 140.6 miles within the 17-hour cutoff were stripped of their timing chips and scooped off the course. It. Was. Over.

Well, it was over for everyone except 34-year-old, first-time Ironman competitor Chrissy Vasquez. Engulfed by the night, emotionally crushed and physically spent, she ran to the sound of each footfall echoing in the silence. She wasn't going to get an official finish. There would be no crowds, no carpet, no silver tape, no medal, no Mike Reilly proclaiming "Chrissy Vasquez, you are an Ironman!" But it didn't matter. She was determined to go the distance.

༄

Chrissy had never considered herself an athlete. In fact, she felt far from it. As a little girl, Chrissy had a typical build, but between the ages of five and six, she experienced a childhood trauma that left deep emotional scars. "I gained a lot of weight," she says, suspecting that it was probably her coping mechanism, protecting her against more pain. As a kid in gym class she finished every race last and described herself as always being the "heaviest student" in her grade. She could scarcely walk a half mile at an 18-minute-mile pace without horrible ankle and shin pain.

As the years went by, Chrissy's weight became part of her identity. For most of her young adult life, her weight hovered around 215 pounds, though at one point, she believes it crept up to about 262. "I was healthy from a physical standpoint, but it was going to catch up with me," says Chrissy. So, in her 20s, she tried to lose the excess weight she had carried nearly her entire life. It turns out, this wouldn't be just a physical challenge but also an emotional one. "I struggle with losing the weight. It's always been who I was," she admits. "Mentally, my whole life I have always been down on myself."

But Chrissy was ready to make a change. "I [was] so sick and tired of being sick and tired." Working with a personal trainer, she lost 40 pounds. Around that time, her friend Stephanie presented her with challenge—a friendly dare, if you will. She invited Chrissy to run a half-marathon with her. Now, Chrissy had never run a single mile, let alone 13.1. But, oddly enough, she accepted the invitation. "Anything I've done in my life, I just go in both feet first," Chrissy says. She enrolled in a running course and could barely run a half mile before her legs were cramping so badly that she had to turn around and head back. The running coach gave her a pep talk, telling her it gets a little easier every time. So she stuck with it, and when race day came, Chrissy didn't back out. It took her 3 hours and 19 minutes to finish the inaugural 2010 Miami Beach Half Marathon. At times the race got really tough, but she finished it. Then she went back for more.

Chrissy ran three more half-marathons that year and then decided to try a triathlon. She signed up for her first sprint distance race in 2011, an indoor tri. She was immediately hooked, registering for four more sprints and five Olympic-distance events over the next two years. Ready to raise the bar, she set her sights on completing the 70.3 miles of a half-Ironman. To date, Chrissy has raced in a total of seven 70.3 events. In some, she earned an official finish. In others, she didn't.

Around this time, Chrissy started blogging about her triathlon experience. Her first post was a hilarious account of trying on a wetsuit, which inspired the blog's name: *Sausage in a Wetsuit*. Readers connected with her authenticity, humor, humility, and grit.

"At races I'm that noticeably slowest, largest, and most out-of-place person there," Chrissy writes with candor on her blog. "It's tough being one of the biggest female competitors out there. The easy thing to do would be to not do it. To not put myself out there for criticism and judgment. But I've already found out so much about myself, and I can't imagine what more there is to find out as I continue this journey."

Chrissy set her sights on going the full distance at the 2013 Ironman Arizona. She was using the race to both challenge herself and also to raise money for the organization Back on My Feet (BoMF). When race day came, her swim and bike went well, but she started to deteriorate mentally and physically during the marathon. "That run ate me alive," she says. The nutrition she ate on her bike ride caused severe gastrointestinal issues. "I was not feeling well. I just wanted someone to tell me to quit. And I was going to quit." But she didn't want to the decision to be her own. She hoped something would happen to force her hand. "I wanted it to be an act of God to take me out," she jokes.

"Then, around mile 15, something clicked in me," Chrissy says. "I started trying." But it was a little too late. By mile 19, she was being followed by the infamous golf cart, the sag wagon, the Ironman "cops" in charge of scooping up racers who weren't on pace to make it to the finish line in the allotted 17 hours. Ironman rules clearly state you are only an Ironman if you finish the race by the time the giant clock reads 17:00:00, and not a second past.

When that golf cart began stalking her, Chrissy knew what was going down. She had been stripped of her chip during a half-Ironman in Kansas, so she knew the deal. Racers aren't forcibly removed from the course, mind you, but they are cautioned that proceeding is at their own risk. Once the race officially finishes, the roads open up to traffic and all race support is gone.

Even though Chrissy now had her reason to quit, something inside her had come alive. "I didn't need an official finish to make my dream come true,"

Chrissy says. "This was about *my* finish. *My* journey." Deflated but not defeated, she made the choice to continue. Emotionally, she had found a reserve tank.

Although still miles away, she could hear the crowd cheering for those final official finishers. Disappointed but unfazed, she pressed on. Eighteen and a half hours after Chrissy started the race, she turned the last corner into what would have been the finisher's chute. It was after 1:00 a.m. and nearly everything was torn down, as if a race had never occurred. Chrissy expected to see a ghost town with a few good friends who had come to cheer her on. To her shock, she was greeted by about 100 cheering people. Apparently, her friends had gathered everyone they could find—lingering spectators, cleanup volunteers, and people waiting in line to register for the 2014 Ironman. (Yeah, they do that.) When these folks heard about Chrissy, they dropped what they were doing to see the woman who refused to give up. "They rolled the carpet back out for me. Pulled across the silver tape," she recalls. "The finish line I got was so special to my story."

Like Julie Moss's crawl across the Ironman Kona finish line, Chrissy's Ironman finish in Arizona actually did more to inspire others than if she had finished "officially." As much as she would love to call herself an Ironman, she understands that she would have just been another finisher running through the chute.

What was most important to Chrissy was meeting her fundraising goal for Back on My Feet. This national nonprofit uses a running-based treatment model to help men experiencing (or at risk for) homelessness get their lives back together. Since 2007, BoMF has assisted more than 6,000 people in 11 major cities across the United States. Her goal was to raise $10,000, but she blew the roof off that by raising $17,500.

Chrissy had heard about BoMF at one of her previous races. "It really struck a chord with me. I have been a volunteer in soup kitchens since I was 14. I've always had a special place in my life for service." A key component of the program are the group runs, led by community volunteers and held three days a week at 5:45 a.m.

BoMF uses running to build discipline, confidence, and self-esteem while also forming a community of support. Chrissy started out volunteering on the periphery. "I was afraid to run with them. I hate holding people back with my slower pace," she says. Soon, she was recruited to lead a new, local BoMF team and realized running with them wasn't intimidating; it was rewarding. "I loved it. It gave me purpose outside of work. I didn't believe in myself. I had to rely on other people to tell me. I want to be that for others."

In the fall of 2013, Chrissy was offered the executive director position for the Indianapolis BoMF program. She is a living testimony to the program's mission—running transforms lives. It certainly transformed hers. "It's not about your pace; it's about your tenacity," she says. Even though she is now in a leadership position, Chrissy still goes out and runs with the group three mornings a week. "If I don't know the faces of who's out there running and their stories, I can't do this job."

Vying for redemption, Chrissy went back to conquer Ironman the following year in November 2014. Unfortunately, once again, the run was her undoing. This time, Chrissy's body revolted as a result of serious dehydration and fighting against record-breaking headwinds (reaching 30 mph) during the bike ride. Incoherent, skin covered with salt crystals, and her body going toxic, Chrissy required immediate medical attention. Her race was over. She suffered another setback while racing in the 2015 Ironman 70.3 Augusta, when she crashed her bike and shattered her clavicle so severely that it required surgery to repair.

"Some would say you've failed twice, time to move on," she tells her fans on her blog. "But I know that it's in me. My journey is still unfolding; it's unique and it's mine. It's been ugly and joyous. It will continue to keep getting better. That much I know."

From a little girl who questioned her worth, Chrissy has grown into an inspiring woman. "Triathlons are like a second chance at life," she says. "I believe everyone is worth another chance. I believe that for myself, too." Her Ironman journey may seem quite punishing, yet if you think about it, it's truly an act of self-love. She simply refuses to give up on herself. She doesn't want you to give up on yourself either.

"The funniest thing about this is I don't love it. The swim makes me anxious; I'm terribly slow. It's a hard day. But I keep coming back to it," Chrissy admits. "I don't know what my goal is, but I'll know when I get there. The transformation is still unfolding."

13

SINK OR SWIM

Here's what I'm going to tell you about your fear.
It's the most boring thing about you.

—ELIZABETH GILBERT

I would rank the act of swimming laps for the first time as one of the most humbling experiences of my life. And I've had plenty of humbling experiences from which to choose. Flat-out humiliating ones too.

While I certainly wasn't an athletic specimen when I started swimming, I considered myself to be in reasonable cardiovascular shape. I was running 3 to 4 miles, three times a week. I could run a 5K in a little over 27 minutes, which wasn't winning anything, but wasn't too shabby for a nonathletic mom who didn't train intensively or push herself very hard. But let me tell you something about swimming. If you're not a swimmer, I don't care what kind of great shape you are in. Swimming. Kicks. Your. Ass. And to add insult to injury, it kicks your ass while you're practically naked and looking like a drowned raccoon.

I could technically swim, if you defined swimming as the ability to organize my arms and legs into something that resembled freestyle, keep myself afloat, and propel myself forward. I could put my face in the water, blow bubbles, and turn my head to the side to breathe. But I never had formal lessons, and I spent my childhood reliant upon the three official strokes of Marco Polo: underwater mermaid swimming, sidestroke, and dog paddle. Anything resembling an actual competitive stroke, like freestyle or breast-stroke, didn't occur until I was 21, when I took swimming as one of my physical education requirements in college. I never swam again after that class, but now, at age 45, I was hoping at least some of it would come back to me.

The main problem with swimming is that it's complicated. Unless you are one of the fortunate ones who spent your youth on a swim team or summers lifeguarding, or had some type of true swimming background, it is a tough sport to pick up as an adult. Learning how to swim involves three main components: proper technique, physical conditioning, and anxiety management.

Let's start with technique. Did you think you knew how to swim "free-style" because you goofed around in the pool as a kid? No, that isn't free-style. That is glorified *not drowning*, and it won't get you more than two laps in the pool before the lifeguard is walking over to your lane offering a kick-board. Breaststroke is another stroke that gets pretty butchered. I didn't have the coordination to even attempt that one (ask my friend Janeen and my daughter Sophia, both of whom tried to teach me. My inability to pick it up blew their minds).

Then there is the head trip. Even if you are not afraid of the water, there is something completely visceral that occurs when your face is submerged while you exert yourself. When you're on dry land and exert yourself, you can pant. You cannot pant in swimming. You must master breath control. So, part of swimming is managing those screaming messages coming from the part of your brain hardwired to find air. Breathing, as it turns out, is kind of important. Go figure.

Before I swam for the first time, I *thought* a lot about swimming. I called it "mental preparation," which sounds way better than "procrastination."

I watched lots of YouTube videos, and I was fortunate in that my youngest two daughters, Ariella and Madelena (ages 6 and 8 at the time) had started a year-round swim program. Sitting in the bleachers, I was able to listen to the technical instruction given by the coaches. At that point, my actual level of expertise wasn't much different than a novice 6-year-old's, so it was just the advice I needed.

> *Courage is like a muscle. We strengthen it with use.*
> —RUTH GORDON

It was my friend Theresa who got me to stop practicing in my head and get my butt into the water by offering (okay, maybe insisting) to meet me at the pool. We met one Saturday morning, right as the gym opened at 7:00 a.m. (Not my idea of a relaxing Saturday morning.) Theresa did her swim workouts with the incredibly athletic Jenn M., who had been a competitive collegiate swimmer and was a phenomenal runner and superstar triathlete. This mother of four had been the overall winner of two Queen of the Hill Sprint Triathlons and ran marathons at a 7-minute-mile pace. She was a machine. Then there was Theresa, a fast runner with no swimming background who jumped into the pool one day, and almost overnight (with insane amounts of hard work and discipline, mind you) became an exceptionally strong swimmer. Case in point, she taught herself how to flip turn. *This* was my audience.

The aim was to feel more relaxed because I was surrounded by familiar faces, but the problem was that I now felt self-conscious and stupid next to these incredibly athletic ladies. It was as if a bright spotlight was shining on me and my ineptitude. Regardless, I had to do this. I reminded myself that they weren't there to judge me; they were there to support me. I was judging myself.

I got in my lane, pushed off the wall, and started.

Eight seconds into what I hoped was freestyle, I started hyperventilating and barely made it to the opposite side. I flailed around in the pool for another 20 minutes, pretending it was swimming, while Jenn and Theresa swam something like 14,000 laps at an Olympic gold medalist's pace. At least they weren't paying attention to my downward spiral. I finally determined that if I stayed in the pool a moment longer I might well drown and so said my goodbyes while they continued on as real athletes do. My shoulders, triceps, and upper back already felt sore. But most sore was my ego.

Humiliated and discouraged, I headed home, stood in a steamy shower, and mentally flogged myself. Who was I kidding? I would never be able to swim. If I couldn't do it in a nice safe pool, how could I do it in a deep lake with no sides to grab? Why was I even doing this? For the book? I could figure out a way to write this book purely from a noncompetitor's perspective. I didn't need to include an experiential component. I could change it up. My personal story was not that interesting anyway.

That's when I gave myself permission to quit, right there with shampoo in my hair. But then a funny thing happened. While one part of me was handing in my resignation, this other part of me was refusing to accept it. I later learned that when people are given a difficult task and then the option to quit, they become more persistent in their goals. I didn't realize it at that moment, but when I told myself to quit, I actually lit my own fire.

The other match lighting that fire had to do with my girls. Motherhood is a privilege I never take for granted and a responsibility I never forget. What kind of message would I be sending them if I threw in the towel? What would I have said to my girls if *they* wanted to quit after their first attempt at something? In fact, the little ones *did* want to quit swimming when they first started, and who was back in the locker room wiping away the tears and giving a stellar Dr. Mom pep talk garnished with sage advice? What would I be modeling to them if I quit on myself now? Equally as important, how could I break a commitment to myself? I had to stick with it. It wasn't about my book research anymore. It was about me.

Once I broke the seal with that first dip in the pool, it was on. I bought a pair of fins and a kickboard (neither of which I really used) and forced myself to the pool during non-peak hours so that I didn't have to share a lane. Every time I sank into that water, I swallowed my pride and just did the best I could. I knew I looked ridiculous to the 22-year-old lifeguard and the really good swimmers who were sometimes in the other lanes. I forced myself not to care. This didn't concern anyone but me. It was "Me versus Me." I was in my own little bubble.

At first, I had to stop and rest at each wall to catch my breath. Soon, I was making it up and back before I had to rest. One day, I came home walking on air because I had made it four continuous laps before having to stop for a breather. I tried to do drills I found on the Internet, but what really worked best for me was swimming as easily, slowly, and continuously as I could without stopping. I wasn't focused on speed; I was focused only on what I hoped was good technique. All I really needed in order to prepare for this triathlon was to feel confident that I could swim 500 yards without stopping or panicking. Period.

The more I improved my technique and conditioned my body, the easier swimming became. Not easy, mind you. Just *easier*. The better I got, the prouder I felt of myself and the more addicted I became to seeing if I could go just a little farther. Because that's the thing about doing something you thought you couldn't. When you *do* it, you look at yourself with new eyes. It had been a long, long time since I had impressed myself. I wondered what other secret awesomeness I might have buried inside me.

I'm always doing things I can't do. That's how I get to do them.
—PABLO PICASSO

Melanie A. laughs when she tells the story of how her boyfriend (now her husband) taught her how to swim for her first triathlon years ago. He knew he had a tough job ahead of him when he discovered Melanie didn't even know how to blow bubbles. "To this day he swears I was the hardest person he ever taught," she says. "The fact that we made it through those lessons without killing each other is, in itself, a miracle. The fact that I actually learned how to swim is a bigger miracle. I still remember how ecstatic I was when I finally swam one lap without stopping. Even the life-guard stood up and cheered!"

When Colleen C. joined the tri-club, she signed up for the open-water swim at the lake to get some experience. "I brought my kickboard, and tried not to panic," she admits. "I wouldn't put my face in the water!" Jayne, fellow tri-club member and a strong swimmer, swam next to Colleen the entire way. "At one point, she told me to try to swim without [the kickboard]. I was in such a panic! I started to freak out, telling her to give me back my board. She said over and over, 'No, you are fine.' When I really started to gasp, she told me to stand up. It was waist high! I laughed so hard!" Since then, Colleen has taken lessons and done more open-water swims, and her panic has diminished. She feels ready to conquer her next goal, an Olympic-distance triathlon.

Amy K.'s swim anxieties have also dissipated with experience, but she still wrestles with them on race day. "I still have a fear that I might panic or something will go wrong during the swim portion of a race," she confesses. Yet she presses on, reassuring herself that she is safe. Mia R. manages her open-water anxiety by swimming without putting her face in the water. "I am too old to be embarrassed anymore. Pride only gets in our way of overcoming our fears," she says. "My first tri was in the ocean with five-foot swells, and it took me a half hour to do the swim, but I did it, and have done two more tris since then."

Better to do something imperfectly than to do nothing flawlessly.
—ROBERT SCHULLER

After weeks of regular swimming, I could finally swim a quarter mile— the distance of the swim leg in the Queen of the Hill. Actually, I could swim nearly a mile without stopping. But my confidence sat in the shadow of the unfortunate reality that this was only half the battle. I wasn't afraid in a *pool*. Swimming in a warm, chlorinated, controlled environment that was only four feet deep was nothing. You were alone in your clearly marked lane with walls to grab and no creatures below. The only choppiness I encountered was caused by the 80-year-old dude aggressively aqua-jogging or some 3-year-old kid getting lessons. (Both were faster than me, by the way.)

At the Queen of the Hill, it was going to be the real deal. Hard-core, straight-up open water. I would be swimming in a cold, murky lake with low visibility and hundreds of legs and arms splashing around me and people bumping into me. With no cobalt-blue tiled line keeping me straight, I would have to learn to "sight" in order to stay on track. Yucky things would brush up against me, like slimy lake plants and other aquatic life I didn't want to think about. Electric eels. Lake snakes. The Loch Ness Monster. Jaws. You see how it all just spirals out of control.

Luckily, the tri-club knew how crucial open-water practice swims and instruction are for newbies. Even for the seasoned triathlete, they are an excellent way to practice sighting or try out a new wetsuit (a good rule is to never roll up to a triathlon in a never-been-worn wetsuit). For the triathlete embarking on her first triathlon, knocking out at least one open-water practice swim before race day is key. You have no idea how you might react your first time in the water. Even the most confident of swimmers can freak. No one, I repeat *no one*, is immune.

Jackie L. never expected that she would feel fearful in open water. She jumped confidently into the lake on the day of her first triathlon, happy and excited, and took off. "I went to breathe and got a mouthful of another swimmer's splash and I panicked," she says. Jackie struggled significantly during the swim but finally made it around the loop and went on to finish the triathlon. She was hooked, but the swim had become a surprising source of anxiety. In her second triathlon, with an ocean swim, Jackie panicked so significantly that she dropped out of the race. Focused on redemption, she returned to the same race the following year. Surrounded by four tri-club friends who stayed by her side, she made it through the swell and finished.

I wondered why she was willing to keep torturing herself when she clearly had so much anxiety that first time around. She says, "I'm extremely stubborn. I don't like to be told I can't do something. I wasn't satisfied until I conquered it." She *did* conquer the swim and in doing so, her self-esteem and self-confidence shot sky-high. Years later, when both she and her husband suddenly lost their jobs, forcing them to relocate to a new state, Jackie knew she possessed the kind of emotional fortitude and tenacity to face these major life changes. She knew it because of triathlon. It showed her that she had the ability to handle tough things and come through them even stronger.

The pride Melanie A. felt when she learned how to swim evaporated quickly when she stared down that lake the morning of her first triathlon. She had never even considered being nervous about the open water, but suddenly she was seized with terror. "I got in the water by sheer force of will and was simply not prepared for an open-water swim with people jostling me around. At one point I just floated on my back, grateful for the wetsuit because I would have drowned without it," she says. "Other waves of very fast swimmers were swimming over me, beside me. One man stopped his race and asked me if I was okay." She *was* okay, and she *did* finish. Melanie has completed countless triathlons since then and feels comfortable in the water.

If you want to learn to swim, jump into the water.
On dry land no frame of mind is ever going to help you.

—BRUCE LEE

ROLLING IN THE DEEP

When I arrived at Lake Gilman for my first open-water practice swim, the dock and bank were filled with women in swim caps and goggles. There were 30 to 40 of them already in the water, at various states of swimming the horseshoe-shaped quarter-mile loop. I signed in under the pavilion, where the back of my hand was marked with the number 90 in thick black permanent marker. Everyone needed to be accounted for. I handed over my $5 fee, shoved another buck in the tip jar for the lifeguards, and walked down the slope leading to the dock. That's when the nerves hit me. It looked so much bigger up close.

I saw a number of women treading water by a floating dock, even more were swimming, and a small group were standing in the shallow water at the second dock, post-swim, getting ready to climb out. Another group of dry women were "on deck," prepping to get in that cold lake. In the center of the action stood Colleen Fossett with a megaphone and a smile. "Okay, ladies, next group enters the water in two minutes!" she called out.

I suddenly felt overwhelmed, gripped by a powerful, unsettling force. Big, fat tears started forming in my eyes, and a lump in my throat threatened to burst forth into an audible sob.

Oh, crap, I'm not seriously going to cry, I thought. I was mortified and confused. My mind was clear, my body felt relaxed, I was engaged in positive self-talk, and yet I was experiencing an emotion that I could neither explain nor stop. *I can't believe I'm crying. This is freakin' ridiculous.* I mentally tried to get myself together, taking slow deep breaths while staying off to the side where no one could see what a dork I was.

Get your crap together, Alicia. You've done harder things than this, I reminded myself, staring down Lake Gilman as if it were an enemy threatening attack. I set my bag on the ground with a slew of others and spotted Anita, a woman whom I recognized from church. As we exchanged hellos I was struck by how calm and casual she was, tucking her curls into a swim cap, smiling away. It was then I realized I was the only swimmer without a cap and one of the few without a wetsuit. "I hope it's not freezing," I said, making small talk. I knew damn well it would be. I'd been forewarned by many. Forewarned that the cold actually takes your breath away, making swimming difficult at first. I had been too cheap to buy a wetsuit; plus it seemed like one more unnecessary hassle.

"Well, you've done this before, right?" she asked.

"Nope. First time," I answered. "And I'm a little nervous . . ." I trailed off as my throat tightened and the tears threatened to burst forth. Damn it.

I crossed my arms tightly around my chest and bounced my knees around, willing myself to get a grip while Anita tried to soothe me with advice about flipping on my back, and how I could get to places where I could stand, and all the plans I could make in the event I panicked. This made me feel much better. We scarcely knew each other, but she took the time to give me pointers when she certainly didn't need to.

Anita explained how it worked. Everyone swam from the main dock out to the floating dock where we would tread water until Colleen gave us the signal over her megaphone to start swimming. Apparently, this helped to control the flow of swimmers and simulated a typical triathlon wave start. Once in motion, we followed the shoreline, keeping the buoys to the right, went around the two lifeboats, and headed back to the place we started. All without drowning. (I added that last part.)

My friend Ashley emerged from her swim, blond hair still matted down from her swim cap. "Hey Ashley!" I waved. "So how cold *is* it?" I was perseverating on the water temperature like a madwoman.

"You want me to be brutally honest or sugarcoat it?" she chirped.

"Brutally honest," I said.

"Okay. There are pockets of freezing cold and regular cold. I'm not going to lie. When you start, you are in a really icy cold pocket, but once you get going and you're completely horizontal, you're in the warmer layer of the water. It gets better as you start moving. You just have to get going." She wasn't wearing a wetsuit, so I knew this was probably an accurate temperature assessment.

"Okay," I sighed. I had been standing on the shore for way too long, and I knew I just had to stop wasting time and just get into that stupid, cold lake. That's when I actually started crying. Like, for *real*, with the sobs and the nose wiping and the shaking and the eyes leaking like faucets. Ashley was up the slope and by my side in a nanosecond offering comfort. "Do you want me to go out with you? I'll swim with you!" she offered with heartfelt sincerity.

I knew she would, but of course I declined. "I'll be okay. I can do it," I choked out, avoiding eye contact. I hoped I didn't sound dismissive and ungrateful. I deeply appreciated her offer and perhaps I should have accepted it. But I had issues. I felt guilty about making Ashley go back in that cold water. And even more than that, I knew I had to do this on my own. No crutch. No coaching. No help. If I couldn't get this done on my own, right here and now, I was screwed on race day.

I marched out onto the dock, quickly descended three little metal steps and, without hesitation, plunged into the most frigid water I've ever been in. Close your eyes and imagine sitting in a bathtub filled with ice water. That's how the "warm spots" felt.

The sudden cold ripped the breath right out of my lungs. My limbs seized up and didn't want to cooperate. Somehow I got myself over to the group of women treading water, waiting for the start signal, my teeth audibly chattering. Colleen counted down "30 seconds until takeoff" over the megaphone and as I waited, it felt like I already used up all my energy just getting to the start point and avoiding hypothermia.

I felt paralyzed by the cold and overwhelmed by the expanse of water. My positive thoughts were getting away from me as the fear and doubt took over. *I can't do this*, I quickly decided and entertained a brief fantasy of swimming back to shore, driving home, drinking some hot chocolate on the couch, and forgetting this whole thing. Why was I subjecting myself to this nonsense? Who cared if I did a triathlon? Nobody. *Nobody freakin' cared.*

Well, one person cared. As much as I hated to admit it, *I* cared. So, I kept treading water and freezing and convincing myself that it would be okay. Sure, I couldn't catch my breath or feel my fingers and I might start to cry again, but I was going to do this.

Colleen signaled us to start swimming. Grateful to be moving, I put my face in the water for the first time. But when I tried to blow out air, my body refused to release it. My respiratory system had clamped down, frozen shut. I blew out bubbles by sheer force, turned my head, and sucked in my next breath. The water was deep brown, like swimming in a cup of tea with no milk and sugar. (Except the tea was ice cold.) When my face was in the water, there was nothing below me but thick, foggy brownness. Nothing in front of me but foggy brownness. It was disconcerting to have no sense of anything around me. No sense of depth, no idea of what's in front or below or behind. My mind could so easily start to freak. So I focused on the one thing I could see—the white skin of my forearm every time it dipped in front of me to take a stroke. As long as I could see that arm pass in front of me, I was safe and in control.

One, two, three, breathe. One, two, three, breathe. I played this on repeat, like a soundtrack for survival. I forced the breath out in violent bubbles, at times audibly screaming under water with each exhale. I focused on that pale arm disappearing and reappearing and swam with as much force and purpose as I could muster. Each time my head turned for a breath, I saw bits of the world, like the shutter on a camera opening for a fraction of an instant and then snapping shut. These glimpses were slowly changing, proof I was moving forward. Otherwise, it was hard to tell.

When I reached the final straightaway, I stopped to get my bearings and saw women not too far ahead standing and chatting in the shallow water by the dock. I could hardly believe it. I was almost there. It felt like forever. It felt like a blink.

I pushed forward, free and clear of all worries. When the water became shallow and I could stand, bare feet sinking into the slimy mud, I started laughing with relief, overwhelmed with a sense of joy and accomplishment. Only moments ago I was bawling and half out of my mind with anxiety, yet 15 minutes later I was busting at the seams with pride.

"Do one thing that scares you each day," Eleanor Roosevelt once said. Well, I don't know if I'd make facing my fears a *daily* endeavor, but I certainly can see the power in it.

Doing the thing you never thought you could do. Showing yourself you're stronger than you realized. Shining brighter than you thought you could shine. That was the feeling. The feeling I had heard so many women describe but had never fully understood until now.

Stop acting so small.
You are the universe in ecstatic motion.

—RUMI

UNFINISHED BUSINESS

"Had it not been for the half-Ironman,
I do not believe I would be here to tell you this story."

AS BARBARA TREAD the frigid waters of Lake Taupo, New Zealand, waiting to start her first half-Ironman, the pain in her left forearm was nearly unbearable. But she was no stranger to pain. Nearly a decade earlier, at the age of 32, Barbara had been diagnosed with rheumatoid arthritis (RA), a painful condition affecting the joints. When she decided to tackle triathlon, she wasn't going to let a little thing like the chronic, nearly debilitating pain of RA derail her. Clearly, Barbara already possessed a will of iron. Now she just needed to cross the finish line of her first half-Ironman—distance race. She was using Lake Taupo as a practice run for the full Ironman, 11 weeks later. The problem was, this race was not going as planned.

Barbara never considered herself much of an athlete growing up, but she started going to the gym and working out as an adult. When she heard some friends talking about doing an adventure race along the Coromandel Peninsula years ago, she was intrigued. So she volunteered as support crew just to be a part of the action. Impressed with the race and the community of athletes, Barbara found the nearest multisport club in her hometown of Hamilton, New Zealand, and volunteered as support crew there too. Several people in that tri-club were training to compete in the 2005 Ironman Taupo. "I decided I had to go and watch this amazing event," she says, and attended that year as a spectator.

"If you ever need an inspirational, emotional experience, go to the next Ironman event. I felt as if I traveled to a new country, where everyone is friendly, supportive, and caring. The event had a profound effect on me and continues to inspire me," she says. It was there, watching 1,200-and-some-odd competitors cross the finish line, that her own Ironman dream was born. She wanted to hear the words of Mike Reilly booming over the loudspeaker: "Barbara Mockford. You. Are. An. Ironman!"

Even though Barbara had zero triathlon experience, a passion awakened after that pivotal day. She was hooked on the idea of finishing that race. "When I do something, it is the largest or the best or nothing at all. I always try for the moon and hope to get to a star, forever the optimist in all things."

"I wanted this whole experience despite my rheumatoid arthritis," says Barbara. "The first thing I did the next day was make an appointment with my trainer to see if it was doable." It was indeed doable, but she would need to be tough. Strike that—tougher. Training for an Ironman was no walk in the park, and doing it with RA was going to be doubly challenging. But pain had become her baseline, and she was quite gifted at ignoring it and pushing through.

During her 11 months of Ironman training, Barbara competed in two cycling races and a Tinman distance triathlon. Now, here she was, ready to knock off 70.3 miles on the road to the "big day," and it was all going to hell in a handbasket.

In the weeks leading up to the Lake Taupo half-Ironman, Barbara had been training through a growing pain in her forearm and an immense fatigue that persisted no matter how much she rested. The morning of the race, the pain was horrendous despite receiving an injection and pain meds from her doctor. The swelling, typical of RA, was nearing the point of deformity. Cursing her arthritis, she steeled her mind and headed out with the rest of the competitors to tread in the freezing cold water, awaiting the start. At the signal, she was off on her swim despite excruciating pain and rising nausea.

The water was so frigid that wetsuits were mandatory and anyone who could not complete the swim in 70 minutes would be pulled out and disqualified. The risk of hypothermia was real. Struggling immensely, Barbara was the second-to-last participant out of the water, followed closely by two race marshals. They escorted her to the first aid tent to warm up, but she knew the cold wasn't the real issue. The crippling pain and nausea were worse than in any RA episode she had ever had. Today wouldn't be her day. Heartbroken, but resolute, she remained positive, staying on to cheer her friends and fellow competitors and focusing on getting better for her upcoming full Ironman only a few months away.

The following day, when the pain and swelling in her wrist and forearm were even worse, Barbara suspected there was something more going on. She headed to the hospital, where X-rays revealed two fractures. There was also something suspicious on the image: a large black area on the bone with things that looked like roots. They suspected a bone infection, which had caused the bone to rot and break. They took a bone biopsy and admitted her to the hospital for multiple tests and observation over three days.

At some point during this process, one of the doctors dropped a bomb on her. They were no longer talking about an infection. They were using the word "tumor." Shocked, devastated, but ever hopeful, Barbara kept herself strong through the limbo of waiting, as more tests were sent off to the Mayo Clinic in the United States to figure out what type of tumor they were dealing with.

During this limbo, her arm was placed in a plaster cast. She and two friends had previously registered for the Tauranga half-Ironman as a relay team, but Barbara certainly couldn't do her swim leg with her arm in plaster. Unfazed, she asked her doctor if she could walk the run portion. "I needed to keep my Ironman dreams alive," she says. Her team was 100 percent behind her.

Barbara walked the entire 13.1 miles of the Tauranga half-Ironman in a pink cast with some unknown tumor splitting open the radial bone of her arm, while she waited to hear if she had cancer and, if so, what her prognosis would be. She finished an hour and fifteen minutes after the official cutoff time. An unofficial finish for her relay team, as per Ironman rules. But people had heard about this amazing woman in the pink cast with the tenacious spirit and were inspired. The CEO of the race's major sponsor was waiting for her at the finish line, and the finisher's tape was pulled across just for her. "[He] shook my hand and put the medal around my neck," she recalls. He told her that while legally she might not have earned the medal, there was no way in hell she didn't deserve it simply for not giving up.

That race gave her a morale boost, but a new challenge was just beginning. After a third biopsy and weeks of uncertainty, the diagnosis was delivered: chondroblastic osteosarcoma. Bone cancer. Barbara refers to it as "death delivered on a platter." After multiple, aggressive cycles of chemotherapy, she would undergo surgery. The doctor told her to prepare to lose her arm just below the shoulder. "I rang one of my friends who had a great sense of humor. He told me all the positive things there were about having one arm, which made me laugh," Barbara writes in her memoir, *An Unshakable Belief*.

Instead of racing in the full Ironman for which she had trained diligently, Barbara began grueling chemotherapy treatments, every three weeks for five consecutive months. Chemo came with horrible side effects, quarantines, blood transfusions, damage to her kidneys and reproductive organs—the list goes on and on. She somehow endured it all and then went into surgery that spring, fully prepared to lose her arm. When she came out of anesthesia, her left arm was still there. They removed the tumor and the carpal bones and then used the fibula bone in her leg to replace the destroyed radius bone. Her arm was saved. Her life, it seemed, was saved too. Saved by the doctors and the treatments and the surgery, but also by her courage, iron will, and strength. She believes her life was also saved by triathlon.

"Had it not been for the half Ironman . . . I do not believe I would be here to tell you this story," Barbara writes in her book. "You get to know your body like you never have before." She draws many parallels between training for an Ironman-distance triathlon and beating cancer. Those personality characteristics that attracted her to the Ironman also served her well in the battle for her life. "Ironman is not for the faint-hearted or the uncommitted. You have to accept to train in the ghastliest conditions of wind, rain, blazing hot sunny days, wind, snow, hail and all other elements of the weather. . . . You have to accept the worst. Train through the worst and be prepared for surprises."

"I think the approach to Ironman of taking one step at a time is what helped," says Barbara. "The strategy, the planning, the preparation, the commitment of an Ironman all contributed to helping me survive."

This plan kicked into high gear when a follow-up scan revealed nodules in her lungs. The cancer was spreading. Her doctor prescribed "palliative care," a treatment approach that focuses on reducing the symptoms to provide comfort rather than a cure. But, Barbara was having none of that. She may not have been able to cross the finish line of an Ironman triathlon, but make no mistake: This woman was made of iron, through and through. She created a customized holistic health plan, followed it to the letter, and months later, her lungs were clear. All traces of cancer, gone.

She has remained cancer-free to date.

Triathlon brought the tumor to her attention, and the daily dedication of training for 140.6 miles gave her the discipline to follow a strict treatment regimen that helped her beat the odds and crush her cancer into oblivion. While she continues to keep the Ironman dream alive, at present she finds great reward volunteering at the events and remaining active in the community that inspires her.

Ever the optimist, Barbara still holds on to the dream of finishing what she started. "Only if I'm 100 percent healthy," she clarifies. It's been a long road, but the journey isn't over. "Mr. Ironman and I, we have unfinished business."

14

WOMEN ON WHEELS

Life is like a 10-speed.
Most of us have gears we never use.

—CHARLES SHULTZ

For many people, biking is inextricably entwined with childhood memories. Feeling like a rock star when we graduated from tricycle to training wheels, bike tricked out with bell and basket. That huge rite of passage when the training wheels came off. The independence of being old enough to ride to a friend's house unsupervised. The exhilarating feeling when you learned to let go of the handlebars without falling or took your feet off the pedals in a seated split while coasting top speed down a hill.

I practically lived on my bike as a kid. A whole gaggle of us rode around the neighborhood in a pack, a collection of glittering banana seats, chrome handlebars, and long streamers blowing in the wind like angel hair. After I outgrew that bike, and my Dorothy Hamill haircut, I graduated to a white-and-red 10-speed that I used to visit friends, skinny legs pedaling in my Dr. Scholl's and cutoff shorts. Once I hit age 15, the bike displayed a fantastic array of cobwebs in the garage, and I could be found either tethered to the phone or lying around in front of the television. I did use an inexpensive, generic beach cruiser to get around while living and working at the beach in my early 20s, biking down the impossibly flat Coastal Highway of Ocean City, Maryland. My bike's purpose then was simple—get me from point A (my waitressing job at the crab shack) to point B (the local bars).

As a kid, the bike represented ultimate fun and freedom. In my young adulthood, it was an inexpensive mode of transportation. But once I bought my first car and became a humorless adult, the bike no longer served a purpose in my life. The fun of it, forgotten. The practicality, irrelevant. The fitness aspect, off-putting. I became a mother, and the only bikes I thought about were the kids' tricycles, and not backing over them as I reversed out of our driveway. By the time I was tackling this triathlon, 20 years had elapsed since my butt sat on the saddle of a bike . . . with one exception.

While Anthony and I were visiting Portland, Maine, we took a ferry to Peaks Island for the day. When we disembarked, we immediately spotted a bike shop where we rented two beach cruisers to tour the circumference of the tiny, scenic island.

I found that I was actually a little nervous about hopping on that bike, although it was as steady, heavy, and safe as a tank. Maybe it was the menacing wicker basket, or the little silver bell. At any rate, I had a wobbly start and feared I might be the one person in the history of humankind for whom "It's like riding a bike" didn't apply.

Eventually, though, I got my bearings, and it ended up being a wonderful ride—the salty sea rushing past my ears as I zoomed down the hills, hair blowing in tangled ribbons behind me. It was thrilling to slice through the air on two wheels, propelling myself forward with the brute force of my quads and hamstrings. So what if I wasn't going Mach speed? It didn't matter—it wasn't a competition. We weren't trying to burn calories or build muscle or cross a finish line. We were sightseeing and chatting, stopping to snap photographs and appreciating breathtaking views along the way. The bike allowed us to experience a new place in a special way.

As much fun as I had, once I returned to the reality of four kids, hectic schedules, and responsibilities, biking returned to that file folder in my mind marked "exercise." Perhaps in other parts of the country, bikes on the open road were more commonplace, but in my neck of the woods the only biking I saw was at the gym, on a stationary bike equipped with a mini-television. They weren't much fun. Once the tri-club throttled up in Mullica Hill, however, women hit the road on fancy five-figure bikes with razor-thin wheels.

I certainly saw the appeal of getting out of the confining thunderdome of a Spin class and into the fresh air. But real biking on a real road was the real deal. There were cars racing by, potholes, wind, and road debris that could cause a flat tire miles from home. Plus, you couldn't fake it on the group rides. People could tell how fast or slow you were. What if I couldn't keep up? I would look like an idiot. I mean, more so than usual. I would have to learn about safety and road etiquette, learn how to shift gears, ride in a group, and fix a chain that might pop off. It all seemed a lot more stressful than that casual ride around Peaks Island. Those girls in pink weren't meandering through the meadow on a heavy, fat-tire bike taking in the scenery. They were racing by at 22 mph like hell on wheels.

But the biggest, most immediate problem I faced with biking was that I did not own an actual bike. Possessing a bicycle seemed like an important detail in my pursuit of triathlon, but damned if I was going to drop a wad of cash on something that might sit in the garage, untouched, for the rest of my life. After all, I wasn't entirely convinced that I would see this triathlon thing through. And if I *did* make it to the finish line, I wasn't imagining an encore performance. The triathlon girls swore that they had never met anyone who crossed the finish line and proclaimed to be "one and done," but I was reasonably confident I'd be a one-hit wonder.

Four weeks before Queen of the Hill, I finally asked my friend Lorri Z. if I could borrow one of her many bikes. She lent me a nice hybrid, a road bike frame with heavier mountain bike tires. What that meant was that I would sacrifice speed for a less threatening ride. I was cool with that.

Once I secured that bike, there were no more excuses. It was time for me to ride.

Begin, and you are halfway there.
—ALFRED A. MONTAPERT

Since I had the annoying problem of having really fit and fast friends, I was too embarrassed to cycle with them and slow them down. As a result, I did most of my bike training alone. That was probably way less fun than group rides, but I was far more emotionally comfortable solo. I figured out how to shift gears and get over hills and manage road distractions. My tush hurt, my neck felt pinched on occasion, and I wasn't sure I was riding hard enough to get a true workout. But I was out there. And the more I biked, the more comfortable I became and the stronger I got. Not faster, just stronger and more confident. Soon, it became sort of fun (that is, when I wasn't huffing up a hill or feeling my whole bike rattle beneath me when an 18-wheeler zoomed by, or when my girl parts weren't going numb).

Biking with friends has its perks, I'm sure. But going alone allowed me to clear my head, enjoy the peace and quiet, and avoid the pressure of keeping pace. My favorite part of my typical 12-mile loop was a stretch of road around the halfway point. It was scenic and flat and devoid of cars. The farmland on either side almost swallowed me up, and I felt so small on this giant spinning globe and overwhelmed with the beauty of nature.

The experience conjured memories of a time eons ago when I never thought twice about cruising around on a bike. Never felt nervous, awkward, or overwhelmed. I simply jumped on my bike as smoothly and effortlessly as I jumped in my car now. Except it felt carefree and energizing and even joyful.

Much to my surprise, training for the bike leg of the triathlon helped me reconnect with the fun of riding. Climbing a hill to zoom down the other side, so fast you felt like you might just fly.

ॐ

The bicycle's popularity is enjoying a resurgence that is evident from coast to coast. Biking is not just something to do competitively. It's an eco-friendly mode of transportation, a fun way to stay fit, and a cool way to explore the world. Today, there are more commuters on bikes, more families going for joyrides together, more century rides for charity, and more events, paths, trails, and parking spaces for bicycles than ever before. Urban transportation, touring the wine country, shredding through the gnarl, pedaling for a cause, or racing in the velodrome—there are so many ways to ride a bike and so many bikes from which to choose.

Today's bike market has something for everyone. There are road, mountain, and touring bikes. There are city bikes, hybrids, and cruisers. You can find bikes designed for fun in the dirt, like BMX, Cyclocross and Fatbike, and bikes designed for competitive track and time trial races. There are tandem bikes, recumbent bikes, freight bikes, sociables, cycle rickshaws, ice cycles, and folding bikes. There are unicycles, prone bikes, sideways bikes, and even electric bikes. But, I was most enthralled with this huge contraption called a "party bike." Also known as a "beer bike," this mobile multipassenger monstrosity is half pedibus/half pub, propelled by humans using bike pedals housed underneath each bar stool. That way you can burn off the calories from the beer as you're drinking it. Ingenious.

> *The bicycle is just as good company as most husbands,*
> *and when it gets old and shabby, a woman can dispose of it*
> *and get a new one without shocking the entire community.*
>
> —ANN STRONG

THE WHEELS OF CHANGE

The history of the bicycle is fascinating. More than just a fun ride, this little contraption of aluminum, tires, and pedals was a symbol of industrial civilization and social reform in the United States. The bicycle initiated the paving of roads, laying the ground for our highway system, and introduced technologies that affected the automotive industry. It also played a major role in eroding the gender barriers of the late Victorian era.

Viewed as a "freedom machine" by American feminist Susan B. Anthony, the bicycle offered women independence, self-reliance, physical fitness, and long-awaited dress reform. She described the power of the bicycle perfectly, saying: "Let me tell you what I think of bicycling. I think it has done more to emancipate women than anything else in the world."

Today we see women on bikes and think nothing of it, but this was not always the case. In fact, it used to be downright scandalous. The bike craze peaked in the 1890s, during the Victorian era, after the Rover Safety Bicycle hit the market with its pneumatic (air-filled) tires and bike chain. The "problem" with this new, more affordable and safer bicycle was that women were now keen on the freedom that came with the bike. This rocked the carefully constructed Victorian societal structure off its axis. Not only was it considered entirely unladylike for a gentlewoman to ride, but it was condemned as indecent and immoral. Clergymen preached about the bike's vulgarity. Doctors wrote of its damage to a woman's pelvis and reproductive organs. Husbands worried that the increasing independence of their wives would cause a rift to the family unit, and young, unescorted women trolling around on a bike would naturally become morally loose.

But the real issue behind all this was that women riding bikes challenged the deeply ingrained social order that hinged on the belief that women were inferior. If women could handle a bike just as well as (if not better than) their male counterparts, then what did that mean? Women riding bikes changed *everything*.

> *Bicycling is the nearest approximation I know*
> *to the flight of birds.*
> —LOUIS J. HELLE JR.

BIKES AND BETTYS

As I watched hundreds of women around me evolve into avid triathletes, I noticed another subculture evolving. A *sub*-subculture, if you will. This subset of women had started out in triathlon but fell in a hard, deep, mad love with cycling. This unbridled passion gave them exclusive membership in another rapidly growing tribe—female cyclists.

After months of chemotherapy for the treatment of invasive breast cancer, Lisa P. was in rough shape. "I was really debilitated," she says. "I couldn't even walk up a flight of steps." Her husband decided to do a bike ride in her honor for the American Cancer Society. "He started training for this bike ride; he couldn't even *ride* a bike," she laughs. But he completed it and was hooked. The following season, he convinced Lisa to start cycling with him. Next thing she knew, she fell in love with the bike too. She became an avid cyclist, mountain biker, and member of the Action Wheels Race Team in southern New Jersey. At age 50, Lisa took up cyclocross, a bike race that takes place on grass and dirt and involves steep hills, quick dismounts, and carrying your bike over obstacles. She absolutely loves it.

When Breigh's husband, Mike, encouraged her to start cycling with him, she had zero interest. She was an avid runner and had been a Division I volleyball player in college, but she was resistant to the bike. "I thought it was the stupidest thing ever," she says, not at all thrilled with his expensive and time-consuming hobby. "I had this irrational fear of getting hit by a car. Then Mike immediately got hit by a car." His injuries were significant, but he healed and was right back at it. For Breigh, his accident confirmed two things: Cycling was both dumb *and* dangerous.

Not one to back down from a challenge, Mike tried another angle. He had recently learned about the MHWTC and shared the news of the brand-new club with his wife. "I don't swim and I don't bike," she told him. "So *that's* dumb." But she eventually caved, joined the tri-club, and started going along on the club's evening group bike rides to cross-train. Cycling came easy to Breigh, and she was quite fast. But she didn't fall in love with it immediately. She rode infrequently, still scared of getting hurt. The following year, she signed up for the Queen of the Hill. She had a new road bike but trained very little on it. Nonetheless, Breigh came in sixth place overall and had one of the fastest bike times in the race. She may have thought biking was stupid and scary, but *she was great at it* even when she was hardly trying. That's when things got interesting.

Breigh started riding with cyclists from the Action Wheels bike shop. "I learned how to rotate group lines, pull, and follow a wheel," she says. She also started making new friends. Good friends. "The social aspect is what hooks you," Breigh explains. By the end of that year, she joined the Action Wheels Race Team, and in 2015, Breigh became the New Jersey Category 4 Road Race State Champion. She has had many cool adventures since, such as biking Nashville's 100-mile ride for the Juvenile Diabetes Research Foundation, riding the Skyline Drive along 220 miles of Shenandoah National Park, and participating in a rigorous cycling tour of Spain alongside Mike and several cycling friends.

Imagine if Lisa P. hadn't let herself hop on that bike or if Breigh hadn't faced her fear of the road and given it a shot. Sure, they might have still been fit and outdoorsy and athletic. But all this amazing stuff would have never happened. I'm not talking about awards and accomplishments, but about all the friends they've made and the places they've seen and the experiences they've had on two wheels. The bonus for both these women is that it was a shared passion with their spouses, allowing for more quality time together and lots of adventure.

Many people shy away from hills.
They make it easy on themselves, but that limits their
improvement. The more you repeat something,
the stronger you get.
—JOE CATALANO

Certainly, not everyone who jumps on a bike will become a state champion or bike 100 miles at a stretch. However, I was becoming more and more convinced that a great many unexpected and wonderful things were hidden behind closed doors. All we needed was the courage to turn the knob and give it a little push.

SHE'S A BRICK HOUSE

The Queen of the Hill was just a few weeks away. I could run the distance. I could swim the distance. I could bike the distance. All that was left was to practice doing two of those activities together. There is a name for this: a "brick."

A brick workout pairs two activities back to back. You can swim and then bike, or bike and then run, or you can do a backward brick, reversing the order. The idea behind the brick is to gain experience transitioning from one event to the next, to become familiar with not only the logistics but the way your body feels. This is most important when transitioning from the bike to the run. Your legs feel like cinderblocks when you start that run after miles of pedaling, which is probably why it's called a "brick." You seriously feel like Frankenstein during the first half-mile, and it's important to experience this *before* race day, if only for mental preparation.

I planned a swim-bike brick a few weeks before the triathlon, after my second open-water practice swim at Lake Gilman. My friend Lori W. joined me. We were halfway through a 12-mile bike ride, cresting a long, undulating hill, when my phone began buzzing in my backpack. "Go ahead, Lori," I puffed, as if she were not already ahead of me anyway. I fumbled in my bag, still biking, and somehow retrieved my phone already knowing who it would be. It was Anthony, as I suspected. I knew what was wrong before he even spoke because he doesn't normally call me when I'm out, especially when he knew I would be a little preoccupied. Carlie either had a seizure, or there was a diaper situation. "Uh, when do you think you'll be getting home?" he asked with a voice dripping both apology and expectancy. Okay, it wasn't a seizure. Which meant . . .

"Dude, I'm on a bike 6 miles away," I panted. He proceeded to tell me what I had already guessed. Code Brown, as we call it. Carlie has been in diapers her entire life, and despite ongoing attempts at toilet training, she will likely be in diapers for the rest of her life. Since she transitioned from little girl to young woman, I have been the sole diaper changer. This makes it difficult to leave the house for long stretches.

Normally I would feel immense guilt kicking in. But the funny thing was, this time I didn't feel guilty. Though the narcissist in me would love to think the world stops spinning when I'm gone, it doesn't. Everyone can and will survive. No one ever died of one dirty diaper.

"I can only get there when I get there," I said, knowing how bad he felt bothering me. He had been a constant source of support on this triathlon journey, and I knew he was simply feeling panicked by the poop and wanted to know my ETA. "Just keep everything as contained as possible. I am going straight home, but let me remind you I need to cover a bunch of miles on two wheels, not four, and I'm not fast."

I caught up to Lori, and we laughed about the whole situation. Lori was also the mother to a daughter with special needs. Our shared experience was something that bonded us from the beginning. We "got" each other. I could tell her every poopy diaper, hazmat cleanup, weird and wacky story without grossing her out or getting the pity stare. That's gold, right there.

As we finished our ride, the sun was quadruple its size, hanging low, just skimming the large cornfield and turning the sky the color of sherbet. It reminded me that even when we're barreling through the hard stuff of life, there is always something beautiful if we only stop to notice. I thought about the parallel between parenting a special child and triathlon. They were both exceptionally challenging, yet the reward far exceeded any difficulty or sacrifice.

With my big race only weeks away, I could finally say I felt reasonably conditioned for all three legs of the triathlon. This particular bike ride reminded me that my mental toughness was never in question. Parenting a child with complex special needs has prepared me well for the tough stuff in life.

If life were a triathlon, I figured at this point, I was already a freakin' Ironman.

UNBROKEN

*"One minute I was riding, then one minute
I'm lying on the road. A man was saying,
'Don't move; you've been hit.'"*

THE LIST OF injuries was extensive: Nearly all the thoracic vertebrae, and several lumbar vertebrae, cracked, broken, or shattered. Spinal cord twisted and bent. Punctured lung. Blown-out fracture of the eye socket. Left hip fractured in two places. Multiple breaks in the left arm.

Her surgeon told her it was a miracle she wasn't paralyzed. It was even a bigger miracle she lived.

"I was training for my first Ironman. It was about 49 days away," says Terry Woods, a Texan, wife and mother of two. "I was at a bike rally, so you'd think it would be safe." It was a beautiful day. The weather conditions and visibility were perfect. The rural little highway was flat, and she was biking on a wide shoulder.

It happened halfway through the 100-mile ride. "This woman came up behind me. People saw her weaving all over the road," she says. "I never saw her. I didn't see it coming." The woman hit Terry at 65 miles per hour, but she remembers none of the impact. "One minute I was riding, then one minute I'm lying on the road. A man was saying, 'Don't move; you've been hit.'

I thought it was a dream. I was disoriented. I couldn't make sense of it." When Terry started her triathlon journey, she never imagined things would end up like this.

☙

Terry discovered triathlon in 2005. "I didn't even know what a tri was," she laughs. "I went to an informal meeting at the YMCA and thought, 'Okay, this is new!'" She learned about the sport, trained, and did her first sprint distance. "I was so excited! Then, I came home and slept for six hours." When she awoke, she immediately registered for more races. That first year, she did four sprints. The next year, she added Olympic distances. Then she took the leap to a 70.3, loved it, and did two more. "I started thinking, 'What's it going to take to do [an Ironman]? I knew I'd be training morning, noon, and night." She sat down and had a heart-to-heart with her non-triathlete but supportive husband. At the time, she was 54 years old, with two children in their 20s who were out on their own. "He was all for it," she says. So, she registered for the 2010 Ironman Louisville and began training in earnest for her longest-distance race.

Now, instead of counting down the days to her big race, she was sprawled across the road, body broken, Ironman dreams shattered. "I couldn't move. It was so incredibly painful," she says. Terry was raced to a nearby hospital and then transported to a Trauma I Center.

The extensive injuries to her spinal column were the most serious, and the reparative surgery was complicated. She sustained compression fractures to 50 percent of the vertebrae in her spine. Her T-11 vertebra (the second-lowest thoracic vertebra) was completely shattered. In a surgery lasting nearly 11 hours, it was removed and a titanium cage put in its place. In addition, two rods were mounted along either side of her spine, extending from her hips to her shoulder blades, and secured with 14 titanium screws. During recovery she needed to wear a body brace all day, removing it only to sleep.

"It was weeks before I could even go to physical therapy," Terry says. Her first hurdle was to get off the pain medication. "One of the things that was almost as painful as the injury itself was the pain of weaning off the narcotics," she admits. "It was excruciating. I literally cried all night long. It's incredibly painful. Your whole body . . . joints, tissue . . . the entire body hurts."

Regaining basic functions took a long time. "I had to learn how to walk again," she says. "It was so painful, I would cry." She worked hard in physical therapy for the next nine months, took one day at a time, faced each little hurdle, and built upon her successes. Her walks, once brief and painful, were getting longer. She began using her indoor bike trainer to ride for five-minute increments.

One pivotal moment in her recovery came in the form of a wonderful gift, as in a literal Christmas gift given to her by her husband. "It was another Garmin," she says. Her original was lost in the accident. She believes it was knocked off her arm because it was never seen again. When she received a new one, it was like gift-wrapped hope. "It meant so much to me. It meant he believed in me."

"I started riding again in April," Terry says. While some might have had a difficult time getting back on the bike, Terry found it surprisingly easy and even comforting. "I love to ride," she says simply. She went out with a local bike group and they rode in a quiet park with low traffic. She surprised herself by riding 40 miles that day.

One year after her accident, Terry was biking regularly and walking. She didn't pressure herself with immediate promises to do another triathlon or to get to the start line of the Ironman she missed. Instead, she was patient with her body and with herself and focused on being appreciative of the lessons she could find in the tragedy and the pain.

"It started calling me again," she says. "I thought, 'I'm going to see if I can do a half-Iron.'" After a successful race at the 2011 Ironman 70.3 Texas, she decided to register for the full Ironman Texas in 2012. She knew the race would be challenging. (I mean, it's challenging under the *best* of circumstances.) "Running does a number on me," she says. "But it's going to hurt no matter what I do—sitting, standing . . ."

Indeed, the run proved to be a great physical challenge. "I was in a lot of pain. I had to literally lie down on my back on the ground for 10 minutes at times," Terry says. "But, I was on cloud nine the entire time!" She made it to the finish line, falling into the embraces of excited friends and family. Terry Woods was an Ironman. Two years earlier, her body was shattered. Now there she stood, unbroken; a huge milestone on a journey that went far beyond the 140.6 miles she endured that day.

Her daughter and son-in-law were in such awe of her, the race, and the inspirational vibe of the entire community that they said they wanted to do one too. "I said, 'I'll do it with you!'" Terry laughs. They all raced in an Ironman together the following year.

"I do at least three races each year. A few sprints and at least one 70.3," she says. Recently, she did a small, non-Ironman-branded 70.3, completely unaware that it was a qualifying race until she received an email inviting her to compete in the Ironman World Championships.

It's been six years since Terry's near-fatal accident. She is changed physically, forever living with the effects of a traumatized spine and chronic pain. Currently, her pain extends from T-8 (around the central region of the spine) down to her hips.

"I had bone stimulation, but the bone didn't grow back," she says. Because bone usually regenerates, the doctors had told her she'd be fine in a year and her life would resume as normal. "But it didn't turn out that way," Terry says. "The doctor called it a 'failed fusion' because it didn't meet the normal healing process."

Despite this life-changing accident, Terry remains happy, positive, sweet, and upbeat. She tells me that she's filled with gratitude for her life, for her family, for the personal growth that has occurred along the way, and for the sport and community of triathlon.

Everyone has a story, Terry explains; something to overcome. We all reach a point where we can feel broken. It's in the act of *overcoming* where we pick up the pieces, reassemble them into something beautiful, and carry on stronger and wiser than before.

Terry feels drawn to triathlon because it's really just a metaphor for life. "You can relate life's difficulties directly to your training," she says. "[Triathletes] know what it feels like to push themselves. They know what change feels like. They recognize there's going to be struggle in changing yourself." Like Terry, when we *over*come we actually *be*come a better version of ourselves. "I love triathlon," she gushes. "I've learned so much about myself and about life."

15

TRAIN WRECK

*The good Lord gave you a body
that can stand most anything. It's your mind
you have to convince.*

—VINCENT LOMBARDI

The acute pain hit me like brass knuckles at the end of my 4-mile run. My knee locked up, and the pain was sharp and fierce. Luckily, I had made it to the end of my driveway when I nearly collapsed. I texted my husband to come outside and carry me in (not as romantic as it sounds). I spent the rest of the day icing and resting my knee and wondering what the hell just happened.

With an 8K race looming on the horizon, I made an appointment with a sports medicine doctor for diagnosis and treatment. I was intent on running, which had less to do with my competitive drive and more to do with my cheapness. (I had already paid the $40.00 race fee, and the thought of wasting that money made me crazy.)

According to the doctor, the increased volume and frequency of running had caused an inflammation under my kneecap. He recommended rest, anti-inflammatories, strength training, and changing my route to vary the pitch of the road. Then he offered some unsolicited advice. "I see a lot of women your age trying to run half-marathons and marathons. I don't necessarily recommend it," he said. "If you like running, that's great. I would just stick with 5Ks."

Wait, women of *my age*? Stick with 5Ks? Okay, I wasn't planning on running a marathon, ever. Maybe a half-marathon one day. But that dude just called me out.

My face must have revealed my inner emotions. "Sorry to disappoint you. That's just my professional advice," he said, smiled sympathetically, and left me sitting alone on that white-papered exam table with what was left of my pride.

By the time I got home, I was fired up. It was bad enough that 22-year-old cashiers were calling me "Ma'am" instead of "Miss." Bad enough I had to buy those eyeglass readers at the dollar store to decipher the tiny writing on the back of an aspirin bottle or the ingredient label on a box of cereal. Now some doctor is telling me *women my age* are too old to run long distances? Clearly, my knee injury was more of a blow to my aging ego than my aging body. For the record, a wounded ego takes longer to heal. Once it did, I embarked on a little investigative work of my own.

Was there medical evidence backing his statement? Was there an ideal amount of running and was there such a thing as "too much?" Are there factors, such as age, that make people more or less injury prone? What I really wanted to know was whether my running career was over before it even started and what, if anything, I could do to avoid that.

I wasn't oblivious to the fact that I started running in "middle age," and that I'd be embarking on my first triathlon at age 45. I suspected this did not bode well, but then I heard about Sister Madonna Buder, a.k.a. the Iron Nun, who became the oldest women to complete an Ironman at the age of 82. She didn't start doing triathlons until she was 52 and to date has amassed an estimated 360 race finishes, including at least 45 Ironmans. Then there's Harriette Thompson, who became the oldest woman to finish a marathon at the age of 92. She didn't begin running marathons until age

76. Okay, you could say these women are statistical anomalies, but it made me wonder if age was such an issue.

Still, I couldn't ignore the other end of the spectrum. When the triathlon craze first hit, it seemed like everyone was gliding along uninjured. As time went on and enthusiasm, ambition, and mileage increased, so too did the number of wounded weekend warriors, irrespective of age. Their injuries went beyond the typical muscle strains, lost toenails, swimmer's ears, and saddle sores. I began to hear stories of hip, foot, and leg stress fractures, foot surgeries, runner's knee, plantar fasciitis, and injuries I've never heard of like piriformis syndrome, patellofemoral stress syndrome, iliotibial band syndrome, and Achilles tendonopathy.

Sometimes, the injuries were acute and healed relatively quickly; other times they became chronic and serious enough to warrant surgery. While you might think this would cause a dip in triathlon participation among these girls in pink, most seemed to simply accept injury as a side effect of their sport. An unavoidable byproduct. Proof of their dedication to their passion. War wounds in the fight to the finish line.

To me, it seemed like a giant rip-off. Here we all were, getting in the best shape of our lives, yet simultaneously experiencing the most aches and pains of our lives! How is that fair?

One thing was becoming clear—there was a fine line between having a body that is a finely tuned machine and one that is a giant train wreck. Were fitness-related injuries just par for the course on the journey to health? Was this the price to be paid for maximizing our full potential? Was it unavoidable, a function of bad luck or bad genetics, or could we do something to minimize our risk and stay injury free?

Why do people say, "Grow some balls"? Balls are weak and sensitive. If you really wanna be tough, grow a vagina. Those things can take a pounding.
—BETTY WHITE

TRIATHLON AND THE LOW-INJURY FALLACY

One of the major selling points of triathlon has long been that it has a low injury rate, thanks to the cross-training. So, imagine my surprise when I did a basic literature search and discovered the complete opposite to be true. It turns out that the incident rate for injuries in triathlon are higher than in any other sport. The *American Journal of Sports Medicine* reports a 90 percent injury rate among triathletes.

"The idea that people can reduce their chance of injury by competing in triathlons may be a fallacy," wrote Sean D. Hammill in an investigative piece published in the *New York Times*. In fairness, triathlon rolls three separate sports together, which makes comparison to a single sport challenging. While the cross-training aspect of triathlon is unarguably beneficial, there is a flip side: Three different sports present three separate opportunities to get hurt. That said, each sport does not carry equal risk. There is one leg of triathlon that accounts for the greatest number of injuries—running.

The Number 1 Perp

Running is responsible for the large majority of triathlete injuries during the race season: 65 percent of all runners sustain injury in any given year, half of which are reoccurrences. The average runner will sustain one injury for every 100 hours of running, and injury risk increases when training volume increases. Some evidence suggests that higher weekly mileage, defined as more than 20 miles per week, increases a runner's chances of injury. However, experience also appears to be an important factor, namely, the less experienced the runner, the higher the injury risk.

Running is so hard on the body because of the vertical force of impact, which is estimated as up to three times your body weight. So, when the foot of a 135-pound woman strikes the ground, the force transmitted through her foot and leg is the equivalent of 405 pounds. Every. Single. Footstrike. Oh, by the way, there are an average of 38,000 footstrikes in a half-marathon and 76,000 in a marathon. That is 76,000 times that *triple your body weight* hammers down on your bones and reverberates up through your body.

Even a runner who logs in a modest 20 miles per week, 52 weeks a year, will take 2 million running steps annually. Yes, impact sports like running can strengthen your bones, but some argue that the running benefits diminish as the mileage increases. In other words, too much of a good thing may not always a good thing for everyone.

Born to Run . . . Or Not

While some people seem to have bodies that cooperate with, and even thrive in, the stress of long and ultradistances, not every body tolerates these stresses the same way. Individual biomechanics play a large role. This includes things like natural strike, pronation, and baseline flexibility. Gender is also a significant factor. Women have a higher rate of sports-related injuries, particularly to the hip and knee. Women are afflicted with runner's knee twice as frequently as men. Plus, women suffer from higher rates of ACL tears because of the female body's alignment and distribution of weight. However, good technique, proper training, the right shoes, sufficient warm-ups and cool downs, strength training, stretching, and enough recovery time between workouts help reduce the risk of bodily harm.

Cycling and Swimming Make Their Mark

The second leading cause of triathlon-related injury is cycling. The most common injuries are "aeroneck syndrome" (a stiff, painful neck resulting from the hyperextension of the head and hunched shoulders), cyclist palsy (hand numbness that occurs from chronic pressure on the ulnar nerve), and piriformis syndrome (a neuromuscular condition that results in hip and buttock pain, numbness, and tingling in the back of the leg and into the foot). Cyclists are also at increased risk for developing urethritis, an inflammation of the urethra, and/or "bicycle seat neuropathy" secondary to the compression of nerves and blood vessels in the nether regions. Time spent on the bike covering long distances increases this risk, but saddle shape, bike fit, rider position, and extra padding can mitigate or prevent these issues.

Swimming has the least impact and therefore causes the least injury. Rotator cuff and swimmer's shoulder (supraspinatus tendonitis resulting from the repetitive motion of the arm) are the most frequently reported injuries and are typically the result of overtraining and/or poor technique.

Other factors that increase an athlete's vulnerability to injury include insufficient sleep, inadequate intake of carbohydrates, and a race season with too many back-to-back races. But the biggest culprit is one that is completely within our control, even though tempering this behavior is challenging for the enthusiastic, competitive, type A triathlete. The biggest factor in triathlon injury? Overtraining.

> *It's when the discomfort strikes that one realizes a strong mind is the most powerful weapon of all.*
> —CHRISSIE WELLINGTON

THE OVERTRAINING TRAP

Laura B.'s foray into triathlon began with an immediate injury. During her first triathlon she fell off her bike, fractured her wrist, and wasn't able to finish. Frustrated, she was even more determined to get back in the game. When her wrist healed, she went full throttle, signed up for a marathon and ramped up her training. Soon, her forefoot began hurting. She pressed on through the pain. "I eventually went to a podiatrist and after two visits, an X-ray, and an MRI, was diagnosed with Freiberg's disease in my third metatarsal."

Freiberg's disease, also known as avascular necrosis, occurs when the blood supply to the bone is cut off, causing the bone to die. The cause? Excessive and repetitive stress to the foot from running. "I was deflated. I worked so hard and was in the best shape of my life at 38 years old. But it was time to stop. I wasn't sure if I'd ever be able to run or do triathlons again," she says. "After healing, and going through a couple of pairs of custom orthotics, two podiatrists, and several pairs of running shoes, I finally was able to take up running and triathlons again. The injuries taught me that stopping is not the same as quitting."

Overtraining is extremely common in all sports, including triathlon. Overtraining is simply an imbalance between periods of intense training and rest. An athlete who is overtrained is not only at higher risk for sustaining injury (it's estimated that 80 percent of injuries are due to overuse) but is also paradoxically diminishing her performance. And yet, up to 85 percent of triathletes are overtrained, according to research.

Here is why overtraining backfires. When you crush a hard workout, you are actually inflicting damage to your muscle tissue in a controlled and purposeful manner. Small amounts of adrenaline are produced during intense training, and the byproduct of this is lactic acid (the thing that makes our muscles feel sore the next day). Our bodies respond to muscle damage with inflammation, which heals the tissue, making it thicker and stronger. That is exactly what training should do—it creates stress on your body, and the adaptation to this stress results in building muscle, improving speed, strength, and endurance.

But *continuous* physiological stress without *ample recovery* creates a daily surge of adrenaline and causes repetitive micro-trauma in the muscles, tendons, joints, and tissues. The result is not stronger, faster, better muscle tissues, but rather tight, brittle, and less effective muscle tissue. Training overload also releases a stress hormone called cortisol, which helps break down muscle protein. When training volume is ramped up without sufficient recovery time, cortisol breaks down *too much* muscle protein. In addition, when cortisol levels stay high over long periods of time, stubborn weight gain around the abdomen, constant muscle soreness, lack of mental clarity, and a less effective immune system often result.

For the enthusiastic or the highly competitive type, resting may feel like a cop-out or a waste, especially when there are only seven days in a week, three sports for which to train, and worries about race day preparation. But it's important to remember that only in recovery does the body properly repair itself, and therefore recovery is an essential part of any training plan.

Beginner's (Un)Luck

Newbie excitement or nervousness can easily morph into an overzeal-ous training routine. Jackie L. learned this lesson when a stress fracture derailed her pursuit of triathlon early on. "It was a newbie mistake," she admits. She had lost 40 pounds when she began training and was excited about her amazing transformation. She was also nervous that the weight would sneak back on if she let a day or two slide. "If you're overweight, you're afraid of not working out," she admits. "Triathlon became my secu-rity blanket." In retrospect, Jackie understands she was training too aggres-sively and not giving herself the necessary recovery days.

When the stress fracture forced her off her feet, it gave her time to reflect. She started working with a trainer, who told her, "If you're tired, you need to rest. The world isn't going to end. Nail your key workouts when you're rested." This was a huge eye-opener for Jackie, and she took the advice to heart, adapting her training regimen accordingly.

Sometimes, overtraining results from simple naiveté. You follow a new training plan, not knowing whether it is too much or too little. The excite-ment of a new endeavor sometimes results in new athletes packing too many races into their schedule and joining too many group workouts because they don't want to miss out on fun with friends. In other instances, overtraining stems from a compulsive personality type or a self-proclaimed "obsession."

"Obsessed" is just a word the lazy use to describe the dedicated.
—RUSSELL WARREN

JANE'S ADDICTION

It's not uncommon to hear triathletes talk about the obsessive, compul-sive, addictive nature of their sport. Indeed, 96 percent of first-time tri-athletes surveyed say they planned to do another one. One-third of first timers said they were planning to do five or more triathlons within a year. Clearly, there is something about the sport that hooks people. But is that harmful addiction or just healthy enthusiasm? For the large majority of tri-athletes, it *is* simply harmless enthusiasm and an admirable dedication that drive them.

A true pathological addiction only afflicts a small percentage of individuals—2.5 percent of the general public, according to one study. However, this rate fluctuates depending on the group being surveyed. A diagnosable exercise addiction has been reported as high as 50 percent for marathon runners, and range anywhere from 20 percent to 52 percent among tri-athletes. In a 2014 study of over 1,000 triathletes, the risk of developing an exercise addiction increased as the number of weekly hours in training increased, suggesting that longer-course triathletes were more likely to meet the criteria of exercise addiction than shorter course triathletes.

When does exercise or training cross the line, and who determines this? How does one make the distinction between commitment and pathology? In 2013, "Exercise Addiction" was added to the fifth edition of the *Diagnostic and Statistical Manual of Mental Disorders*, the standard classification manual of mental disorders used by US mental health professionals. There are several criteria needed to make an official diagnosis, but the key feature is that the exercise is uncontrollable, is excessive, and leads to significant impairment or distress in either social, work, or emotional functioning.

"Exercise addiction is difficult to diagnose," says clinical and sports psychologist Mitchell Greene, PhD of Greenepsych Sport Psychology. "Perhaps the biggest clinical indicator that someone is being destructive rather than dedicated is if they feel like the exercise is controlling them, rather than the other way around." Yet typically, the exercise-addicted triathlete sees little problem. "Generally, someone with exercise addiction is very good at rationalizing their behavior," Dr. Greene explains. They will usually argue that if they are addicted, at least it's a "healthy addiction," unlike drugs, alcohol, or gambling, and therefore unproblematic.

But experts don't necessarily agree with the "healthy" addiction argument. Those who compulsively exercise typically end up overtraining and tackle longer and longer distances, both of which increase risk for injury.

Longer course training may also increase the risk of chronic inflammation, endocrine problems, compromised heart health (arrhythmias, arteriosclerosis, and "athletic bradycardia"), plateauing weight, premature aging, gastrointestinal issues (such as running-induced ischemic colitis), and, in women, pelvic floor prolapse.

There is also a serious medical condition called the "female athlete triad" that afflicts women and girls who exercise too much and eat too little. This syndrome consists of three interrelated medical conditions: chronic energy deficiency, menstrual disturbances (such as a cessation of menses), and loss of bone density. The long-term health consequences include immunosuppression, fertility problems, iron deficiency, stress fractures, and osteoporosis, all of which may be irreversible without prompt treatment.

So, while triathlon is indeed a very healthy sport, it could be argued that when it comes to any kind of "true" addiction, there is no such thing as a "healthy" one.

Training is what you are doing while your opponent is sleeping in.
—BRIAN OWEN

OVERTRAINING SYNDROME

USA Cycling certified coach and multiple Ironman Kona Championship qualifier Jesse Moore of Moore Performance Coaching has seen his share of athletes suffering from something called "overtraining syndrome" (OTS). A retired competitive "Cat 1" cyclist with a degree in exercise physiology and a long career in competitive running and bike racing, Jesse combines his scientific background and personal experience to help other athletes become their very best. He has coached professional athletes, top ten Tour de France finishers, Ironman triathletes, and amateur athletes. He sees the pitfalls of overtraining across the board.

"We have seen overtraining and learned a lot from it," Jesse says. OTS is the result of overtraining, which Jesse explains succinctly as the result of an intense, heavy stimulus coupled with under-recovery. Red flags for OTS include a notable dip in performance, immense emotional and physical fatigue, above-average and near constant muscle fatigue, overuse injuries (such as Achilles tendonitis and plantar fasciitis), and a lack of motivation to train. The advice that rings loud and clear, from both professional athletes and trainers, is to listen to what your body is telling you, reduce your intensity, and rest. "Getting people to listen is the challenging part," admits Jesse. "It can be a long process back. I've had people with broken arms and collarbones who bounce back faster than from overtraining syndrome." But an athlete can absolutely recover. To do so requires insight and a willingness to change the behaviors in question. It's best to prevent overtraining from occurring in the first place. How can we do that and still set goals for ourselves? By training smarter, not harder.

Take care of your body. It's the only place you have to live.
—JIM ROHN

TRAIN SMARTER, NOT HARDER

Jesse has seen both ends of the spectrum through his career—those who reach their competitive heights and those who are crawling their way out of an overtraining hole. He believes there are four important keys to maximizing performance and minimizing burnout: time management, quality training, sufficient rest, and smart nutrition.

Time Management

"Make sure your training fits your life, not your life fit your training," advises Jesse. With three sports to juggle, the biggest challenge is finding a balance between training, recovery, relationships, career, and life. Jesse believes the most important first step in training is sitting down with a pad of paper, a pen, and a calendar. He begins by asking them to add up the number of hours they need to train each week. "Then, we pull 20 percent off that." Why? He wants them to see the big picture. "Have a three-year plan," he explains. "Ask yourself, 'Can I handle this race load for three years? Is it sustainable?'"

In addition, Jesse finds it more effective to rotate through one discipline each week instead of focusing equally on all three sports weekly. "A lot of people think they need to run much more than they do," he says. This isn't the first time I've heard this. Since running causes the most damage to the body, avoiding a running overload seems intuitive. This doesn't mean you will be inadequately trained when you hit the pavement at your next race. Jesse says that swimming and biking improve your running speed and endurance. "You just have to make sure the bikes and swims are quality."

Quality over Quantity

"A lot of people just want the volume. I see that most often in beginners," says Jesse. Instead of ticking off mile after mile at a slow and steady pace, he suggests making workouts count. This is accomplished by doing shorter distances at a higher intensity. He also believes in the importance of strength and mobility training. "It's a higher priority than people make it," he says. Often times, Jesse will knock a bike, run, or swim off the training schedule in favor of adding a strength and mobility workout. "We're losing muscle mass and mobility. Women in particular have a loss of lean muscle mass and bone density in middle age."

Resting Requirements

"There's a mythology of needing to be crushed all the time," Jesse says. "Rest as hard as you train. A rested body can break new ground." As already discussed with overtraining, muscle is not built during workouts; it's built during rest. To skip a recovery day or to cram too many hard, high-intensity workouts into the week takes all that work you just did and basically flushes it. Instead of celebrating a new PR or age-group victory, you may end up frustrated with a subpar performance or home on the couch nursing a nagging injury.

"There is going to be a certain amount of fatigue and soreness. If it goes on for days and days, it's a problem," says Jesse. "For the recreational person, I'd be careful with chronic fatigue. You will become burned out." Jesse's goal is to keep people passionate and joyful about triathlon and not turn training into a killjoy. "You got to make it to race day healthy. I'd rather you be undertrained, but love it."

Necessary Nutrition

"My observation is that women do not eat enough or the right things during training and racing to maintain an optimal energy level," says Gretchen Cooney, USAT-certified coach and owner of Bucket List Training. "Many are worried about gaining weight, eating and drinking products that may not be ideal as part of their everyday nutrition plan."

Jesse has similar concerns as he watches triathletes avoid entire food groups, often leading to inadequate nutrition. "The nutritional landscape has changed a lot. People are going low-carb, especially women," Jesse says. Those who restrict their diet too much may not be getting enough energy and, depending upon the severity of this behavior, may end up with the female athlete triad. Another problem with calorie restriction, or inadequate intake of certain nutrients, is that it signals the body to increase cortisol, a hormone that has a negative impact on muscles and bone. More cortisol in your system can increase the risk of stress fractures.

In contrast, there are those who follow the "I do triathlons to eat whatever I want" motto. These women may change little about their diet, or even increase their calories because of increased hunger. But are they the right calories? Having a hunk of cheesecake and a few glasses of wine may replace the 1,000-plus calories you just burned, but does it replace the nutrients lost? Probably not. Both under- and over-consuming have a negative impact on nutrition, which, in turn, hurts performance and health, and increases vulnerability to injury.

Here's the good news: Triathlon doesn't have to turn your body into a train wreck. Fortunately, there's a lot of great advice out there from professional athletes, experienced coaches, and lifelong age-group competitors. If we seek out this advice, rest when we need to rest, and stop and recover when we feel pain, it's a sport that can be enjoyed for decades.

> *You don't need to get scared away from endurance sports.*
> *You just need to train for endurance the right way.*
> —BEN GREENFIELD

Nancy Reinisch of the Roaring Fork Women's Triathlon Team is a great example of someone who has been able to successfully maintain longevity in this sport. She has been doing triathlons for 30 consecutive years and has sidestepped all the typical injuries. She says this is neither accidental nor lucky. "I do it by keeping it all in balance. My longevity is due to careful training, nutrition, and support," she says.

"In order to stay in this sport you have to be realistic about your goals. If it's about getting fit and having fun doing it, you can do this year after year." Nancy sees a lot of what she considers the beginner's mistake of doing too much too quickly. "Many triathletes get into the sport and start right out doing an Ironman. Silly! Take the time to work up to it," she advises. "I did my first 70.3 two years ago." She was 60 years old and had decades of experience before she even attempted that distance. Her conservative approach to triathlon does not mean she isn't competitive. A decorated and passionate triathlete, Nancy has stood on the podium many times and even qualified to compete with Team USA in the 60–64 age group at International Triathlon Union World's Chicago in 2015, proving triathlon is an excellent way to take care of your body throughout your lifespan. With over 90 races under her belt, she certainly knows what she's talking about. "My goal is to reach 100 triathlons by the time I turn 65," she says. "For me, that will be epic!"

50-50

"You want to live large after you beat cancer."

HER SURVIVAL ODDS were 50-50, at best. At 41 years of age, Jenn Sommermann was diagnosed with Stage III ovarian cancer. Seventy-two hours later, she was whisked into surgery, which was followed by six months of chemotherapy. "It was 18 months of hell," Jenn remembers. Now a survivor of ten years, she believes she beat the odds because of her excellent medical treatment, positive attitude, and triathlon.

Jenn did her first triathlon at the suggestion of a friend who thought it would be a unique way to celebrate their 40th birthdays. They registered for the all-female Danskin sprint tri in Seattle and raced among 5,000 women. Crossing that finish line, Jenn knew she was in love. "I had to do more! I just loved the competitive aspect. I loved the vibe."

Over the next two years, Jenn thrived on the joy and focus the sport offered. "I love the training. I love the motivation to get up at 5:00 a.m. for something. I am pretty much a solo artist. [It's] a great way to feel like you're part of something while you're on your own." Though she never considered herself an athlete, triathlon clicked with her disposition. "I am Type A. Super, *super* Type A," she explains. "You gotta be pretty buttoned up to excel at this sport. It's an exercise in organizational acrobatics."

Little did she know that the multisport she loved would save her life, not once but twice, literally and metaphorically.

The symptoms of ovarian cancer are subtle and vague, easily explained away and ignored: immense fatigue, increased frequency of urination, fullness, indigestion, bloating, and back pain. Nothing that seemed too out of the ordinary. By the time she grew concerned enough about her symptoms to seek medical advice, things had progressed. That's the sneakiness of this disease and why it's known as the silent killer.

Shortly before her 42nd birthday, Jenn received the news: She had ovarian cancer. It was advanced, spreading rapidly, and required swift and aggressive treatment. Despite the gravity of the diagnosis, Jenn's spirit was far from broken. She was a triathlete to her core, after all. That meant she was determined, relentless, and strong. That meant she had all the qualities of a survivor.

One day, as she sat in the hospital getting her chemotherapy infusion, Jenn flipped through a triathlon magazine and saw an ad for the (now defunct) US Women's Triathlon Series. What caught her eye was that the race series benefited the Ovarian Cancer Research Fund (OCRF). It was at that moment, lying in a hospital bed, that Jenn promised herself she would race the entire series the following year. That was the goal she needed, something tangible on which to focus during a dark, uncertain time. It gave her purpose and hope. "Attitude is a large part [of recovery]. I treated this like it was a triathlon. It was the race of my life."

In 2008, Jenn kept the promise she made to herself and competed in all three races as part of OCRF's Team Hope. Her pledge was to raise $500 for each race, but she ended up raising a grand total of $15,000, making her the top fundraiser on the special team of survivors. This incredible accomplishment put her on the radar of OCRF's president, who thought Jenn had the perfect attitude and charisma to be a great spokesperson.

"She proposed I do a tri in all 50 states," recalls Jenn, who was immediately keen on the idea. "You have an opportunity to make a huge impact," she says. "It seemed like putting a positive spin on cancer."

In 2009, at the age of 45, Jenn Sommermann announced her 50 by 50 by 100 campaign—50 races in all 50 states to raise $100,000 for ovarian cancer research. She would tackle this lofty goal before turning 50, which gave her five years. She had already knocked off Massachusetts in 2007, and California, Illinois, and Washington in the 2008 US Women's Triathlon race series. Four down, 46 to go. In 2009, she raced in five more states and then competed in 11 states in 2010, 2011, and 2012. In 2013, Jenn raced in her final eight states: Alabama, Kentucky, Iowa, Oregon, Michigan, Wyoming, South Dakota, and—saving the best for last—Hawaii.

Racing on a teal bike in her teal OCRF tri-suit, Jenn spread her message at every event. Raising awareness and educating women was, and still is, an important aspect of her campaign. Every woman she educates is a life touched, a seed planted that could someday mean the difference between early detection and a death sentence.

Not only did Jenn surpass her campaign's fundraising goal, but she had quite an adventure over those five years. She was quarantined after contracting "swamp rot" in Louisiana, endured a sleet and hail storm in Alabama and a tornado in Ohio, and confronted a stubborn moose in Alaska. Finally, on November 24, 2013, her adventures came to a celebratory conclusion at the finish line of the Lavaman Triathlon. A large group of family and friends came to cheer her on, their toenails painted teal in a show of support. She had raised a total of $107,115 in those five years. Every penny went directly to OCRF.

Jenn's campaign was entirely self-financed. She had no sponsorship money and turned all "in-kind donations" into cash donations. For instance, if she was comped a race fee or hotel accommodations, she added the cash equivalent toward her fundraising goal out of her personal savings. Jenn estimates that her out-of-pocket expenses for registration fees, shipping her bike, and travel were about $10,000 per year. "A misconception with the campaign was that I was independently wealthy, didn't work, and had all the time in the world," she laughs. In fact, none of that was the case. She worked three jobs while training, making speeches, doing press interviews, and coordinating the logistics of her race schedule, which sounded like a three-ring circus and continued even through the off-season.

The sacrifice wasn't just financial. "I didn't see my husband for five years," Jenn confesses. However, they both believed that this opportunity was a gift. It was bigger than her. They recognized the reward was in the number of lives saved.

After her 50 by 50 by 100 campaign ended, the big question was "What's next?" Her answer was quite introspective. "New beginnings will make themselves known," she wrote on her blog, *Triathlete for a Cure*. That they did.

In October of 2015, she and her husband downsized their lives, moved from Long Island to Florida, and took full-time jobs as the crew on a mega-yacht. They are also excited about planning a trip to Japan. "We live big," she says. "You want to live large after you beat cancer."

Jenn is currently on a hiatus from racing, though far from retired. "I was so defined by my cancer for so many years, when it was over I was ready to close the door." She still swims with a masters group and runs when she can, but living on a boat full-time makes training and racing a challenge. Nonetheless, triathlon is in her soul. "It's still who I am. I define myself as a triathlete; that's the first thing I say about myself. It's there for me. If I take off 10 years, it's still there for me."

Jenn is eight triathlons away from becoming a distinguished member of the USAT Century Club, a club that recognizes athletes who reach the "100 race" milestone. That is pretty awesome. But what is most awesome is that Jenn has beat the odds and continues to live cancer-free. She has not only survived, but thrived. I don't think cancer knew who it was messing with.

16

CHARITY, CAUSES, AND CURES, OH TRI!

Racing for a cause allows our athletes
to take triathlon from a self-centered sport
and change it to a selfless endeavor.

—DAVE DESCHENES

In 1998, Australian David Holleran set the world record for the longest triathlon when he swam 26 miles, biked 1,242 miles, and ran 310 miles over a period of 18 consecutive days. On May 5, 2016, a 47-year-old single mother more than doubled that distance. She covered 3,762 miles over the course of 65 consecutive days, and she did it all to raise awareness for a cause close to her heart.

Norma Bastidas began her quest to complete the world's longest triathlon on March 1, 2014, in Cancun, Mexico, when she started to swim. Norma swam six to ten hours a day, every day, enduring near-constant stings by jellyfish larva that wormed into her wetsuit. Her face, lips and mouth were painfully swollen to near-disfigurement by the saltwater of the Caribbean Sea. She swam a total of 122 miles over nearly three weeks, although only 95 miles would be officially counted due to a GPS malfunction the first day.

When the swim ended on March 20, Norma began the second leg of the world's longest triathlon. She cycled a total of 2,932 miles, traveling from

Mexico through the Southern United States. She road 11 hours a day, covering anywhere from 100 to 120 miles at a clip, for 27 straight days. When she reached LaGrange, Georgia, Norma ditched the bike and began to run. An experienced ultramarathoner, Norma ran 30 to 40 miles per day. She ran through near-constant rain, suffering from infected foot blisters and severe digestive issues that caused a dramatic 20-pound weight loss. Unfazed, Norma just dug deeper, running straight through the night to complete her last 96-miles. When she finished, she had run a total of 735 miles.

Norma's extraordinary journey came to a ceremonial and emotional end when she finished at the National Mall in Washington, D.C., on May 5, her birthday.

Norma Bastidas didn't embark on this journey for fame, money, or a place in the history books. Her triathlon served one purpose: to raise awareness of, and put an end to, human trafficking. Starting in Mexico and ending in Washington, D.C., Norma's triathlon followed a known human-trafficking route. Finishing at the US Capitol symbolized Norma's hope to unify two major cities in two different countries for one important issue. Everything she endured—the pain and the exhaustion—was in honor of the hundreds of thousands of humans trafficked across international borders. Most are young girls who are lured, kidnapped, forced into sexual slavery, and horrifically abused.

Norma has a personal connection to this issue. Born and raised in Mazatlan, Mexico, Norma was one of five children being raised by a single mother. As a teenager, Norma was manipulated and misled into taking a modeling job in Japan. Longing to escape poverty and help her family, she accepted what seemed like a great career opportunity. Instead, she found herself trapped in a trafficking ring, sold to the highest bidder, and abused, beaten, and drugged. Thankfully, Norma was able to escape, but the ordeal left deep emotional scars. She turned those scars into strength, devoting her life to helping other children and adolescents who are trapped, abused, and sold.

Norma's awe-inspiring triathlon journey is an example of how this sport can be used to draw attention to an important cause. Even on a local scale, women use triathlon to rally communities, offer hope, raise money, increase awareness, and ignite change. Like Norma, often the cause comes first, and the triathlon follows.

CAUSE TO TRI

"My first triathlon was in honor of my mom who was battling ovarian cancer," says Jennifer M. In 2007, the now defunct SheROX triathlon series was supporting the Ovarian Cancer Research Fund, which piqued her interest. "When I first heard about the race, I was overwhelmed by taking care of two small kids and caring for my sick mom. I didn't have enough time to train, but made a promise to myself I would do it the following year. I started training slowly, still overwhelmed with everything, but it was a great stress reliever."

Jennifer registered for the 2008 race, but unfortunately her mom didn't live to see it. She passed away in November 2007. "I made it to the finish line because of her," Jennifer says. Since that race, she has been hooked. Now a mother of four, Jennifer has amassed many triathlon finishes, including a half-Ironman. She continues to raise money for cancer research through Relay for Life and continues competing in triathlons because she loves them.

"I've always carried a picture of my mom in my triathlon transition race bag. She is who I look at before a race, and at some races I glance at it during my transitions to keep me going when it gets rough," she says. "I know what she went through was a heck of a lot harder than what I'm feeling during these races, and the thought of her sees me to the finish line."

> *There is no exercise better for the heart*
> *than reaching down and lifting people up.*
> —JOHN A. HOLMES

Jennifer M. is just one of thousands of women tackling a triathlon in honor of a loved one, in support of a charity, to advance research, or to raise awareness for a cause near and dear to the heart. In an online survey commissioned by Eventbrite, more than one-third of all endurance race participants said the reason they race is "to raise money for a specific charity or good cause." Running USA's National Survey reported that 42 percent of their respondents participated in a race because of its connection to a charity.

So why triathlon? There are so many creative ways to raise money for charity—Beef and Beer parties, fashion shows, bake sales, raffles, dances, bowling, and merchandise sales that will give you anything from tote bags to candles in exchange for your generous contribution. Heck, you can just write a check to your favorite organization without breaking a sweat. Why subject yourself to a long, difficult race? Especially if you're not an athlete, nor have you ever been?

THE MARTYRDOM EFFECT

I'm not the only one trying to figure this out. Many studies have examined that very question and what they found is this—it is the very act of overcoming pain that adds symbolic value to a goal. "There is copious evidence that people derive meaning and value from their hard-earned accomplishments and the pains they endure on the road to goal achievement," write Christopher Olivola and Eldar Shafir in their paper "The Martyrdom Effect." The sacrificial endeavor of running a marathon or completing a triathlon gives it a deeper meaning.

Because the triathlon itself is such a powerful metaphor for overcoming adversity, it resonates deeply with those who race for a cause or a cure, in honor of someone, or in memory of someone. Taking on triathlon means overcoming obstacles, just as we fight to overcome pain, disease, or tragedy. For some, it's a way to feel closer to that pain and, in turn, to that person or group of people who are suffering. As it is for Jennifer M., a difficult race is the opportunity to symbolically embody the fighting spirit of the person you loved and lost.

Apparently, people are more inspired to donate to a fundraiser if someone is embarking on a physical challenge. This is probably why organizations like Team in Training and Race for a Cure are so wildly successful. The Ironman Foundation also emphasizes and encourages charity among its athletes, providing over $30 million in grants, donations, and program support to a wide variety of nonprofit organizations.

STRENGTH IN NUMBERS

For many triathlon clubs, charity is part of the group's culture. Since its inception, the MHWTC has been committed to fundraising, community outreach, charity, and volunteering. Those goals are even part of the club's mission statement. During its first five years, the MHWTC selected one specific cause to focus on annually, such as ovarian cancer, melanoma, or autistic spectrum disorders. It created an awareness campaign, raised money, and donated substantial checks to an organization related to the selected cause.

In 2014, the club broke new ground when it focused on ending the stigma and discrimination against mental illness. They raised $20,000 for the nonprofit Bring Change 2 Mind (cofounded by award-winning actress Glenn Close and her sister Jessie). However, it was the awareness and education piece that made the biggest impact on the club members and the community at large. Glenn and Jessie Close were so inspired by the club's work that they traveled to Mullica Hill to speak at a mental illness educational workshop and kick off a charity race the following day. That was exciting, but even more thrilling was watching the stigma around mental illness start to crumble before our eyes. Conversations began as people shared personal and familial struggles with depression, anxiety, schizophrenia, addiction, and suicide. Things once whispered in secret were being discussed openly.

In total, the MHWTC has donated over $50,000 to various charities thus far. In addition, it is actively engaged in a variety of service projects, fundraisers, and drives. From aiding families after the devastation of Hurricane Sandy in 2012, to helping schools reduce bullying, to collecting running shoes for the homeless, to supporting the local farm industry, to its bike safety initiative, the women of the MHWTC are dedicated to serving the community they love. Since becoming a 501(c)(3) nonprofit in 2015, the MHWTC initiated a scholarship program for high school students and established need-based stipends for club members facing tough life challenges. The club's philanthropic spirit earned it the Gloucester County Chamber of Commerce Non-Profit Club of the Year Award in 2015.

The MHWTC isn't the only all-female tri-club harnessing the power of triathlon to promote positive change. In fact, female triathletes appear to have a major philanthropic streak! Moira Horan, founder of Jersey Girls Stay Strong, cofounded the Shark River Paddle Battle, a charity race that has raised more than $10,000 for St. Jude's Children's Hospital and a local respite program for women in cancer treatment. The Southern California–based TriLaVie has raised more than $25,000 for Exceeding Expectations, a program helping at-risk children living in the inner city of San Bernardino redirect their lives through triathlon. The Pink Ladies of Wilmington, North Carolina, have raised more than $35,000 for local charities including the Miracle League of Wilmington and the Special Olympics.

The Roaring Fork Women's Triathlon Team in Colorado makes sure charity begins at home. They hold a fundraiser at the start of every tri season to benefit women who can't pay the team's registration and/or race fees. "The same women will pass down old bikes, helmets, clothes, and other equipment to the new women to help them get started," says cofounder Nancy Reinisch. That is our best charity!" The team members have also volunteered as guides for Nancy Stevens's Tri-It Camp for the Blind.

TRI FOR A CURE

When a charitable heart combines with a passion for triathlon, it's a formidable match and a powerful force. Julie Marchese of sheJAMs is an excellent example of this.

Triathlons were not in Julie Marchese's plans. Neither was breast cancer. She has faced both, and both have changed her life. Then, she went on to change even more lives.

Before Julie co-founded the sheJAMs tri-club in Maine, she was an active volunteer on the Maine Cancer Foundation's Board of Directors. She gravitated toward this organization after her mother was diagnosed with breast cancer. But, in the middle of her tenure, irony struck when Julie received her own diagnosis. After treatment, Julie celebrated by completing her first triathlon with a group of friends. "Crossing that finish line changed my life forever," she says. "I got a real trainer and a real bike and worked out every day. There was an athlete deep down inside of me." When the Maine Cancer Foundation started brainstorming an event to replace its golf outing, Julie suggested her newfound obsession—triathlon. She pitched the idea for Tri for a Cure to the Board, it was approved, and she and her friend Abby Bliss became the race directors. "We didn't know what we were doing," Julie laughs. "But we were doing it. It was being in the right place at the right time with the right cause."

The first Tri for a Cure Maine was held in 2008. They were given the benchmark of raising $35,000. Julie and Abby left that goal in the dust, raising a whopping $275,000. The support for that race was tremendous right out of the gate. "We had committees of 30 to 40 people at the meetings," Julie says. She estimates there were close to 600 volunteers on race day. The race has been raising an average of $1 million per year ever since. In total, Tri for a Cure hit the $10 million mark in 2016, making it one of the largest fundraising triathlons in the nation. It is the largest all-female triathlon event in the state of Maine.

The racecourse consists of a .33-mile bay swim, 15-mile bike ride, and 3-mile run along the scenic shores of Cape Elizabeth and South Portland. Many of the competitors are survivors. The rest are friends and family racing in support of, or in honor of, loved ones.

The first three years, registration was first-come, first-served. "The 1,400 spots would sell out in three minutes," Julie says. Now, the race is so popular, they have gone to a lottery system. Although there is a mandatory $500 fundraising requirement, it doesn't seem to deter anyone. Instead, it's a tremendous draw because it allows each racer to feel like they are truly making a significant difference. "It's huge. We work on it year-round. We have bands, nice prizes, parades in the morning, and lots of community support. They embrace it." Racers flock from all over the country, dedicated to the cause. Some years, they have participants from more than 20 different states represented.

Julie's philanthropic spirit seeps into everything she does. So when she cofounded sheJAMs triathlon club, it was another opportunity to give back. The members of SheJAMs sponsor a family every Christmas, participate in Habitat for Humanity, and created the "Stitch Out Cancer" Pink and White Scarf Project, knitting and distributing over 2,000 scarves to the women participating in the Tri for a Cure race. On a larger scale, they hold three charity races annually. "Each year we ask our members what nonprofits they would like to see us support, and we get their feedback." These charity races have raised money for Girls on the Run, Easterseals' Veterans Count Program, and the Maine Centers for Women, Work, and Community. In 2015, sheJAMs debuted the Power of SHE 10K, the only all-female 10K in the state of Maine. Proceeds from this race have supported organizations like the Maine Women's Fund and Crossroads addictions treatment center.

SheJAMs has recently partnered with the Lobsterman Triathlon, one of the oldest Olympic Triathlons in Maine. The sheJAMs LobsterJAM is an all-female Olympic-distance triathlon and aquabike, held as a "race within a race." "We will be the fundraising arm of this event," explains Julie. Each participant is required to raise a minimum of $100 for the Maine Cancer Foundation. "This is to get those who have never done a triathlon before to give it a try for a good cause."

GALS FOR CAL

For the Massachusetts-based women of Gals for Cal, one important cause was the reason for coming together and tackling triathlon. This dedicated triathlon team was inspired by the love of a little boy and the hope for a cure for Duchenne muscular dystrophy (DMD).

"As an infant he was slow, but he was a triplet," says Cindy Quitzau about her son, Cal. When he was a preschooler, she noticed he'd trip and fall a lot. He also struggled to walk and climb on playground equipment. His prominent calves, like "little walnuts" in infancy, became even more enlarged as he grew, which, she would find out later, was a red flag. After a battery of tests, the diagnosis she feared was confirmed. Her 6-year-old boy had Duchenne muscular dystrophy, a rapidly progressive, genetic, muscle-wasting disease.

DMD is the most common fatal genetic disorder diagnosed in childhood. It's one of nine types of muscular dystrophy, primarily affecting boys, and presently has no treatment or cure. Currently, there are 20,000 boys living with Duchenne in the United States. Life expectancy is around 20 years.

"My son had been diagnosed with Duchenne. I wanted to do something," Cindy remembers. A few friends came to her with the idea of doing a triathlon. Neither Cindy nor her friends were triathletes, so she was taken aback. "I laughed," she says. At that point, her only image of a triathlon was the Ironman. "I said, 'You guys are crazy! I can't do that!' None of us could even run a mile!" But when she learned there were shorter distances, the wheels in her head began turning. Maybe it would be a way to channel her energy into something positive. She could use the triathlon to raise awareness and money for DMD, a disease that was sorely underfunded.

In 2009, the Quitzau family created a triathlon team affectionately named Gals for Cal. Twenty friends joined Cindy; they all signed up for the Danskin Women's Triathlon, trained hard, and fundraised their hearts out. Most of them wouldn't have called themselves athletes. A large majority didn't even know how to swim or bike. Cindy had to teach herself how to swim at the age of 48. She was so terrified of the open water that she recruited a friend to swim that leg of the race for her.

They all made it to the finish line of the triathlon and raised a whopping $25,000 for the Jett Foundation. It was beyond Cindy's wildest dreams.

"We blew ourselves away," she says. "The bond, the encouragement, and the support—it was so much fun."

The next year, their team doubled in size. Cindy conquered her open-water fears and did the full triathlon. By 2011, there were 85 women of all fitness levels from the New England area racing for Gals for Cal. "We sort of mushroomed. One year we had 100 girls doing the race. We seem to attract newbies, and we love newbies," says Cindy. The growing ranks reflect how deeply Cal, Cindy, and the Quitzau family inspire the people around them to make a difference. "People like to be involved in things that make them feel good."

In 2016, the Gals for Cal raced together for a ninth season, and it was their biggest one to date, raising more than $76,000. Overall, the Gals for Cal have raised more than half a million dollars for individuals living with Duchenne muscular dystrophy and their caregivers.

Cindy continues to expand her reach into the Duchenne community by helping to improve the quality of life for families touched by DMD. In 2017, the Gals for Cal are locking arms with the Jett Foundation, and together they will help fund families needing costly equipment that insurance may not cover. "This area is a huge unmet need in our community," Cindy says.

The younger generation has also gotten involved. In 2015, about 20 kids did their first triathlon to support the Gals for Cal. From there, the Kids for Cal team was born and has participated in several New England youth triathlons. Fathers didn't want to feel left out, so Team D.A.D.S. (Dads Against Duchenne) was formed. It seems many people crave being part of something bigger than themselves.

Triathlon gave Cindy an outlet and a purpose during a difficult transition into the world of Duchenne. The triathlon, for her, was more than a race. It became a symbol of overcoming struggle, of pulling together as a community, and of making a difference in the lives of other families going through the same thing. It became a kind of support group.

"I was the only mom [of a child with Duchenne] on the team the first year," Cindy says. Now, she estimates there are about ten mothers of boys with DMD in Gals for Cal. "It's become a support to the moms and the families. Taking care of yourself as a special mom is important. The challenges are enormous. We can help ourselves while helping someone else."

Triathlon also kept Cindy's body strong when she needed it most. In 2012, at the age of 50, she suffered a major stroke. Paralyzed on the left side of her body and unable to walk, she had a long road of rehabilitation ahead. She had three children to care for at home, one with DMD and another with Down syndrome, so she had a lot of reasons to get strong again. Cindy applied the tenacity and mental toughness to her rehabilitation that she learned through triathlon. "After I had the stroke, I temporarily couldn't walk. But Cal can't walk at all. It gave me some empathy," she says. After working hard in therapy, she learned to walk again and use her left arm. Though she's regained a lot of her physical strength, running is still a challenge due to spasticity in her left foot, and she has not been able to race since. "Physically, I'm fine. But I have these little deficits." She has a new brace to help with "foot drop" and some custom orthotics to support her fallen left arch. "[I] just got back on skis so I am looking forward. No time to look back!" she says.

Cal lost his ability to walk at the age of 12, and uses a motorized wheelchair to get around. But soon he will lose his upper-body strength, too. Cardiac and respiratory problems associated with DMD typically begin in adolescence. Yet nothing stops a now 15-year-old Cal from coming out to cheer the Gals on at their race. "The whole Gals for Cal [team] has helped him emotionally," Cindy says.

Survival into adulthood is becoming more common with advanced medical technology, so Cindy stays hopeful, though realistic. "It will take his life. We just don't know when." Until then, the Gals will be swimming, biking, and running to help fund a cure for this disease with Cal cheering them on.

"I wish every Duchenne mother was surrounded with this kind of support," Cindy says. "I honestly don't know how I would be coping with the monster that is Duchenne without this tribe of women."

Life is either a daring adventure or nothing. To keep our faces toward change and behave like free spirits in the presence of fate is strength undefeatable.

—HELEN KELLER

I didn't have a specific cause or higher purpose in doing my own triathlon, but knowing how noble the triathlon could be drew me closer to it. I wouldn't be racing for something larger than myself this time, but one day I might. And that was an exciting prospect.

TEAM WINTER

"The day my dad was diagnosed,
I knew I had to shift my focus."

WINTER VINECKI is an accomplished and decorated triathlete. She has competed in the world's toughest marathons on all seven continents and holds three marathon world records. She has wins at the Spartan World Championship and the Pacific Northwest XTERRA and is the 2016 women's Grand Prix title holder in NorAm aerials skiing. She is also a passionate philanthropist who started a nonprofit and has raised approximately half a million dollars for prostate cancer research. She is an inspirational speaker, advocate, ambassador, and a 2018 Winter Olympic hopeful as a member of the US Ski Team for Aerials Freestyle.

Did I mention she has accomplished all of this at the ripe old age of 18?

❧

Winter grew up with her parents and three brothers on a large farm in rural Michigan. Her family was active, sporty, and outdoorsy. Her parents taught her she could live life to the fullest, without limits. There were no boundaries put on what she and her brothers could accomplish if they set their minds to it.

Winter set her mind to it, alright. She began skiing and competing in triathlons at a young age. Her mother, Dawn, was her role model in triathlon. "I watched my mom compete. It was kind of a family event," she says. Winter grew up cheering for both her mom and uncle at various running races and triathlons nearly every weekend. One day, a 5-year-old Winter saw other children doing a kids' tri. "I thought, 'I want to do that too!'" She lined up at her first race in Canada with her water wings on. "None of the other kids had water wings, so I threw them off!" she laughs. By the age of 7, Winter was traveling all over the country to compete in the USAT triathlon series and to run 5K races. They had to travel because triathlons for kids (and adults) were pretty scarce in rural Michigan. In fact, there weren't many triathlon races for kids *anywhere*.

"She was this 9-year-old, training and racing with other adults, mostly men," Dawn says. Winter would run with her uncle. She'd train for her open-water swims with her uncle and mom. This tiny little girl was right there, keeping up lap for lap with the grownups.

Although her accomplishments are many, perhaps what stands out most about Winter is her heart. Trophies, medals, wins, and breaking records are not what fuel her fire. Instead, it's love, family, tribute, and hope. When you strip it all away, she's simply one girl racing for the love of her dad.

Winter's father, Michael, was a musician and never much of an athlete. Inspired by his wife, and seeing the growing interests of his sporty kids, he started running. Soon, he bought a bike with plans to begin racing. Then life delivered a huge blow.

Winter was only 9 years old when her dad received the worst possible news. At 40 years of age, this loving father of four small children was diagnosed with a rare and aggressive form of prostate cancer. The odds were not in his favor.

Instead of crumbling, Winter channeled her emotions into action. She wanted to do something productive, something positive, something to honor her father, as well as the one-in-six men who are diagnosed with prostate cancer. Shocked by the lack of awareness of prostate cancer, she formed

Team Winter, a 501(c)(3) nonprofit dedicated to raising awareness and money for a cure. I remind you, she was only 9 years old!

They found the perfect race to kick off Team Winter's fundraising—the 2008 Athletes for a Cure Triathlon in Disney World, Florida. One small issue, it was an Olympic distance—1.5K swim, 40K bike, and 10K run—and she was only 9 years old. What could they do? Dawn registered her daughter and hoped for the best. Then the race director called. The rules stated that Winter was too young to participate, and they weren't sure if an exception could be made. When Dawn explained their story and the goal of Team Winter, he was supportive. Athletes for a Cure found a way to convince the USAT to let Winter compete.

Some might have had reservations about Winter's ability to handle the race distance, but Dawn and Michael had no doubts. "He knew, like I knew, since she was a baby, she was capable of doing anything," says Dawn. Winter herself was calm about the whole thing too. She was trained, strong, determined, and focused. Dawn swam the 1.5 kilometers alongside Winter. The race directors brought in two elite, world champion triathletes, Karen Smyers and Simon Lessing, to bike and run with her.

Winter came in third in the "19-and-under-female" age group. Most importantly, she exceeded her fundraising goal of $10,000. Inspired by Winter's heart and soul, all the competitors at the Athletes for a Cure Triathlon that year competed for Team Winter in an unprecedented symbolic display of unity. So, in total, the entire field of triathletes raised over $100,000 for the Prostate Cancer Foundation.

Winter's dad, undergoing treatment at the Mayo Clinic at the time, traveled to Orlando to see his daughter cross the finish line. It was the last race he would attend. Sadly, he didn't make it to his 41st birthday, dying only 10 months after he was diagnosed.

Winter competed in the IronKids series, cinching the National Triathlon Champion title in 2010 and 2011 at the age of 11 and 12, respectively. Because of her athleticism and character, she was selected as the IronKids ambassador, a role she served in for four years.

Her focus and drive continued to center around building Team Winter, curing prostate cancer, and honoring her father. And while most kids (and adults) would want to showcase their trophies as reminders of their hard work, Winter gave them away. She sent her IronKids trophies to someone fighting prostate cancer. "I wanted to give hope to the families," she says.

When Winter was 14 years old, she decided to set a new goal: run a marathon on every continent before her 15th birthday. Seven races on seven continents, all for Team Winter and in memory of her father.

She started this journey in April 2012 in Eugene, Oregon. First marathon ever? Still only 13 years old? No sweat. She finished the course in a time of 3:45:10 and placed fourth in her age group. One down, six to go. But, the marathons to follow were some of the most grueling, challenging, and magnificent marathons the world could offer.

Winter had turned 14 by the time she arrived on her next continent—Africa. There, she was the third-place female finisher overall in the Amazing Maasai Marathon in Kenya. Battling scorching heat and tough terrain, Winter conquered the course in 4:04:00. Then she headed to the bottom of the globe for the Antarctica Marathon in March; getting there was almost as perilous as running the race. Winter braved the treacherous terrain, running 26.2 miles in temperatures of negative 22 degrees. She didn't just survive this run; she crushed it, finishing third overall among females and setting the world record for the youngest person ever to run a marathon in Antarctica.

In June, Winter tackled the Inca Trail Marathon to Machu Picchu in Peru, which is known as one of the most difficult marathon courses in the world. She chewed it up and spit it out, setting a new course record when she crossed the finish line as the first place female.

In August, Winter took second place overall among females in the Sunrise to Sunset Marathon in Mongolia, and then that fall she completed her final two races on the two remaining continents: New Zealand's Great Barrier Island Wharf to Wharf Marathon (counted as Australia), and the Athens Classic Marathon in Greece. Her collective 183.4 miles of running (not including the hundreds of miles in training and travel) ended auspiciously on November 10, 2014, at the Panathenaic Stadium in Athens, home of the first modern Olympics. On that day, Winter set a second world record when she became the youngest person to run a marathon on all seven continents. She and her mother Dawn, who ran every marathon with her, became the first mother and daughter duo to run seven marathons on seven continents.

There is a photograph of a smiling Winter crossing her final finish line in Athens, looking neither sweaty nor winded, arm raised in the air with a finger pointing straight up to the heavens. It is a gesture to her father, and a pose often seen in Winter's finish line photos. She knows he's at every race. "I can feel him watching down on me," she says.

There is no doubt Winter's father is a huge source of inspiration. Her other source of inspiration? Her dedicated and inspiring mom. There is no denying the apple did not fall far from the tree. Strong, confident, caring, athletic, compassionate, well-spoken, and filled with positive energy, this devoted mother of four is an active triathlete and busy physician. She has been by her daughter's side every step of the way.

Winter is currently focused on training for the 2018 Olympics, not for triathlon but in Aerial Freestyle, an event where skiers ski off a ramp, performing twists and turns in the air before landing. As I mentioned, Winter began skiing at a young age. She was invited to Park City, Utah, to train with the Fly Elite Team at the age of 12. Now at 18, Winter was just named to the 2016–2017 US Ski Team. Although training as an Olympic hopeful is her primary focus right now, Winter certainly hasn't retired from triathlon. She confesses that she still has an Ironman finish on her bucket list.

Whatever Winter is up to, she always uses her athletic abilities to get the word out about prostate cancer. I don't think she'll quit until a cure for the disease that took her father is found. To date, Team Winter has raised half a million dollars for the Prostate Cancer Foundation to help that cause.

Winter Vinecki demonstrates the power that one person has, regardless of age. "Triathlon has taught me you can do anything you put your mind to," she says. "It empowers you."

17

TRI: THE NEXT
GENERATION

Anything or anyone that does not bring you alive
is too small for you.

—DAVID WHYTE

When our swim club advertised a Splash and Dash race for kids ages 5 through 12, my daughter Madelena begged to do it. I had reservations. At the time she was a very new swimmer. That was my fault; I had neglected to enroll any of my kids in swimming lessons, so they were very late bloomers in the water. (I remember bringing Sophia to a pool party in kindergarten, and she was mortified to be the only 5-year-old still wearing water wings.)

I wasn't sure she was conditioned to swim the five consecutive laps required of this Splash and Dash race. And if she couldn't, would she start to freak out? Cry? Give up? I wondered if I should protect her, tell her we can't register for the race, think of some excuse (it was at 7:00 a.m. on Father's Day, after all). But another part of me realized I was projecting all of my personal crap onto this situation.

First, she would be in a pool, not an ocean, surrounded by adults and lifeguards. Second, she could rest between laps to catch her breath. Third, letting her tackle something that was beyond her comfort zone would stretch her limits and end up being a positive experience. How do we know what we are capable of if we never try to do anything? I didn't want her to wait until she was 40 to start discovering she had more inside her than she realized (*Ahem*). Lastly, if her own mother didn't believe in her, how could I expect her to believe in herself?

This mental roller-coaster ride took approximately 90 seconds. Then I registered her for the race and hoped to pick up a few pointers myself (and maybe that last little kick of inspiration) for my own triathlon the following weekend.

Age is no barrier. It's a limitation you put on your mind.
—JACKIE JOYNER-KERSEE

TRI'ING YOUNG

Years ago, simply *finding* a multisport event for children was nearly impossible. Just ask young athlete Winter Vinecki and her mom, Dawn. "There were no triathlons or tri-clubs to join in rural Michigan," Dawn recalls. "All they had were adult tris, and that was part of the problem." Another problem? They didn't make tri-wear for children. Dawn would buy "Adult, Extra Small" tri-tops for her daughter and cinch them tight with rubber bands.

When Winter became the IronKids Ambassador, youth triathlon was still obscure. "It was instrumental having Winter as an ambassador," says Dawn. By making appearances, speaking at schools, and teaching kids about triathlon, she gave more exposure to the sport. Winter appreciates how much the sport has grown among young athletes at all levels of competition.

Now, races for kids abound. When triathlons became more popular among adults, the enthusiasm trickled down to the children cheering their parents on from the sidelines. Increased interest sparked more races and more opportunity for young athletes of all abilities to experience the sport's many benefits.

Tris for Youth

Triathlon participation among kids is on the rise. USAT reports remarkable growth among its youth membership. In 2005, members between the ages of 7 and 17 represented less than 1 percent of USAT members. By 2012, their share of membership had risen to 35 percent.

USAT has been encouraging young triathletes by offering camps and races across the country. In 2015, there were over 750 USAT-sanctioned events held for youth across the country. IronKids, a branch of Ironman, holds over 50 events around the globe each year for children between the ages of 6 and 15. The age-appropriate distances focus on fun and fitness over competition. For the more serious young triathlete, USAT offers a Triathlon Athlete Development Program in which selected talent and Olympic hopefuls train at the elite level.

Tris for Teens

Triathlon is rising in popularity among teens and young adults as well. High school participation has increased from around 13,700 to nearly 58,000 competitors. In February 2016, the USAT announced its High School Triathlon Program, designed to expand opportunities for athletes aged 13 to 19 and to increase the number of high school triathlon clubs across the country. These efforts include the inaugural USAT Triathlon High School National Championships in South Carolina, launched in the spring of 2016.

Tris as an NCAA Emerging Sport for Women

Triathlon clubs have been sprouting up in the hallowed halls of colleges and universities. There are approximately 160 active triathlon clubs on college campuses and 1,200 students competing in USAT's Collegiate Club National Championships. In January 2014, the National Collegiate Athletic Association (NCAA) adopted women's triathlon as an "emerging sport." To be considered a championship sport, at least 40 varsity teams must be established within a 10-year period. To facilitate this, in 2015 the USAT Foundation began awarding multiyear grants, totaling $2.6 million, to eligible schools in Division I, II, and III that are launching NCAA women's varsity triathlon programs.

> *Play is the highest form of research.*
> —ALBERT EINSTEIN

HEALTHY BODIES, HEALTHY MINDS

The American Heart Association recommends that children get at least 60 minutes of moderate to vigorous aerobic activity every day. *One hour* minimum, each day. Not just activity, but "moderate to vigorous" activity. These recommendations begin at age 2. Sounds easy, but living in an age of video games and handheld electronics, children tend to spend more time in front of a screen than running and playing. Case in point, one-third of all American girls do not meet this minimum standard.

Coping Skills

Exercise in childhood goes beyond health and fun. Physical activities help children cope with stress by tempering cortisol levels, a hormone that is released in reaction to stress. According to a study of 8- and 9-year-olds published in *Pediatrics*, regular exercise during an after-school program had positive effects on both executive functioning and stress. The children who received the most physical activity in the study had the lowest cortisol levels when exposed to a stressful situation. In addition, the more physically active children showed rapid improvements on a cognitive test.

A Match Made in Heaven

While triathlon may not sound like an ideal sport for children, if you think about it, it's a match made in kid heaven. When kids play, what do they do? Zip around endlessly on their bikes. Splash in the water for hours making up games. Run around playing tag or just . . . running . . . for no apparent reason. Triathlon is like the grown-up version of the best day in a child's life! It's no wonder adults find triathlon fun. It reconnects them with the long-lost joys of a childhood past. And it's no wonder that kids are being drawn into it in larger and larger numbers—in many ways, it's a natural fit.

Too Much Too Soon?

With 12.7 million kids and teens meeting the criteria for obesity, one could argue that the emphasis should be on getting more kids out there moving than worrying about kids overdoing it on exercise. But, as we've already discussed, the fact that a little exercise is good and a lot of exercise is great doesn't take away the potential for overload. Where is that point? No one really knows for sure, and it is probably different for everyone.

Both prepubescent and pubescent girls, like adult women, can fall victim to the female athlete triad, stress fractures, overuse injuries, and overtraining syndrome. To think youth is a buffer to injury would be erroneous. Furthermore, overuse injuries may have a more profound impact on a young girl whose bones are still growing and body is still changing. Sometimes these injuries can end a career in sports before it even begins.

But these caveats are more relevant to girls competing at a high level of competition. For those using triathlon as a hobby, a fun way to build confidence and self-esteem, these types of risks are minimal.

Diversification Trumps Specialization

A hot topic in youth sports is the debate over hyper-specialization versus diversification. Hyper-specialization (focusing on a single sport played year-round regardless of training volume) appears to be the most common practice in the United States right now, and the philosophy most encouraged by society and coaches. This philosophy trickles down to parents anxious to make sure their child isn't left sitting on the bench. Tiger Woods specialized at a very young age, and look how he turned out, right? However, Tiger Woods is more of a statistical outlier than the norm. Most research does *not* support early specialization; the reason being it is correlated with more negatives than positives in the long run.

Studies show that kids who hyper-specialize too young have an increased risk of a serious overuse injury. A study conducted by Loyola University found that young athletes who hyper-specialize have a 37 percent increased chance of becoming injured. In that same study, 60 percent of youth who were injured were hyper-specialized, and the large majority of injuries were due to overuse. Kids who hyper-specialize are also more likely to suffer emotional burnout: quitting the very sport they used to love until they had to do it 24/7/12.

At some point, young athletes who want to take it to the next level *should* specialize. But most experts recommended that parents and coaches hold off on this until at least age 12 or, more conservatively, age 15. Instead, diversification in sports is encouraged. Enter triathlon, stage left. It's three sports rolled into one which means instant, built-in diversification.

Research supports diversification in sports, reminding athletes, parents and coaches that it doesn't "ruin" a child's chances of excelling in a single sport. It may seem counterintuitive, but playing multiple sports at an early age actually has a positive effect. Kids who diversify during their childhood appear to experience greater athletic success down the road. Just look at Winter Vinecki as a perfect example. She skis, runs, does Spartan races, swims, and cycles.

And It's Self-Esteem for the Win!

Whether a young girl goes on to be the next Winter Vinecki or simply enjoys the sport of triathlon for the fun and challenge, there is one guaranteed side effect: a whole lot of self-esteem.

Girls face tremendous pressure as they navigate through the tween and teen years. Body image issues, insecurity, social pressures, bullying, dating pressures, and eating disorders plague young girls in today's world. Sports, whether competitive and organized or fun and recreational, have a long history of acting like a buffer. Triathlon in particular has a uniquely transformative power. Why? Probably because it's freakin' *hard*! When something is really hard and you do it anyway, it provides a serious boost in self-esteem and confidence. Think of the feeling grown women get crossing their first finish line, and then imagine what happens when a young girl, at a vulnerable time in her development, has that same experience. That, my friends, is a gift. A gift that two very special organizations have shared with girls who may have otherwise never had the opportunity.

> *The more difficult the victory, the greater*
> *the happiness in winning.*
> —PELÉ

GIRLS IN THE GAME TRIATHLON TEAM

Founded in 1995, Girls in the Game has had a powerful impact on the lives of girls on the south and west sides of Chicago. Their mission is to promote sports and fitness opportunities, along with nutrition, health education, and leadership skills in girls living in socioeconomically disadvantaged urban areas. To date, the organization has empowered more than 40,000 girls through their innovative programming. Outcomes data show that even after a single season in the program, 70 percent of girls show significant improvement in self-worth and nearly 90 percent demonstrate perseverance and determination.

Miranda Hauser is a volunteer who started out with the organization in their after-school program. "We'd help them with their homework, do a fun fitness activity, and give them a hot meal," she says. After being exposed to a wide variety of sports and fitness activities year-round, the girls develop confidence and leadership skills, learn about nutrition, and practice teamwork.

The Girls in the Game Triathlon Team is a summer program designed for girls between the ages of 7 and 14. "With P.E. being cut, and funding for girls sports going down . . . we saw the need and took advantage of it," says Miranda. A triathlete herself, Miranda started volunteering as a coach with the team eight years ago.

The large majority of the girls in the triathlon program are from low-income areas and don't have bikes and/or helmets, so the program provides them when necessary. "There are girls every year who come in and don't even know how to ride a bike," says Miranda. "They come in not knowing how to swim."

Most of the girls who join the triathlon team are already involved in the Girls in the Game program. Sign-up is voluntary, and the program is free. But because it's grant-funded, space is limited to no more than 14 girls each season. "A lot of years there's a wait list," Miranda says. Many of the girls have such a positive experience that they keep coming back.

The 10-week training program provides coaching and conditioning to prepare the girls for a local race. They meet for two hours of coached sessions every Tuesday, spending a little time on each discipline. The coaches incorporate games to make training fun and focus on individual improvements instead of competition. Though the girls come from different schools in the area, they develop a bond through training.

"They all cross the finish line," Miranda says. Even more importantly, they develop mentoring and leadership skills that are very evident on race day as they encourage each other. "We promote that you cheer on your team. The older girls who finish earlier will run back and run with the younger ones. There's a positive vibe."

Miranda never ceases to be amazed by the boost of confidence triathlon gives the girls.

"One of the girls was dead last," Miranda remembers. They were worried that she might get upset, or give up, so they kept asking her if she was okay as she struggled through the course. The girl kept smiling and trucking along. "She said, 'I'm going to finish!'" Miranda recalls. And she did. "It was cool to see her confidence." She may have been the last to cross that finish line, but she was so proud of herself.

That's one of the many empowering things about triathlon. We all run our own race. We are heroes in our own stories. These girls, at a tender age, are rewriting their own stories the moment they cross that finish line because now they've learned what they're made of. They've learned there are no limits to what they can do and who they can be.

That transformation is what keeps Miranda active on both the triathlon team and the Girls in the Game Advisory Board. "It's so fun to see the first day of the pool, and the confidence that happens over time," she says. "You'll see girls who are really into it, especially the girls who have done it before. You'll see them mentoring the new girls. Some of them come in completely unmotivated. Even *they* get excited on the day of the race . . . [to see] the smiles on their faces . . . it's incredible."

> *Strength does not come from physical capacity.*
> *It comes from an indomitable will.*
>
> —MAHATMA GANDHI

I-TRI GIRLS

Theresa Roden felt transformed even *before* she crossed the finish line of her first triathlon in her 40s. "I was an overweight kid," she says. "I was always the last picked for every kickball game. Weight was something I've dealt with my entire life." When she was pregnant with her daughter, Theresa's mother died and she grieved by turning to the comfort of food. "I packed on the pounds," she remembers, estimating her weight as approximately 230 pounds. "I was miserable. It was the lowest of the lows."

Five years after her daughter was born, Theresa happened to be at the beach during the Block Island Triathlon. Watching the men and women running by her, she felt inspired. "The craziest thought came into my mind. I said, 'I'm going to do that next year.'" She recruited some friends, and they trained together for that entire year. "They were in better shape, but I was a better swimmer and biker." This gave her a huge surge of confidence, and she began to connect with the idea that there was an athlete inside her.

Perhaps she was capable of more than she realized. "For the first time I was actually kind to myself. The transformation that happened on the inside changed the way I ate, changed everything."

When Theresa arrived at the starting line of the Block Island Triathlon that following year, she had already transformed herself both inside and outside. Finishing the triathlon changed her life forever: "I crossed the finish line, and it was phenomenal."

The feeling of empowerment Theresa received from triathlon ignited a spark. She had to share this feeling. At first, she pulled other friends into the sport. Then, when Theresa's own daughter hit those muddled middle school years, a lightbulb went off. "If I could have learned how good it feels and how empowering it feels as a 13-year-old, think of how different things would have been," she says.

Armed with a background in education, a passion for triathlon, and a compassionate spirit, Theresa developed the i-tri program for girls, complete with a tailored, comprehensive curriculum. She approached the administration at her daughter's school and, with their enthusiastic support, piloted her program with a group of 12 students from the East End of Long Island. Her daughter was in that original group.

The community i-tri girls serves is diverse: 50 percent identify themselves as a minority and 10 percent of the population lives below the poverty level. "The majority of residents are working class. There is a big population of immigrants," Theresa says. The decision to target this community was absolutely intentional. Adolescent girls, under the best of circumstances, struggle with acceptance, self-esteem, confidence, and body image. For girls from disadvantaged economic backgrounds with extra socioeconomic stressors and limited resources, these transitional years can be even tougher.

"Our goal was to bring girls together from different socioeconomic classes, religions, and ethnic backgrounds. Once you're an i-tri girl, you're an i-tri girl. None of that matters." Unlike the Girls in the Game Triathlon

Team, where sign-up is open to any interested girl, the i-tri girls are selected through a screening process and can join only through invitation. "I was looking for a girl who didn't consider herself an athlete, going through a tough time, with low self-esteem and body image issues," says Theresa. To identify those at-risk girls, she created a survey that was administered to sixth, seventh, and eighth graders. She also received input from the school social worker. "We created a list of girls," Theresa says. "[They were] invited to a meeting. We explained things, tried to inspire them. They could opt in or opt out." No one was forced; they had to enter freely. She also requires full support and participation from the family. Without that, the program can't succeed.

Once a girl chooses to sign up, everything is free. "We don't want any girl selected to not be able to afford to participate," says Theresa. The program consists of weekly group lessons designed to teach girls self-respect, self-confidence, positive body image, and healthy lifestyle choices. The customized curriculum includes self-esteem workshops, family outreach, nutrition education, and physical fitness. Once a week after school, the girls are introduced to things like Zumba, yoga, kickboxing, and spin classes. On Saturdays, they do their triathlon training, which involves swimming, biking, and running at the local YMCA.

The program culminates with the Hamptons Youth Triathlon at Sag Harbor. The race, designed for ages 10 through 17, consists of a 300-yard swim in the bay, a 7-mile bike ride, and a 1.5-mile run.

When the first i-tri group completed the program and crossed that finish line, Theresa knew her program was impacting lives. "It was absolute magic," she says. "None of these girls would have had the confidence or believed they had the ability to go out for a team," says Theresa. "Now, they're on a team. The camaraderie is like nothing I've ever seen."

Now entering its seventh year, i-tri has four different groups running in four schools. A total of 150 girls have gone through the program. "We have never had a girl who has been in the program and not been able to finish the race," Theresa says. Nearly all program alumni come back to mentor the new girls. Those girls from the pioneering years are now in high school and return as coaches, eager to mentor the newcomers.

Girls who were selected for the program were the quieter, less "popular," more insecure girls at the school. They were typically left out and left behind. After going through the i-tri program, they carry the confidence from triathlon into other areas of their lives. "The more work we do, the more we realize we're making a mental health impact," says Theresa. "As much as it's about triathlon, there are so many bigger things that happen."

These girls also develop into leaders. The principal at the high school once pulled Theresa aside and told her, "I don't know what you're doing, but these girls coming over, they are incredible."

The gift that Theresa Roden has given to these girls? Simply helping them unlock their potential.

Whether you think you can, or think you can't, you're right.
—HENRY FORD

PEP TALK FOR TWO

After two weeks of daily practice on her new swim team, and the day following her 7:00 a.m. time trials, Madelena woke up early Sunday morning with her game face on.

Actually, she had no game face. She was exhausted and nervous.

"I don't want to go. . . . I'm so tired," she whined, buried under her covers. Remember, no one had forced her to sign up for this Splash and Dash. It was her own idea, but like a lot of us, sometimes ideas that seem good at the time bite us in the backside later.

"You know what I think? I think you're nervous. And that's okay," I said. "It's totally normal to be nervous and when that happens, you feel like you don't want to do it. But I think you'll regret it if you don't go. If you let your fears stop you, you'll stop yourself from having so many great experiences in life. I think this will be one of them."

She admitted to the nerves and the self-doubt.

"Mom," she said. "What if I come in first?"

"I'll be incredibly proud of you," I replied.

Her eyes got big and her tone serious. "But, what if I come in last?"

"I'll be incredibly proud of you."

She went through a handful of places; 12th, 53rd, 2nd, 16th. My answer stayed the same. "Maddie, just setting a goal and seeing it through, just stepping up and doing it, finishing what you started . . . *that* makes you a winner. If you show up at that start line, there is no way you can lose. You only lose if you never try."

A good reminder for both of us.

Until you face your fears, you don't move to the other side,
where you find the power.

—MARK ALLEN

COULD, WOULD, SHOULD, DID

"I never thought in a million years I could do it."

JESSICA CAPPELLA was an active, working mother of two young boys who loved going to the gym to kickbox and lift weights. "I was in the best shape of my life," she says, "but I noticed my legs were starting to get weaker and I had back pain all the time." Initially, she blamed her weight-training routine. When things didn't improve, she consulted a doctor, who suspected a herniated disc and sent her for a diagnostic MRI.

"I got a call two hours later that I had a spinal cord tumor that spanned five vertebrae, from L1 to L5," she says. "Two days later, I was in the hospital having surgery."

"The surgery went really well," Jessica says. "But, when I woke up, I couldn't move my right leg at all."

Nothing. No feeling or movement from the mid-thigh down. Incomplete paraplegia, a complication neither she nor her doctors had anticipated. Everyone was surprised, and Jessica felt blindsided.

In addition to her unexpected leg paralysis, Jessica experienced other postsurgical difficulties, including seizure-like activity, adrenal failure secondary to the steroids she was given, and a fluid collection that developed at the operative site. These complications led to a tough recovery. She spent four months in the hospital. "No one could figure out why I couldn't move my right leg. They said, 'Let's give it 6 months.'" Despite all of her hard work at McGee Rehabilitation Hospital, the feeling in her leg never returned.

Jessica's first year of recovery was filled with adjustments, the most notable being that she was now wheelchair-bound. She transitioned from an active, busy, and independent life to navigating life from a chair, relying on help from others, and managing chronic pain and neuropathy. She also had to leave a fulfilling career as a critical care nurse and say goodbye to the kickboxing classes and workout routines she loved. Parenting two young boys presented practical challenges, as well. Her youngest has a mitochondrial disease that causes a variety of medical, developmental, behavioral, and neurological conditions, including blindness, cognitive impairments, epilepsy, permanent tube feedings, and thyroid disease.

Jessica continued to suffer from pain, neuropathy, and muscle weakness after surgery. Pain management was an ongoing challenge, as they tried to find medications with the fewest side effects. "I was pretty out of it the first year," she says.

A year later, Jessica underwent a second surgery to remove scar tissue that had caused a tethered spine. "Before the second surgery, I begged my doctor to take off my leg so I could get a prosthetic," Jessica confesses. Though being an amputee would not have been easy, she felt a prosthetic would give her the ability to live a life that more closely resembled the one she had left behind. It would allow her to engage in athletics the way she used to, which she fiercely missed. Unfortunately, she was not a candidate. To be successful with a prosthetic requires strength in the supporting muscles. Her hip and right buttock were simply too weak, and the window of time for improvement had closed. "Usually, your first year or two after a spinal injury is when you make improvements," Jessica says. In other words, despite all her hard work and hope, this was probably about as good as it was going to get.

"I missed activity, a lot," Jessica says. One evening she and some friends were watching television together when an ad for Guinness beer came on. The commercial opened with a bunch of guys on a court playing an intense game of wheelchair basketball. "At the end, all the guys stand up out of their chairs, except for one. They were all playing in wheelchairs for their one friend. I said, 'I love that commercial.'"

Little did she know, this 60-second television ad had given her friends an idea. "They gave me a membership to the tri club and said, 'You're doing a triathlon, and we will all do a leg with you.'"

After getting the green light from her doctors, the next step was figuring out how to train. "I was excited, but didn't know how I was going to do this." With the help of her family and friends, she figured it out. To swim, she secured a child's water wing around her right ankle to buoy her leg. Her husband made her an adaptive bike with an extended pedal to support her right leg while she powered herself almost exclusively with her left. She used an elliptical for further conditioning, because she could strap her foot to the pedal and pull with her arms. For the run, Jessica would require her wheelchair. However, the act of leaning forward to push the chair for 3 miles was extremely painful for her back. So her friends set up a fundraising page, raising over $3,000 to purchase a lighter racing chair.

Three friends trained with her, one to accompany her on each leg of the triathlon. Although they were registering as a relay team, Jessica would actually be doing the entire race. Team Cappella talked with Michelle Powell, the Queen of the Hill Race Director, to work out the necessary accommodations under USAT guidelines. Jessica was going to be the first challenged athlete to ever race the Queen of the Hill, and everyone was thrilled to make it happen.

Requesting special accommodations was difficult for Jessica. "I wanted to be treated like everyone else," she explains. Her biggest fear? That the other women racing would think she was getting off "easier" or didn't deserve special treatment. "I was afraid people would look at me and be angry or annoyed that I was racing," she says. Of course, nothing of the sort happened. On race day, she encountered only encouragement, positive energy, and support. People were far from annoyed; they were inspired.

Jessica's family, her friends, and even the staff from McGee came to cheer her on, clad in matching blue T-shirts with "Team Cappella" printed across the front. On the back, four simple words: "Could, Would, Should, DID."

Not only did Jessica cross that finish line, but she did so with a time of 1:17:13, ranking her 27th out of 302 finishers overall. Officially registered as one of 17 relay teams, this finishing time earned Team Cappella a second-place relay team win. At the Queen of the Hill, everyone who stands on the podium is "crowned" with the race's signature rhinestone tiara.

"It was an amazing experience. My girlfriends were a huge support," Jessica says. "I never thought in a million years I could do it. Then proving to myself that I could? It gave me that boost to go on."

Today, Jessica can walk with the support of a full brace, which extends from her upper thigh to her toes. It's a big improvement from total reliance on a wheelchair. "I'm ambulatory for small things. I need the chair for longer distances," she says.

Adjusting to a new way of life hasn't been easy, but Jessica remains grateful and positive. Sometimes, when she has a tough day, she thinks back to that June day in 2014, the day she did her first triathlon. "I look at my little tiara to remind myself when I get in the dumps," Jessica says. It reminds her of a time when the impossible became possible. Reminds her that there is strength in friendship, strength in family, and a bottomless strength inside her.

18

QUEEN OF THE HILL

You never climb a mountain, get to the top
and say, "I should have just been content
to stay where I was."

—A 1997 NIKE AD

y 4:45 a.m. I have given up on sleep. My alarm is set for 5:00 anyway, so I quietly rise from bed. I have been wide awake since 3:30.

I had laid out everything I needed the night before, an uncharacteristically obsessive-compulsive thing for me to do. Usually, I fly by the seat of my pants, completely disorganized, forever missing one sock, a set of keys, half my brain. This morning, I am so together I don't know what to do with myself. I simply have to make a breakfast smoothie, hydrate, meet up with my neighbor Lorri Z., and cycle to the lake with her. I am grateful for her pre-race company, a welcome distraction.

When I arrive at Lake Gilman, about a mile from my home, it is buzzing with activity. Hundreds of ladies in matching pink and black tri-suits are walking their bikes from the satellite parking to the lake. Orange cones are being lined up in the street, and cop cars with their lights blinking block the intersection, closing the roads to traffic. A giant inflatable arch has been erected at the finish line, and the computerized chip timing system is being set up by a some tech guys. Underneath a large, rustic pavilion, the Queen's brunch is coming together as someone tests the sound system.

The backdrop to all this commotion is a serene, tree-lined lake. Still and glassy, it reflects tree branches and the puffy clouds of a warm summer sky. This morning, the lake is accessorized with several enormous orange inflatable pyramids floating on the surface of the water, marking a horseshoe-shaped swim course. I feel a sinking in my stomach and a tightness in my chest when I look out over Lake Gilman. But I also notice that the feeling is not as bad as the first time I faced my open-water fears weeks ago. I am grateful for those two practice swims.

For some reason, the last buoy looks farther away than it did before. "That's just perception," a volunteer assures me when I ask her if the course is different. "It's still a quarter of a mile," she laughs. "Don't worry."

Lorri and I join the slow trickle of women pushing their bikes up the hill to the transition area. The smiles, the exclamations of "Good luck," the hugs, the enthusiastic "Are you ready?" and "How do you feel?" lilt through the air. The pre-race atmosphere feels more like a love fest than a competition. Even the strongest competitors sport a friendly game face.

As I enter the triathlon area, or T-zone, a young volunteer writes the number 106 on both my upper arms. My race age is then written on the back of my right calf. A little too boldly, in my opinion. Your "triathlon age" is typically one year older than your actual age. "I'm really 45," I say to the 13-year-old girl body-marking me. She giggles, but I'm imagining in her mind she's all like, *Okay, lady. Forty-whatever! You're just an old mom.* Indeed, I was just an old mom. But an old mom getting prepped to rock a freakin' *triathlon!*

I find what I think will be a good spot on the bike racks. When I see my friend, Heather S., we embrace in an excited hug. She recalls me swearing—*swearing*—that I would never, ever do a triathlon years ago at that crazy book club, which gives us a good laugh. Her comfort, ease, and joy on race day are infectious. She's here for the party; she feeds off the positive energy and smiles the entire race without a hint of anxiety. "Girl," she told me once, "I paid a bunch of money to race in this thing, and then paid for babysitting. I don't have my kids. I'm with my friends. I'm going to *enjoy* myself." Words to live by.

We take a few pre-race selfies with our cell phones. She squeezes in another hug, wishing me luck as we part. She knows this day is a big deal for me.

I head back down the hill to the lakeside, get my hair French-braided at the braiding tent, relieve an anxious bladder in the pink porta-potties, and make it in time for the pre-race meeting. This is where Colleen goes over the rules: Where to exit the water, where you can mount and dismount the bike, a warning to be careful on the final bike hill because it is extremely steep, and to walk your bike up and down from transition with helmet on and fastened.

And don't die. Well, I added that last part.

A little girl sings the national anthem. Now, it's getting real. I'm feeling nervous, but then I see her. A woman out on the dock being helped from her wheelchair into the water. I didn't know who she was at the time, but I later learned it was Jessica Cappella, the young mom whose leg was paralyzed after the removal of a spinal tumor. I didn't know her or her story that day, but I did know this—seeing her made me stop feeling so nervous and incapable and start feeling grateful.

As a challenged athlete, Jessica starts her swim first. Then the first wave is called to the water. Each age group wears a different colored cap to represent their wave. My cap is white, and I am in the last of eight waves. I'm not happy about being one of the last people in the water, as it means that the large majority of people will already be done and celebrating by the time I drag myself across the finish line. It will also be hotter on the run, the cheering crowd will be smaller, and my family will have to wait longer for my arrival. "Well, fewer people will pass you!" Anthony laughed when I complained about the situation. Always looking on the bright side, that one. "And we will be there at the finish line, no matter how long you take," he added. That was all I needed to hear.

The other thing about being in the last wave is that you get to sit there waiting while your anxiety builds. I watch as hundreds of women jump into the lake, wave by wave, until finally mine is called. Many swimmers are already finishing, exiting the water, and running up the hill to start the bike leg before I'm even wet. The lake is filled with splashing arms and legs, but emptying fast. We white caps descend a small slope and queue up to be funneled through makeshift gates. Michelle Powell is in the small group of race staff standing at the edge of the dock. She gives me a smile and a heartfelt "Good luck." I feel better seeing her there.

"Shout out your number as you jump in," she instructs. I glance at my arm as I hear the splash of the woman in front of me.

"One-O-Six!" I push the words out, but my voice sounds thready and floats off into the breeze. I take a step and cross the blue-and-red timing mat. I'm at the edge of the dock. The start of my journey. There are 12 women behind me and about 13 miles ahead of me. This is it.

You must do the things you cannot.

I'm airborne for scarcely a second and then plunge into darkness. The cold water hits me with a fierceness, but it's not nearly as cold as the weeks before. My breath is not stolen, and I'm able to get my arms and legs moving easily. Once I get going, the temperature actually feels quite comfortable.

I swim. Steady, even, and calm. The swim is completely uneventful, from a swimming standpoint. The one bonus of going into the water last is that you're not swimming on top of people. I have lots of elbow room. I only bump into someone once, a woman resting on her back to whom I apologize as sincerely as one can with goggles and a swim cap on. I'm hyperfocused on the act of swimming, sighting, and staying relaxed. Everything else ceases to exist. It's just me in the water, moment by moment, stroking, breathing, sighting. I don't exhaust myself; I don't get competitive with myself. I'm not trying to win anything. I'm just trying to survive. I just want what Meredith Atwood of *Swim Bike Mom* calls "a good finish."

Looping around the third buoy and swimming the final straightaway, I'm flooded with an intense feeling of relief. With every turn of my head, I watch the shoreline change, see the faces of the crowd looking on, the sunlight streaming through the shallower waters. I see women standing and exiting the lake. I right myself, feet squishing into the lake floor, and wade toward the steps with a goofy grin plastered across my face. For me, that 12-minute swim might as well have been the entire race. The hardest part was over. Doubts about being able to finish a triathlon are gone. I'm on land now, and I've *got* this.

With the weight of the world off my shoulders, I let out a whoop of joy that explodes from the center of my soul. I throw my fists in the air and can't stop smiling. Michelle is on the shore yelping enthusiastic congratulations, and we quickly embrace. I jog up the slope and see a man in a blue shirt, face blocked by a camera, and a little girl with a small homemade sign standing by his side. It's Anthony and Sophia, cheering me on. "Go, go, go!" he urges, but I have to stop and kiss them both.

I am on such a high, that I forget my dorky white swim cap is still on my head until I get to the bike. It isn't breaking any rules, mind you. It's just that I look like a Q-tip in every post-swim photo.

I run up the hill to T-1, where we transition from swim to bike. The transition area is a ghost town. The bike racks are nearly empty, and it's oddly quiet. The upside of being at the tail end of a race is that you can find your bike really easily. Mine was literally the only one in the entire row. The downside is that it makes you think you're dead last. Maybe I *am* dead last! I feel a sinking in my stomach and a frenzy start to rise. What if I *am* last? I think to myself, and start to panic. I hear the sweet Southern drawl of Heather S. in my head. *Who cares, girl! Just have fun!*

The bike is the longest part of the race, especially for me because I am slow. I would like to blame it on the fact that I'm riding a hybrid, not a light road bike, but I'm just not one of those people with strong cycling legs.

For a long time, I don't see a single soul. Then I spot a few cyclists far ahead of me. I am still convinced I might be in last place because I don't see anyone behind me for miles. Then, I start passing a few people. A few people pass me. I'm not out here alone, and I'm relieved. I see my friend

Karen who hangs with me for a while and we have fun chatting before she takes off. It's nice to have a little company for part of the ride.

The bike takes me a slow 45 minutes, but I enjoy every minute. As I come down the final hill back to T-2, volunteers are shouting at everyone to slow down and dismount from our bikes. "Someone crashed here earlier," I'm told as I run my bike up the hill toward the racks. "Who was it?" I call over my shoulder. "Christylynn!" they say. "I think she broke her collarbone. It was pretty bad." Mother of three. Exceptional cyclist. Competitive athlete. Super-sweet person. Damn. That girl could have made it onto the podium.

I return my bike to the racks, waving and smiling at everyone I see, and start the final leg of my journey, the 5K run. My favorite part is last, which is good because that's when you need to dig deep. Despite my happy heart, by the time my feet start hitting the blacktop, exhaustion is kicking in. My legs are heavy and burning from the ride, and it is difficult to get my stride going. But the nice thing about the run is that I don't feel as alone. Since it is an out-and-back course, I get to see all the runners on the other side of the road as they loop around. We exchange happy hoots of encouragement.

I am surprised to see so many women struggling on the run. It is my comfort zone. I might be tired, I might be thirsty, I might be hot, my legs might feel like lead, but I won't crash or panic or sink. Most importantly, I won't stop.

I am moving at a decent clip, but my body is feeling the effects of lack of sleep, repetitive adrenaline surges and crashes, low fuel, and a morning of swimming and biking over 10 miles already. It is starting to take real effort to push myself closer to the finish line. I offer encouraging words to those who look like they need it as I pass them. "You got this," I pant, jogging by. Every time I say these words to someone else, it reminds me that I got this, too.

Despite the exhaustion, I have a goofball smile pasted across my face the final quarter mile. I turn into the home stretch, running across a small overpass bridge lined with enough cheering people to make it an emotional experience. I know I'm crossing that finish line pretty late in the race. I originally worried about this being a buzzkill, but when I get to the home stretch I could have finished to chirping crickets at midnight and it wouldn't have mattered. I'm not running those final yards on asphalt. I am running on air.

Anthony and Sophia are at the finish line wearing giant grins. Next to Anthony stands my friend Theresa, who came in eighth overall and has been waiting for me, gives me a heart-felt hug, screaming congratulations. "She wouldn't leave until you crossed that finish line," Anthony told me later. It was a small gesture, but I'll never forget how much that single act of kindness meant.

That is what it's all about. *That* is the stuff that keeps us coming back for more. It goes beyond the act of swimming, biking, and running. It's the joy, it's the challenge, but above all it's the outpouring of support and friendship. I know triathletes have a reputation of being Type A, driven, and competitive. There may be truth to some of that, but I can honestly say that triathletes are some of the most warm, kind, supportive, enthusiastic, empowering, positive, giving, and inspiring people I've ever met, and I've talked to a lot of them from all across the country. Whether you are a first timer or a 30-year veteran, whether you dabble or whether you are obsessed, you are always, *always* welcomed.

> *A river cuts through rock, not because of its power,*
> *but because of its persistence.*
> —JAMES N. WATKINS

I cross the finish line of my first triathlon in 1 hour, 34 minutes, and 22 seconds. My swim and bike sucked, but I was thrilled to make a personal record on the 5K with a time of 27:10. The three overall winners were 40, 46, and 54 years old, respectively. The youngest racer that day was 14, and the oldest, 75. I myself placed 158th, which put me right in the middle of the pack and in the middle of my age group too. So, mathematically speaking, pretty average.

But being "average" in this pack of women was an honor. For a first-timer non-swimmer who was an undertrained and inexperienced cyclist riding a hybrid bike, I didn't feel the least bit "average." I felt like the Queen of that dang Hill. Queen of the entire universe! The best part was everyone else did too.

We are halfway through the award ceremony when someone yells to Colleen. The final triathlete is running in. Everything screeches to a halt. "The last runner is coming in, everyone! Let's go!" Colleen shouts. People jump off the podium, and everyone runs down the slope to holler and cheer for a 40-year-old woman finishing her first triathlon. She completed the course in 2:43:22, over an hour and a half after Jenn M. broke the tape for the win. If you saw the two of them side by side, you wouldn't be able to tell who came in first and who came in last. The pride in their eyes was identical.

The ceremonies are over, and I have successfully stuffed my face and drunk my mimosa. (Okay, five mimosas. They were in tiny cups.) It is time to roll out. I grab my bike, throw my knapsack over my shoulder, and head down the hill to bike home. Anthony had already left with Sophia to see the remainder of Ariella and Madelena's swim meet. I am planning to sprint over there too and catch the tail end of it. I see my friend Jayne as I'm leaving, and we walk down the hill together.

I had heard through the grapevine that Jayne had a tough race. First, she lost her timing chip in the lake and had to swim back to retrieve it, costing valuable time. Then she had a technical malfunction on the bike when her brake, unbeknownst to her, was rubbing against her wheel, slowing her considerably. "I'm bummed," Jayne says. "This was my comeback year."

Last year, Jayne had trained hard for the Queen of the Hill but was knocked out of commission when a large mass was discovered in her uterus. Instead of racing, she ended up recovering from an unexpected hysterectomy. The recovery wasn't easy, but she got her body back in action. She wanted to prove to herself that she was fit, healthy, and back in the game.

She was fit and healthy, alright. But the game hadn't played fair today. I ask her about her race, and instead of complaining, she tells me a story.

"After I finished the race, I started walking home," she says. Jayne, like me, lives close to the lake. Upset and disappointed, she didn't feel like sticking around for all the post-race festivities. As she's walking back, there are many women still finishing up the run. "I see this woman, and she's running slowly, but she looks like she's struggling," Jayne says. "I don't know why, but I just asked her if she wanted some company while she ran." As they plodded along, they got to chatting and Jayne learned that the woman has cancer and is currently in the midst of treatment.

All of a sudden, Jayne's entire perspective about her bad race day changed. "She started to cry; then I started to cry," Jayne says. This woman is so grateful for Jayne's support that she tells her 'I think God put you here in my path today to help me.' Jayne saw it a little differently. "I told her, 'No, it was *you* who were put in *mine*.'"

Nothing in life just happens.

—GOLDA MEIR

Crossing that finish line in June 2014 was one of the most amazing moments of my life. I felt so many different things that day. Confident. Proud. Happy. Joyful. Hungry. Not metaphorically hungry, but actually hungry for copious amounts of food. But was I hooked? That was the million-dollar question, and my friends were dying to know my answer. Did I, the person who said she would be "one and done," get hooked?

There is no doubt that I was changed by triathlon. You finish a triathlon, and it's like this newfound strength is bursting from inside. You get a glimmer that maybe, just maybe, you can do even more than you ever dreamed. I thought I had lost myself under the piles of laundry and dirty dishes in the sink, but I found myself again when I laced up my running shoes and covered 13.25 miles by land and by sea. (Okay, lake. Work with me here.)

Triathlon brought a new level of health and fitness into my life for which I am grateful. It brought new friendships into my life, for which I am even more grateful. Never have I been part of something so big and so special. Never have I felt so inspired and uplifted by those around me.

And yes, I will even admit that at some point during the day (probably after I emerged from the lake), the triathlon actually started becoming fun. You heard that right—FUN. I admit it. But hooked? Even though I had been told 1,000 times that I would go home and start signing up for 10 more races, I didn't. The only thing I wanted to do when I got home was eat, shower, eat some more, drink a beer, and sleep. And not train for anything the rest of the summer. Or perhaps ever again.

I received a text the next day from Lydia, asking if I wanted to join her for some triathlon at the beach in a few weeks. I couldn't think of anything I wanted to do less, but of course I said that nicely.

I guess the bottom line is this. While I enjoyed my triathlon immensely and was pretty certain that I would do another at some point in my life, I didn't feel that addictive pull so many people have described. But you know what? That is okay. I'm allowed to be who I am, and they are allowed to be who they are. The great thing about triathlon, as I learned through this process, is that there is no *one* type of triathlete, no *one* body type, no *one* personality, no *one* mold to fit in to. It attracts all sorts of women, it welcomes all sorts of women, and it's here for you in whatever way you need it to be.

When I began my research, I was trying to understand triathlon the way you figure out a puzzle or crack a code. After writing this book, my head understood so much more about women who tri. After I experienced triathlon firsthand, my *heart* understood even more. But, the thing is, I never needed to understand triathlon. I needed to understand myself *through* triathlon. And I did just that.

I now understood what Elysa Walk of Giant Bicycles said during her TEDx talk. After cycling 900 kilometers around the perimeter of Taiwan over eight days, she said, "I had rediscovered joy within the challenge of my adventure." That was my biggest takeaway from this whole process. Joy is not something that happens to us, shows up like good luck, or is hard-wired in our DNA. As Elysa explains it, joy is the byproduct of surmounting our biggest obstacles. It doesn't come from the *avoidance* of difficult, pain-ful, and flat-out impossible things. It comes from the act of *surviving* them. When we stare down our worst fears, crest that mammoth hill, complete that 1,000-mile journey by hook or by crook, limping, crawling, dragging ourselves to the finish—that, she says, is the secret of genuine, unadul-terated joy. Like glimpsing the dark side of the moon, we know ourselves through and through. We know in our moment of greatest weakness that we can muster our greatest strength. But we will never see our true power unless we give ourselves the chance.

> *There are too many people praying for the mountains*
> *of difficulty to be removed, when what they really need*
> *is the courage to climb them.*
>
> —UNKNOWN

One of my favorite quotes lives on a plaque at my alma mater, McDaniel College. It's by Dr. Ira Zepp, human rights activist and professor emeritus of religious studies. He said this:

"We must learn when to be water and when to be rock."

Water and rock. Each powerful beyond measure, one in its fluidity, its ability to take any shape necessary; and the other in its durability, its ability to stand its ground without bending or breaking.

Flow and endure. Relentless and rooted. Powerful and unwavering. Run-ning fast, holding steady. We must learn when to be water and when to be rock.

A lot like triathlon. A lot like life.

Life looked different now that I had conquered a triathlon. For one thing, I used to think those women were crazy. Now I know the truth. They *are* crazy, but in the best possible way. Crazy like when you kick off your shoes and dance like no one is watching, sing karaoke completely sober, or do something totally unexpected—get a tattoo, go skinny-dipping, rappel down a mountain, bungee jump, skydive, spontaneously book a trip to a remote island.

Crazy, like that time you did a triathlon.

That kind of crazy that puts your world into hi-def. And if you find your tribe of people who inspires you to live out loud like that? Never let them go.

Those girls in pink might have a little bit of crazy in them, but I would argue that we all do. Or, at least, we should.

Maybe I need a little more crazy in me.

Maybe you do too.

It always seems impossible until it's done.

—NELSON MANDELA

THOSE GIRLS IN PINK

*You have within you right now
everything you need to deal with whatever
the world can throw at you.*
—BRIAN TRACY

I t's the perfect day for a run. Sunny skies, a bite to the air—neither too cold nor too hot. What makes it most perfect, though, is that I am kidless. I throw on one of my many pink tri-club shirts, pull my laces tight, and start to run.

I've been running for five years now. There is something meditative about running for me. It doesn't start out that way, though. When I begin, I feel the sting of each inhale ripping through my windpipe, feel the slap of my feet against the asphalt and the mild burn of lactic acid rushing to my muscles. My lungs struggle, my heart races, my throat burns, and my muscles tingle. It's in those first steps when my mind tells me to stop. But then I get through that wall, easing into my stride. My shoulders relax, my breath is controlled, the little aches disappear, and I ease into a hypnotic groove.

When I run, I don't listen to music. Instead, I tune my ears to the gossip of the birds, the symphony of crickets in the woods, the bubbling of the streams, and the rustling of the leaves. I try to focus on these sounds to keep my head quiet and aware of the present. This works some days. Other days, my mind won't shut off. Today, May 4, is an anniversary of sorts. So today, I'm feeling reflective.

I crossed the finish line of my first triathlon in June 2014. Six months later, I was diagnosed with breast cancer. It was five weeks after my 46th birthday, two weeks before Christmas, and a year after having my very first (very belated) mammogram. Until that moment, I believed triathlon had been my greatest challenge. Little did I know I'd be up against an even bigger challenge and the stakes of not making it to *this* finish line were much higher. What I would soon realize was that triathlon had prepared me well for this journey. It had given me the mental toughness I needed.

I noticed a tiny lump close to my armpit in the weeks following the Queen of the Hill. I chalked it up to swollen lymph nodes secondary to swimming in the lake. Had I not been assigned to write a magazine feature story on breast cancer the year prior, I probably would have never noticed this little lump. But something changes inside of you when you interview 10 women and write their survivor stories. I began doing monthly self-exams for the first time in my life and finally scheduled my first mammogram.

Invasive ductal carcinoma, Stage I. I caught it early: It was tiny and non-aggressive, and my lymph nodes were clean. My prognosis was excellent. My tumor, well-behaved. Thankfully, I was the most vanilla case of breast cancer you could get.

I had a lumpectomy and lymph node dissection in January, followed by six consecutive weeks of daily radiation. And I have to take a pill for five years. Thankfully, I dodged the chemo bullet. As far as cancer goes, I got off easy. But even "easy cancer" sucks and takes over your life for a while. There were lots of unpleasantries, but I won't bore you with those details. People endure way worse, so I have no complaints.

But here is the significant thing. When I found out what my course of treatment was going to be and when it would all end, I said something shocking. I said, "I'm doing a triathlon to celebrate." Triathlon? Celebrate? Did I say that? Yes, I did. I not only said it, I said it with conviction. There was something symbolic about doing this race. I wanted to do it to feel strong again. I wanted to do it to feel alive again. I wanted a goal, something to fight for. Some tangible proof of my recovery. I wanted to do it for the women I met in the radiation waiting room during those six weeks who couldn't do the things that I could.

I needed to do it because *Screw you, Cancer.* That's why.

Back in September, before my diagnosis, my friend Janeen asked me if I'd consider doing the Queen of the Hill with her. It was going to be her first triathlon, so she was nervous and overwhelmed. I happily agreed, and we planned to train together and race together. It would be fun! Well, then I had to go and get stupid cancer and that wrecked everything. I couldn't do the group swim sessions with her, or much of anything until late spring. But we managed some running and biking together closer to the race, and even a brick workout and practice swim in the freezing lake. Mentoring her distracted me from my out-of-shape, jacked-up body. It was exactly what I needed.

I "graduated" from cancer treatment on May 4, 2015, and ended up doing not one but two sprint triathlons over two consecutive Saturdays in June. My first race was the Brian Ballard Memorial Triathlon at my swim club, the same race where Madelena did her first Splash and Dash. This year, it was a family affair. Three of my girls did the Splash and Dash, and I tackled the triathlon.

My race wasn't pretty. I could barely finish the measly nine pool laps and was so crushed by the unrelenting hills on that bike ride that I suffered major charley horse cramps in my calves during most of the run. It wasn't a run, really; it was a hobble. I came in third to last. Ask me if I cared. A swim, bike, and hobble were nothing compared to the five months of shenanigans I had just been through. All that mattered was that I was out there, I was strong, and I was not going to quit on this race or on myself. I needed to feel that. My girls needed to see that.

My second race that June was Queen of the Hill. Once again, I would have to face the dreaded open water. On race day, I found that I was less nervous and more excited than last year. However, I started to unravel once

I got in that lake. This year, the swim was tough for me, and I mean physically tough. Thanks to the surgery and six weeks of radiation, I had been out of the pool for too long. Because I was never a swimmer, I didn't have that muscle memory or that second-nature technique. I wasn't anywhere near as conditioned as I had been the year before. And because it was physically tough, I couldn't keep my head together. I had to flip on my back and grab onto buoys. At one spot, it was shallow enough to stand, and I took advantage of that, pretending I was treading water. I was concerned that I might actually drown at several points. For real. In a nutshell, I was a hot mess. But despite all this, I made it around the loop. I'd like to think it was my strength of will, but I am certain it was only by the grace of God.

When I got to the transition area, I was thrilled to see Janeen there, though a little surprised. "You're still here!" I laughed. She is a few years younger than me, so she had started in the wave right before mine. Plus, she was a strong swimmer. I had promised I'd try to catch her on the bike, but now here she was! Although, looking a bit discombobulated.

"Yeah, I might have checked my phone to see how my daughter's swim meet was going," she confessed. Texting from transition. I had to laugh. "Alright," I said. "Grab that bike, sister. We're *going!*"

"You don't have to stay with me," Janeen reassured me as we rode. Of course, I knew she was fine on her own. She would race and she would finish and she would have fun. But I really wanted to. Mostly, I enjoyed her company, but I also remembered what it was like to be new and unsure. I remembered how much it meant to me when I saw Theresa waiting at my first finish line to cheer me in, even though she had finished 100 hours ago. I knew how much Janeen struggled with the run, and that she felt underprepared. The run was her one weak spot, and although it was my relative strength, I never considered ditching her for a PR when she needed someone most. After all the kindness and unwavering friendship she had given me during the past five difficult months, supporting her through a little run was the least I could do.

After a pretty relaxing bike ride, we reached her arch-nemesis—the run. The run for her is like the swim for me. I wanted Janeen to have a run she could feel good about, to try to do it without stopping, no matter how slow we went. So, my strategy was to talk *nonstop* to keep her distracted. Fortunately, talking is my strong suit. If there were a talking triathlon, I'd be the world champion.

Janeen remained uncharacteristically quiet during that run, but she did the whole 3 miles without stopping to walk, and I did the whole 3 miles without stopping my talk. When we crossed that finish line, almost in perfect synchrony, we hugged, and she broke down in tears, thanking me profusely for sticking with her. Until that moment, I hadn't realized how much it meant to her to have me there.

My first Queen of the Hill was all about me. The second Queen of the Hill was about being there for someone else. That second year, I experienced firsthand what kept the founding mothers of the Mullica Hill Women's Tri Club motivated, enthusiastic, and passionate. I could begin to imagine how helping an entire group of women reach their goals, knowing that in some small way you encouraged them, inspired them, and supported them, was beyond rewarding. It's pretty special to know you played a small part in someone else's journey.

> *Our deepest fear is not that we are inadequate.*
> *Our deepest fear is that we are powerful beyond measure.*
> *It is our Light, not our Darkness, that most frightens us.*
> —MARIANNE WILLIAMSON

In the two years since I did my first triathlon, and the two years since I've been cancer-free, many things have changed and nothing has changed. The tri-club is still kicking ass and taking names. As an official nonprofit, they now have a board of directors. I sit on that board, a seat at a table I never thought I would occupy. I'm certainly the least decorated, least knowledgeable, and least "triathlony" person in the bunch. Their race calendars are packed. They mountain bike on the weekend, do CrossFit and yoga between all the swimming, biking, and running, and can be found competing in all the big local running races. Several of them have even done Ironmans and half-Ironmans! Meanwhile, I'm running 2–3 miles twice a week if I'm lucky, holed up writing like a recluse, and chauffeuring my peanut gallery to their various activities every day after school, while being a full-time caregiver to my eldest daughter, who recently turned 21 and graduated from her special school district. But when I start wondering how I'm even qualified to be on this board, I remind myself of one important thing. When we talk about triathlon, we're really talking about empowerment. Triathlon is the vehicle for change, and if you believe in that mission, if you support that goal, then it doesn't matter if you do one tri a year or 12.

> *There is no passion to be found in settling for a life*
> *that is less than the one you are capable of living.*
> —NELSON MANDELA

Remember that first local 5K race I did with my friend Theresa? I have done it every year since. My second year, Sophia ran it with me at the age of 8. A few years ago, Madelena and Ariella (ages 9 and 7, respectively) joined us, along with my husband, nieces, a sister-in-law, and my 65-year-old mother-in-law, who had never done a 5K in her life. She won first place in the "60 and Overs" category. Okay, she was the *only one* in that group, but still, she was so proud of herself, and we were all beaming with pride and happiness for her. I remember back to that cold day in 2011 when I raced it alone. It's much more fun as a family affair.

It might have been a coincidence, but when I started challenging myself with running and triathlon, my girls seemed to come out of their safe little comfort zones as well. My husband gives me full credit, which I may not deserve. I hope that watching me do intimidating, scary, challenging things, without caring what I looked like or how I performed, has had a positive influence. I do believe it has, in some small way. But, at the end of the day, these girls are the ones taking the risks, testing themselves, and pushing past their boundaries. What I love about confidence is how it causes a chain reaction.

At the age of 7, Ariella was confident enough to participate in an open-water swim of three-quarters of a mile across a lake. She was the youngest competitor in the group. Anthony and his father were in a canoe shadowing her. Apparently, shortly into the swim she freaked out. Anthony told her several times that she could climb in the boat, that she had tried her best and should have no regrets. She refused again and again, crying as she swam but refusing to give up.

"The determination on her face . . . I've never seen anything like it. I'll never forget it," he told me later. To have had that at 7 is pretty inspiring.

Sophia (the most conservative and cautious of them all) faced her fear of roller coasters when she finally got on her first one at the age of 11. She also tried out for the travel soccer team and started swimming noncompetitively, facing her fears of going off the starting blocks. Madelena, who suffers from stage fright, challenged herself by trying out for a speaking part in the school choir concert. She got it, and on the night of the event, she nailed her lines. Since then, she has given several speeches in front of large rooms. She's always nervous, but she does it anyway. I tell them that's what courage is. It's not the lack of fear that makes us brave. It's feeling scared but doing it anyway.

Anthony won't admit it, but he seems to have picked up running shortly after I did. According to him he's "always run," but I've known him for 18 years, and I don't recall him running with any consistency until recently. Whatever. I know the truth. I inspired him just a little. That's nothing in comparison to all he inspires in me.

Another person who became inspired? My sister-in-law recently started running, completely out of the blue. She had never run in her 45 years of life and suffers from a bad back. Now, she's addicted. Last fall, she was working toward running a mile. When I saw her at Thanksgiving, her running had progressed. "I'm up to 1.5 miles now," she said with a sparkle in her eye. "You don't understand, Alicia. I never thought I could run a mile. My goal is to be able to run a 5K and now I'm halfway there."

Here's the thing: I *did* understand. That was me, five years ago. Other people may forget that once you doubted yourself. Once you threw your fists in the air like Rocky and almost cried with pride when you made it three quarters of a mile at a turtle's pace around the block without stopping. Other people might forget that once you were a beginner, but *you* never forget.

"And once you get to 3 miles? You are going to realize you can run 5 miles, then more and more," I said. She looked at me as if I were nuts and laughed. "No, no, no. Five miles?! I don't think I could do that." I smiled and shook my head because I already knew the truth. I knew she could do it. *She* just didn't know it yet.

That's the thing with pushing ourselves beyond what we believe is our breaking point. The moment we choose strength in a time of challenge, we understand that strength is always a choice.

For me, strength has a color, and that color is pink. Pink is universally recognized as the color of breast cancer awareness. It's also the color of my tri-club. Interestingly, it is the latter with which I most identify. The pink magnet on the back of my minivan is not in the shape of the breast cancer ribbon. It's a simple oval with the words "Mullica Hill Women's Tri Club" stamped in the center. It reminds me that I'm part of something bigger than myself. It serves as my badge of courage, of survival. We're all survivors of something, and triathlon is the tangible proof of what we can endure. Triathlon shows us that we can shoot straight through the center of our fear and our pain and come out the other side all the better for it. And we might even gain some new friends along the way.

Last summer, I raced in the Queen of the Hill for a third time, this time as a duathlete. I wasn't willing to put the time in at the pool and decided the whole event would be less nerve-wracking and more fun if I cut out the whole open-water swim. I did it with a new friend, who was also new to multisport, so it was just about finishing and making sure she had a good race. It was all fun, no stress, and still a great feeling of reward, which is just the way I like it.

I may or may not have any more triathlons in me. Life is filled with unpredictability and change, so I can't pretend to know where this winding road will take me. There's only one thing I can tell you with absolute certainty. In my heart, I'll forever be one of those girls in pink.

Resources

CHAPTER 1: A SPANDEX REVOLUTION

2 *Julie Moss seems to hit a wall:* Zieralski, Ed. "Julie Moss' Agony in Defeat Was Appalling, but Love's Labor Made Her a Star." *People.* October 11, 1982.

3 *Though she came in second place that night:* Mallozzi, Vincent M. "Triathlon: Winner Who Didn't Finish First." *New York Times.* October 18, 2003. http://www.nytimes.com/2003/10/18/sports/triathlon-winner-who-didn-t-finish-first.html.

3 *a regular girl who became a hero:* Moss, Julie. "Triathlon." In *Chicken Soup from the Soul of Hawai'i: Stories of Aloha to Create Paradise Wherever You Are.* Edited by Jack Canfield, Mark Victor Hansen, Sharon Linnea, and Robin Stephens Rohr. Deerfield Beach, FL: Health Communications, 2003, 209–215. See also Mackinnon, Kevin. "Ironman Looks Back: Hall of Fame Member Julie Moss." *Ironman.* Last modified on February 25, 2013. http://www.ironman.com/triathlon-news/articles/2003/06/julie-moss-%E2%80%93-back-to-kona-to-celebrate-her-defining-moment.aspx#axzz4ADwea5rV.

5 *2.3 million Americans competed in a triathlon:* USA Triathlon. "SGMA Report: U.S. Triathlon Participation Reaches 2.3 Million in 2010." TeamUSA. August 17, 2011. https://www.teamusa.org/USA-Triathlon/News/Articles-and-Releases/2011/August/17/SGMA-Report-US-Triathlon-Participation-Reaches-23-Million-In-2010.

5 *well over 4 million:* "Number of Participants in Triathlons in the United States from 2006 to 2015." *Statista.* https://www.statista.com/statistics/191339/participants-in-triathlon-in-the-us-since-2006.

5 *representing more than half of the newcomers to the sport:* "Women-Only Triathlons." *Tri-Eva.* http://www.tri-eva.com/racing.

CHAPTER 3: A TRI IS BORN

15 *running, cycling, and canoeing*: "Triathlon." Wikipedia. Last modified May 6, 2016. https://en.wikipedia.org/wiki/Triathlon.

16 *Les Trois Sports*: Triathlon Historian. "History of Triathlon: 1900s Through 1920s France." Triathlon Facts. September 21, 2012.

16 *Jack Johnstone, is credited with brainstorming a multisport event*: Johnstone, Jack. "The Story of the First Triathlon." 2008. *Triathlon History*. http://www.triathlonhistory.com /Home.

17 *Technically speaking, the Mission Bay triathlon*: Trageser, Claire. "San Diegans Remember World's First Triathlon 40 Years Ago—at Mission Bay." *KPBS*. December 11, 2014. http:// www.kpbs.org/news/2014/dec/11/san-diegans-remember-first-triathlon-40-years-ago/.

19 *Some time after competing*: Baker, Erin. "Famous Triathletes: John Collins." *Triathlon Facts*. 2012. http://triathlonfacts.com/famous-triathletes-john-collins/.

19 *The most well-known version*: "The Ironman Story: An Interview with Judy and John Collins." *Always Happy Travels*. 2014. http://alwayshappytravels.com/the-ironman -story-an-interview-with-judy-and-john-collins/.

19 *In one article, Judy's version clarifies*: Docherty, Rob. "Birth of the Ironman." *XTRI*. 2011. http://www.xtri.com/features/detail/284-itemId.511707699.html.

24 *Ironman might have remained an unconventional, maverick race*: McDermott, Barry. "Ironman." *Sports Illustrated*. May 14, 1979.

PROFILE. ANDREA PEET

30 *12 races in 12 months*: Peet, Andrea. Team Drea.com. http://teamdrea.com/blog.

For Further Reading
Jeff, Heather. "Making Her Mark." *Runner's World*. March 25, 2015. http://www.runners world.com/run-matters/making-her-mark.

Cate, Heather. "The Race Not Chosen." *She Is Noble*. http://sheisnoble.com/nomination /andrea-lytle-peet/.

CHAPTER 4: THE LONG AND SHORT OF IT

33 *"the new marathon"*: Sloane, Matt. "Everyday Athletes Embracing Triathlon." *CNN*. November 10, 2010. http://www.cnn.com/2010/HEALTH/11/09/triathlon.popularity/.

33 *"the new golf"*: Kelly, Julie. "Triathlon Continues Upward Trend." *Bicycle Retailer and Industry News*. February 13, 2013. http://www.bicycleretailer.com/industry-news/2013 /02/13/triathlon-continues-upward-trend#.Vo3GPpMrLJw.

33 *"from maverick to mainstream"*: Ford, Bonnie D. "Outside the Lines: Trouble Beneath the Surface." *ESPN*. October 18, 2013. http://espn.go.com/espn/feature/story/_/id/9838319 /trouble-surface.

33 *on-road and off-road triathlons rank:* Sports and Fitness Industry Association. "2014 Sports, Fitness and Leisure Activities Topline Participation Report." wwwsfia.org.

33 *one of the five fastest-growing sports around the world:* "Top 5 Growing Sports." *The Glide Slope.* Last modified December 4, 2016. http://www.theglideslope.com/runway /top-5-growing-sports/.

33 *One way to view the growth of triathlon:* United States Olympic Committee. "USA Triathlon Annual Membership Report—2014 Update." *TeamUSA.* August 2016. https:// www.teamusa.org/usa-triathlon/about/multisport/demographics.

34 *In 2010, triathlon participation was reported at 2.3 million:* USA Triathlon. "SGMA Report: U.S. Triathlon Participation Reaches 2.3 Million in 2010." *TeamUSA.* August 17, 2011. https://www.teamusa.org/USA-Triathlon/News/Articles-and-Releases/2011/August/17 /SGMA-Report-US-Triathlon-Participation-Reaches-23-Million-In-2010.

34 *By 2015, it reached 4.24 million:* "Number of Participants in Triathlons in the United States from 2006 to 2015." *Statista.* https://www.statista.com/statistics/191339/participants -in-triathlon-in-the-us-since-2006.

34 *triathlon's journey toward being a full-fledged, NCAA Championship sport:* "NCAA Triathlon." *USA Triathlon.* https://www.temusa.org/USA-Triathlon/About/Multisport /NCAA-Triathlon.

35 *78 percent of USAT members participate in sprints:* "USA Triathlon Annual Membership Report—2015 Update." TeamUSA. 2015. https://www.teamusa.org/usa-triathlon /about/multisport/demographics.

35 *A lesser known distance dubbed the Tinman:* "History." Tinman Hawaii. http://www.tin manhawaii.com/index.php/history.

36 *The Olympic might be considered "the most perfect":* Lindsay, Marc. "10 Olympic Distance Triathlons in 2015." *Active.* 2015. http://www.active.com/triathlon/articles/10-olympic -distance-triathlons-in-2015.

38 *The XTERRA race series:* "About." *Xterra.* http://www.xterraplanet.com/about/.

For Further Reading
Thom, Kara Douglass. "The Evolution of Triathlon." *ExperienceL!fe.* August 2005. https:// experiencelife.com/article/the-evolution-of-triathlon/.

CHAPTER 5: WHO'S DRINKING THE KOOL-AID?

41 *a defining moment in sports history:* Mackinnon, Kevin. "Ironman Looks Back: Hall of Fame Member Julie Moss." *Ironman.* February 25, 2013. http://www.ironman.com /triathlon-news/articles/2003/06/julie-moss-%E2%80%93-back-to-kona-to-celebrate -her-defining-moment.aspx#axzz4ADwea5rV.

45 *the mind of the endurance athlete:* Van Dusen, Allison. "Inside the Endurance Athlete's Mind." *Forbes.* September, 22, 2008. http://www.forbes.com/2008/09/22/endurance -race-training-forbeslife-cx_avd_0922sports.html.onality.

45   *more effective modulation of pain:* Geva, Nirit, and Ruth Defrin. "Enhanced Pain Modu-
     lation Among Triathletes: A Possible Explanation for Their Exceptional Capabilities."
     PAIN 154, no. 11 (2013): 2317–2323.

45   *endurance athletes viewed the intensity of their pain as a function of their own percep-
     tion:* Kress, Jeffery, and Traci Statler. "A Naturalistic Investigation of Former Olympic
     Cyclists' Cognitive Strategies for Coping with Exertional Pain During Performance."
     Journal of Personality and Social Psychology 87 (2007): 266–281.

46   *suffering as the primary reward:* Atkinson, Michael. "Triathlon: Suffering and Exciting
     Significance." *Leisure Studies* 27, no. 2 (2008): 165–180.

47   *significant gender differences:* Lovett, David M. "An Examination of the Motives to Par-
     ticipate in Sprint Distance Triathlon." PhD diss., University of New Mexico at Albu-
     querque, 2011.

47   *Motivation fell within three predominant themes among the women surveyed:* Waddel,
     Alexis. "A Qualitative Analysis of Motivation of Elite Female Athletes." Master's the-
     sis, San Jose State University, 2010. http://scholarworks.sjsu.edu/cgi/viewcontent.cgi
     ?article=4826&context=etd_theses.

CHAPTER 6: NO NUTS, JUST GUTS

59   *women had been banned:* Sebor, Jessica. "The History of Women's Running." Active
     .com. http://www.active.com/running/articles/the-history-of-women-s-running.

60   *on penalty of death:* Penn Museum. "The Women: Were the Ancient Olympics Just for
     Men?" *The Real Story of the Ancient Olympic Games.* http://www.penn.museum/sites
     /olympics/olympicsexism.shtml.

60   *the passage of Title IX:* "A Title IX Primer." *Women's Sports Foundation.* August 1998. http://
     www.womenssportsfoundation.org/home/advocate/title-ix-and-issues/what-is
     -title-ix/title-ix-primer; US Department of Justice. "Overview of Title IX of the Education
     Amendments of 1972, 20 U.S.C.A SS 1681 Et. Seq." Last modified August 7, 2015. https://
     www.justice.gov/crt/overview-title-ix-education-amendments-1972-20-usc-1681
     -et-seq.

60   *Today, it's about 1 in 2.5:* Feminist Majority Foundation. "Gender Equity in Athletics
     and Sports." 2014. *Feminist Majority Foundation.* http://www.feminist.org/sports/titleIX
     factsheet.asp.

61   *compared to 37 percent in 2015:* "USA Triathlon Annual Membership Report—2014
     Update." *TeamUSA.* Last modified August 2015. https://www.teamusa.org/usa-triathlon
     /about/multisport/demographics.

61   *Female representation in North American Ironman events:* Mackinnon, Kevin. "Ironman
     CEO Update: Here We Grow Again." *Triathlon Magazine Canada.* February 2, 2016. http://
     triathlonmagazine.ca/news/ironman-ceo-update-here-we-grow-again/.

61   *111 million Americans tuned in:* "USA Triathlon Annual Membership Report—2014
     Update." *TeamUSA.* Last modified August 2015. https://www.teamusa.org/usa-triath
     lon/about/multisport/demographics.

61 *Aiton created Tri-For-Fun in 1988:* Murphy, T. J. "How Triathlon Got Hot." *ExperienceL!fe.* 2004. https://experiencelife.com/article/how-triathlon-got-hot/.

62 *women-only triathlons:* Bruning, Karla. "The Top 10 Women's Races." *Shape.* 2016. http://www.shape.com/fitness/cardio/top-10-womens-races.

62 *Fastinistas:* Bowen Shea, Sarah. "Fastinista!" *Runner's World.* July 13, 2011. http://www.runnersworld.com/running-apparel/stylish-female-runners-are-fastinistas.

62 *"Athleisure" has surpassed denim sales:* Sutherland, Amber, and Rosenbaum, Sophia. "Athleisure Trend Sends Denim Sales Plummeting." *New York Post.* August 12, 2014. http://nypost.com/2014/08/12/athleisure-trend-sends-denim-sales-plummeting/.

63 *Athletic apparel for women:* Crann Good, Alice. "Fit for Life: Activewear Goes Chic for Day and Night." *Pensacola News Journal.* May 19, 2015. http://www.pnj.com/story/life/2015/05/18/fit-for-life-activewear-goes-chic-for-day-and-night/27549663/.

63 *Consider the sports bra:* Cattel, Jeff. "The Origin of the Sports Bra Is Too Good." *Greatist.* October 28, 2014. http://greatist.com/discover/sports-bra-history.

63 *"shrink it and pink it":* Logan, Linzay. "Putting a Stop to 'Shrink It and Pink It.'" *Competitor.* Jan 8, 2013. http://running.competitor.com/2013/01/shoes-and-gear/putting-a-stop-to-shrink-it-and-pink-it_64316.

64 *Women spend more time volunteering:* Kurtzleben, Danielle. "CHARTS: New Data Show Women, More Educated Doing Most Volunteering." *U.S. News & World Report.* February 27, 2013. http://www.usnews.com/news/articles/2013/02/27/charts-new-data-show-women-more-educated-doing-most-volunteering.

64 *TNT has raised more than $1.4 billion:* The Leukemia and Lymphoma Society. "About Team in Training." *Team in Training.* http://www.teamintraining.org/firsttimehere/.

For Further Reading
Kelly, Julie. "Triathlon Continues Upward Trend." Bicycle Retailer and Industry News. February 13, 2013. http://www.bicycleretailer.com/industry-news/2013/02/13/triathlon-continues-upward-trend#.Vo7lMpMrLJw.ooo.

Marino, Vivian. "Fitness: Call Her Nuts, or Call Her Ironman." *New York Times.* June 6, 2004.

Olivola, Christopher, and Eldar Shafir. "The Martyrdom Effect: When the Prospect of Pain and Effort Increases Charitable Giving." *Advances in Consumer Research*, vol. 36, edited by Ann L. McGill and Sharon Shavitt. Duluth, MN: Association for Consumer Research, 2013, 190–194.

Rueckert, Linda, and Nicolette Naybar. "Gender Differences in Empathy: The Role of the Right Hemisphere." *Brain and Cognition* 67 (2008): 162–167.

PROFILE. NANCY STEVENS

70 *Team Nancy made history:* Milholm, Joelle. "Stevens Competes in Triathlon World Championships." *Post Independent.* September 25, 2006. http://www.postindependent.com/article/20060926/SPORTS/109260021.

70 *Tri-It Camp:* Milholm, Joelle. "Blind Triathletes Come to Town to Give Multisport a Try." *Post Independent.* April 22, 2007. http://www.postindependent.com/article/20070423 /VALLEYNEWS/104230019; Mica, Roman. "Blind Triathletes Take the Lead at Inspiring Others." *Active.* Accessed on January 25, 2016. http://www.active.com/triathlon /articles/blind-triathletes-take-the-lead-at-inspiring-others.

CHAPTER 7: SIGMA TRI

78 *Today, there are more than 1,000 triathlon clubs:* "USA Triathlon Annual Membership Report—2014 Update." *TeamUSA.* Last modified August 2015. https://www.teamusa .org/usa-triathlon/about/multisport/demographics.

80 *Maslow is best known . . . Hierarchy of Needs:* Burton, Neel. "Our Hierarchy of Needs." *Psychology Today.* May 23, 2012. https://www.psychologytoday.com/blog/hide-and-seek /201205/our-hierarchy-needs.

81 *40 percent of endurance sport competitors:* "Endurance Sports Participant Study." Eventbrite. https://eventbrite-s3.s3.amazonaws.com/marketing/britepapers/Endurance_ Report_Survey.pdf.

82 *women make just about* anything *into a social opportunity:* Waddel, Alexis. "A Qualitative Analysis of Motivation of Elite Female Athletes." Master's thesis, San Jose State University, 2010, http://scholarworks.sjsu.edu/cgi/viewcontent.cgi?article=4826 &context=etd_theses.

CHAPTER 9: RUN WITH IT

99 *Americans love to run:* Running USA. "2015 State of the Sport Report—U.S. Race Trends." *Running USA.* July 13, 2015. http://www.runningusa.org/2015-state-of-sport-us-trends; see also "2015 National Runner Survey" (requires payment). http://www.running usa.org/2015-national-runner-survey.

100 *Today's core runner:* "State of the Sport—Part I: Core Runner Profiles." *Running USA.* April 21, 2013. http://www.runningusa.org/index.cfm?fuseaction=news.details &ArticleId=1539.

101 *36,000 times* less often *per day:* Fasano, Giacomo. *Revolutionary Powercycles: The Science of Sweat.* Amazon Digital Services, 2015, p. 84.

101 *jogging a total of just 3–6 miles per week:* Lee, Duck-chul et al. "Leisure-Time Running Reduces All-Cause and Cardiovascular Mortality Risk." *Journal of the American College of Cardiology* 64, no. 5 (2014): 472–481.

103 *The Broad Street 10-miler in Philadelphia:* Independence Blue Cross and Philadelphia Parks and Recreation. "Broad Street Facts." 2012–2016. http://www.broadstreetrun .com.

104 Runner's World *named it one of the fastest 10-mile courses:* "Course Information." 2017 Blue Cross Broad Street Run. http://www.broadstreetrun.com/eventinformation/course info.cfm.

104 *the first Broad Street 10-Mile Run in 1980:* "Broad Street Run." *Wikipedia.* Last modified May 2, 2016. https://en.wikipedia.org/wiki/Broad_Street_Run.

107 *running is called a gateway sport:* Topper, Hilary. "Running, the Gateway Sport to Triathlons for Women Triathletes." *A Triathlete's Diary Blog.* October 26, 2016. http://www.atri athletesdiary.com/running-the-gateway-sport-to-triathlons-for-women-triathletes/.

PROFILE. LISA HALLETT

111 *Lisa and fellow military wife . . . cofounded:* "About." *Wear Blue: Run to Remember.* http:// www.wearblueruntoremember.org/history/.

112 *Lisa Hallett's story and her organization:* Ward Barber, Jennifer. "NBC Show Preview: Lisa Hallett's IRONMAN to Remember." *Ironman.* November 6, 2014. http:// www.ironman.com/triathlon/news/articles/2014/11/lisa-hallett-nbc-preview.aspx #axzz4AcLRkVwV; Williams, Doug. "Running as a Way to Cope with Loss." ESPN. November 12, 2014. Accessed March 10, 2016. http://espn.go.com/sports/endurance /story/_/page/veterans20141110endurance/endurance-sports-running-healing -power-army-widow-lisa-hallett-others.

CHAPTER 10: TRI GIRLS AREN'T CHEAP DATES

118 *a sport most people can't afford:* Dreibus, Tony C. "Triathletes Stung by Killer Fees." *Austin Fit Magazine.* Last modified October 1, 2015. http://www.austinfitmagazine.com /October-2015/Triathletes-Stung-By-Killer-Fees/.

118 *ranges from $126,000:* USA Triathlon, mentioned in Hanc, John. "When Amateur Ironmen Pay for the Elite Treatment." *New York Times.* February 12, 2016. https://www .nytimes.com/2016/02/14/your-money/when-amateur-ironmen-pay-for-the-elite treatment.html.

118 *to $174,000:* Lewis, Kate. "Is Rapid Growth Endangering the Ironman and Endurance Sports?" *The Glide Slope.* October 14, 2014. http://www.theglideslope.com/runway/is -rapid-growth-endangering-the-ironman-and-endurance-sports/.

118 *jumps to around $247,000:* World Triathlon Corporation's 2015 survey, mentioned in Hanc, John. "When Amateur Ironmen Pay for the Elite Treatment." *New York Times.* February 12, 2016. https://www.nytimes.com/2016/02/14/your-money/when-amateur -ironmen-pay-for-the-elite-treatment.html.

118 *triathletes are typically "highly professional and advanced socioeconomically":* USA Triathlon and Tribe Group. "The Mind of the Triathlete™: Market Research Report." 2009. PDF.

118 *start-up and ongoing costs:* "Triathlon Gear List." *Fitness Fatale.* July 10, 2011. http://fit nessfatale.com/2011/07/10/triathlon-gear-list/; "The Cost to Be Called an Ironman." *Fitness Fatale.* September 24, 2011. http://fitnessfatale.com/tag/how-much-does-an -ironman-cost/; "The Cost of Zero to Ironman." *Fitness Fatale.* July 18, 2012. http://fit nessfatale.com/2012/07/18/the-cost-of-zero-to-ironman/.

122 *The Escape from Alcatraz triathlon:* Osborn, Katy. 2015. "Triathletes Aren't Happy It'll Now Cost $750 to 'Escape' from Alcatraz." *Time.* October 27, 2015. http://time.com /money/4088862/triathlon-alcatraz-price-increase/.

124 *average registration fee for running races:* Warrenfeltz, Jim. "How Much Does Running Cost over a Lifetime?" *Runner's World.* July 22, 2013. http://www.runnersworld.com /run-the-numbers/how-much-does-running-cost-over-a-lifetime.

124 *$5,000 per year on triathlon-related travel:* Active Marketing Group. "The Triathlon Market." *Active Network Rewards.* http://www.activenetworkrewards.com/AssetFactory .aspx?did=352.

125 *professionals with discretionary income:* Karol, Gabrielle. "The True Costs of Training for Triathlons." *Fox Business.* July 16, 2013. http://www.foxbusiness.com/features /2013/07/16/true-costs-training-for-triathlons.html.

For Further Reading
Hutheesing, N., and Bloomberg Rankings. "The Real Cost of Completing a Triathlon." *Bloomberg.* November 10, 2012. http://www.bloomberg.com/consumer-spending /2012-11-05/the-real-cost-of-completing-a-triathlon.html.

PROFILE. ERIN BRIGGS

128 *anti-NMDA receptor encephalitis:* The Anti-NMDA Receptor Encephalitis Foundation. www.antinmdafoundation.org; Autoimmune Encephalitis Alliance. http://www.aealli ance.org.

CHAPTER 11: SWIM, BIKE, RUN . . . DIVORCE?

131 *Psychologist and triathlete Dr. Pete Simon coined the phrase:* Simon, Peter. "Divorce by Triathlon." *Balanced Training Solutions Blog.* July 2010. http://balancedtrainingsolutions .blogspot.com/2010/07/divorce-by-triathlon.html.

131 *the stress and strain triathlon can cause:* Helliker, Keven. "A Workout Ate My Marriage." *Wall Street Journal.* Last modified February 1, 2011. http://www.wsj.com/articles/SB100 01424052748703439504576116083514534672.

131 *"compromised social lives":* Mallett, Clifford J., and Stephanie Hanrahan. "Elite Athletes: Why Does the 'Fire' Burn So Brightly?" *Psychology of Sport and Exercise* 5 (2004): 183–200.

132 *25 percent of members are single, widowed, or divorced:* "USA Triathlon Annual Membership Report—2014 Update." *TeamUSA.* Last modified August 2015. https://www.team usa.org/usa-triathlon/about/multisport/demographics.

133 *couples reporting the most strain were those in which only one person:* Lamont, Matthew J., Millicent Kennelly, and Erica Wilson. "Selfish Leisure? Competing Priorities and Constraints in Triathlon Event Travel Careers." Tourism—Creating a Brilliant Blend: Proceedings of the Council for Australian University Tourism and Hospitality Education Conference, Adelaide, SA School of Management, University of South Australia, Adelaide, SA. February 8–11, 2011.

134 *the comfortable dynamic in her marriage shifted off its axis*: Atwood, Meredith. "Beginner's Luck: Room For Two?" *Triathlon*. July 22, 2015. http://triathlon.competitor.com /2015/07/features/beginners-luck-room-for-two_119547.

142 *Mothers who were less physically active*: Hesketh, Kathryn R., et al. "Activity Levels in Mothers and Their Preschool Children." *Pediatrics* 133, no. 4 (April 2014): e973–e980.

142 *women exercise less once they become mothers*: Firger, Jessica. "When Moms Exercise, So Do Kids." *CBS News*. March 24, 2014.

143 *"exercise can be both a selfish and an unselfish act"*: Stevens, Eric C. "Prioritizing Your Fitness Isn't Selfish, It's Necessary." *Breaking Muscle*. http://breakingmuscle.com /sports-psychology/prioritizing-your-fitness-isnt-selfish-its-necessary.

144 *"If training for long-distance triathlons"*: D'Avanza, Jessica. "How to Keep (or Salvage) Relationships While Training for Triathlons." *rUnladylike*. February 12, 2014. http:// www.runladylike.com/2014/02/12/balancing-triathlon-training-and-relationships/.

For Further Reading
Etxebarria, Itziar, Maria Ortiz, and Aitziber Pascual. "Intensity of Habitual Guilt in Men and Women: Differences in Interpersonal Sensitivity and the Tendency Toward Anxious-Aggressive Guilt." *Spanish Journal of Psychology* 12, no. 2 (2009): 540–554.

Lacke, Susan. "Triathlete Love: You Tri, Your Spouse Doesn't." *Triathlete*, March 30, 2015. http://triathlon.competitor.com/2015/03/features/triathlete-love-you-tri-your -spouse-doesnt_114336.

CHAPTER 12: TRIATHAPHOBIA

152 *"80 percent of triathlete performance has to do with psychological factors"*: Waddel, Alexis. "A Qualitative Analysis of Motivation of Elite Female Athletes." Master's thesis, San Jose State University, 2010. http://scholarworks.sjsu.edu/cgi/viewcontent.cgi ?article=4826&context=ctd_theses.

153 *Dr. Larry Creswell . . . triathlon-related fatalities*: Creswell, Larry. "Japan and Triathlon Fatalities." *The Athlete's Heart*. February 25, 2016. http://www.athletesheart.org/page/2/.

153 *the mortality rate in triathlon*: "Your Chances of Dying." *Best Health Degrees*. http://www .besthealthdegrees.com/health-risks/.

155 *54 percent of women are afraid of getting hit*: Braker, Sarah. "New Research on Women's Bicycling Participation Reveals Insights—and Some Surprises." *People for Bikes*. May 28, 2015. http://www.peopleforbikes.org/blog/entry/new-research-on-womens -bicycling-participation-reveals-insightsand-some-sur.

158 *"Finishing last . . . doesn't define you"*: Moritz, Amy. "Dead Last: The Power of Showing Up." *The Accidental Athlete*. September 26, 2012. http://www.amymoritz. com/2012/09/26/dead-last-the-power-of-showing-up/.

158 *"We mistakenly assign real risk to our internal fears"*: Brooks, Lauren. "Don't Let Fear of Failure Get in the Way of Your Dreams." *Breaking Muscle*. http://breakingmuscle.com /sports-psychology/dont-let-fear-of-failure-get-in-the-way-of-your-dreams.

PROFILE. CHRISSY VASQUEZ

163 *BoMF has assisted more than 6,000 people*: Gonzalez, Gabby. "'Back on My Feet' Cele-
brates Four Years of Helping Homeless Men and Women." *Fox 59 News*. March 11, 2015.
http://fox59.com/2015/03/11/back-on-my-feet-celebrates-four-years-of-helping-home
less-men-and-women/.

165 *"Some would say you've failed twice"*: Vasquez, Chrissy. *Sausage in a Wetsuit*. http://www
.sausageinawetsuit.blogspot.com.

For Further Reading
Hein, Lindsey. "Athlete Highlight: Chrissy Vasquez." *Out for a Run*. October 25, 2013.
http://lindseyhein.com/20131025-41/athlete-highlight-chrissy-vasquez/.

PROFILE. BARBARA MOCKFORD

183 *"all the positive things . . . about having one arm"*: Mockford, Barbara. *An Unshakable
Belief: Keeping the Ironman Dream*. Kenosha: Expanded Technologies, 2012.

For Further Reading
Tri Survivor. www.trisurvivor.nz.

CHAPTER 14: WOMEN ON WHEELS

190 *Susan B. Anthony*: Angus, Hilary. 2015. "Three Women Who Changed the Course of
History on Bicycles." *Momentum Magazine*. March 5, 2015. https://momentummag
.com/three-women-changed-course-history-bicycle/.

190 *condemned as indecent and immoral*: Hoefer, Carsten. "Social Change: Suffragettes
and Workers on Bikes. *Crazy Guy on a Bike*. Last updated April 18, 2009. http://www
.crazyguyonabike.com/doc/page/?page_id=46873.

190 *rocked the carefully constructed Victorian societal structure*: Zheutlin, Peter. "Annie Lon-
donderry: Women on Wheels: The Bicycle and the Women's Movement of the 1890s."
2006. http://www.annielondonderry.com/womenWheels.html.

For Further Reading
Angier, Natalie. "The Bicycle and the Ride to Modern America." *New York Times* science blog. July 13, 2015.

O'Malley, Soren. "The Importance of the Bicycle to the Early Women's Liberation
Movement." *CrankedMag*. 2006. https://crankedmag.wordpress.com/issues/issue-4
/the-importance-of-the-bicycle-to-the-early-womens-liberation-movement/.

PROFILE. TERRY WOODS

195 *The list of injuries was extensive*: Woods, Terry. "Shattered, Crushed and Untethered."
TeamUSA. May 11, 2016. https://www.teamusa.org/USA-Triathlon/News/Blogs/My
-Story/2016/May/11/Shattered-Crushed-and-Untethered.

CHAPTER 15: TRAIN WRECK

204 *rate for injuries in triathlon are higher than in any other sport*: Burns, Joshua, et al. "Factors Associated with Triathlon-Related Overuse Injuries." *Journal of Orthopedic and Sports Physical Therapy* 33 (2003): 177–184.

204 *90 percent injury rate among triathletes*: O'Toole, Mary L., et al. "Overuse Injuries in Ultraendurance Triathletes." *American Journal of Sports Medicine* 17 (1989): 514–518.

204 *"The idea that people can reduce their chance of injury by competing in triathlons may be a fallacy"*: Hammill, Sean. "Triathletes, On Your Mark . . . Whoa!" *New York Times*. November 24, 2009. http://www.nytimes.com/2009/11/26/fashion/26fitness.html.

204 *Running is responsible for the large majority of triathlete injuries*: Zwingenberger, S., et al. "An Epidemioloigical Investigation of Training and Injury Patterns in Triathletes." *Journal of Sports Science* 32, no. 6 (2014): 583–590.

204 *one injury for every 100 hours of running*: Sports Medicine and Athletic Related Trauma (SMART) Institute. "Sports Specific Safety: Cross Country Running." http://health.usf.edu/nocms/medicine/orthopaedic/smart/pdfs/sports_specific/cross%20country.pdf.

204 *injury risk increases when training volume*: Vleck, Veronica E., and G. Garbutt. "Injury and Training Characteristics of Male Elite, Development Squad, and Club Triathletes." *International Journal of Sports Medicine* 9 (1998): 8–42.

204 *higher weekly mileage . . . increases a runner's chances of injury*: Cosca, David D., and Franco Navazio. "Common Problems in Endurance Athletes." *American Family Physicians* 76, no. 2 (2007): 237–244.

205 *Women have a higher rate of sports-related injuries*: Lauretta, Ashley. "Do Women Face Injury More Than Male Athletes?" *Women's Running*. Last modified July 13, 2016. http://womensrunning.competitor.com/2016/06/health-wellness/injury-prevention/women-athletes-injured-more_60166#DcKpBRv2ke3HZpBRv2ke3HZpKV.97

205 *higher rates of ACL tears*: Horowitz, Steven. "ACL Injuries: Female Athletes at Increased Risk." *MomsTeam*. Last modified August 7, 2014. http://www.momsteam.com/health-safety/muscles-joints-bones/knee/acl-injuries-in-female-athletes.

205 *The most common injuries are "aeroneck syndrome"*: Silder, Amy, Kyle Gleason, and Darryl G. Thelen. "Influence of Bicycle Seat Tube Angle and Hand Position on Lower Extremity Kinematics and Neuromuscular Control: Implications for Triathlon Running Performance." *Journal of Applied Biomechanics* 27 (2011): 297–305.

207 *"80 percent of injuries are due to overuse"*: Dalek, Brian. "The 5 Most Common Triathlon Training Injuries." *Men's Health*. April 27, 2015. http://www.menshealth.com/fitness/triathlon-injury-prevention.

207 *up to 85 percent of triathletes are overtrained*: Migliorini, Sergio. "Risk Factors and Injury Mechanism in Triathlon." *Journal of Human Sports Exercise* 6, no. 2 (2011).

207   *Why overtraining backfires:* Fitzgerald, Matt. "How to Avoid Overtraining." *Triath-lete.* January 10, 2011. http://triathlon.competitor.com/2011/01/training/how-to-avoid -overtraining_18585.

208   *96 percent of first-time triathletes . . . One-third of first timers:* "Active Network and Triathlon America Reveal Key Findings on the Triathlon Community." *Active Network.* February 20, 2012. http://www.activenetwork.com/news-and-events/active-press-releases /2012/active-network-and-triathlon-america-reveal-key-findings-on-the-triathlon -community.

209   *For the large majority of triathletes:* Youngman, J., and D. Simpson. "Risk for Exercise Addiction: A Comparison of Triathletes Training for Sprint-, Olympic-, Half-Ironman-, and Ironman-Distance Triathlons." *Journal of Clinical Sport Psychology* 8, no. 1 (2014): 19–37.

210   *"female athlete triad":* Nazem, Taraneh G., and Ackerman, Katheryn E. "The Female Athlete Triad." *Sports Health* 4, no.4 (2012): 302–311.

211   *overuse injuries:* Andersen, C. A., et al. "High Prevalence of Overuse Injury Among Iron-Distance Triathletes." *British Journal of Sports Medicine,* 47, no. 13 (2013): 857–861.

PROFILE. JENN SOMMERMANN

216   *The symptoms . . . are subtle and vague:* Birch, Jenna. "The Subtle Signs of Ovarian Cancer Every Woman Should Know—Explained by Survivors." *Yahoo! Health.* September 11, 2015.

217   *Jenn Sommermann announced her 50 by 50 by 100 campaign:* Ovarian Cancer Research Fund. "Jenn Sommermann: Triathlete for a Cure." http://www.ocrf.org/news/jenn sommermann-triathlete-for-a-cure. See also *Jenn Sommermann: Triathlete for a Cure.* www.jennsommermann.blogspot.com.

CHAPTER 16: CHARITY, CAUSES, AND CURES, OH TRI!

219   *Norma Bastidas began her quest to complete:* Williams, Doug. "Record Triathlon Brings Awareness." *ESPN.* May 28, 2014. http://espn.go.com/sports/endurance/story/_/id/1099 4589/endurance-sports-norma-bastidas-mega-triathlon-set-record-worthy-cause; Wilson, Jacque. "Woman Tackles World's Longest Triathlon." *CNN.* April 18, 2014. Accessed March 20, 2016. http://www.cnn.com/2014/04/18/health/worlds-longest-tri athlon-bastidas/; Grossman, Sarah. "Trafficking Survivor Completed World's Longest Triathlon to Help Other Victims." *Huffington Post.* June, 1, 2016. http://www.huffing tonpost.com/entry/norma-bastidas-human-trafficking-triathlon-recordus_574df5a2e4 b02912b24116be.

222   *survey commissioned by Eventbrite:* "Charity Beats Vanity in Motivating Adults to Participate in Endurance Events and Races." *Eventbrite.* July 24, 2012.

222   *So why triathlon?:* Internicola, Dorene. "Another Reason Charity Is Good for Your Heath." *Huffington Post.* Last modified February 1, 2014. http://www.huffingtonpost .com/2013/12/02/charity-races_n_4370489.html.

222 *"The Martyrdom Effect"*: Olivola, Christopher, and Eldar Shafir. "The Martyrdom Effect: When the Prospect of Pain and Effort Increases Charitable Giving." *Advances in Consumer Research* 36, edited by Ann L. McGill and Sharon Shavitt. Duluth, MN: Association for Consumer Research, 2013, 190–194.

223 *Ironman foundation:* Ironman Foundation. http://www.ironmanfoundation.org/.

PROFILE. WINTER VINECKI

For Further Reading:
Reeder, Alyssa. "Teen Triathlete Winter Vinecki Teamed Up with Athleta to Raise Cancer Awareness." *Teen Vogue.* March 8, 2013. http://www.teenvogue.com/story/winter-vinecki-cancer-awareness-athleta.

Roemeling, Alisha. "Salem Teen Marathon Runner and Aerial Skier Winter Vinecki." *Statesman Journal.* 2014 http://www.statesmanjournal.com/story/news/2014/10/08 salem-teen-marathon-runner-and-aerial-skier-winter-vinecki/16924203/.

Vinecki, Winter. "Team Winter." *Newton Running Blog.* https://www.newtonrunning.com/blog/tag/team-winter/.

CHAPTER 17: TRI: THE NEXT GENERATION

239 *USAT has been encouraging young triathletes:* "USA Triathlon Annual Membership Report 2015 Update." *USA Triathlon.* https://www.teamusa.org/usa-triathlon/about/multisport/demographics.

239 *750 USAT-sanctioned events held for youth:* "2015 Membership Report 2015 Update." *USA Triathlon.* https://www.teamusa.org/usa-triathlon/about/multisport/demographics.

240 *60 minutes of moderate to vigorous aerobic activity every day:* American Heart Association. "The AHA's Recommendations for Physical Activity in Children." *American Heart Association.* Last modified March 22, 2013. http://www.heart.org/HEARTORG/HealthyLiving/HealthyKids/ActivitiesforKids/The-AHAs-Recommendations-for-Physical-Activity-in-Children_UCM_304053_Article.jsp#.WHMjOxsrJDM.

240 *one-third of all American girls do not meet this minimum:* American Heart Association. "Cardiovascular Health Promotion in Children: Challenges and Opportunities for 2020 and Beyond: A Scientific Statement from the American Heart Association." *Circulation,* 134 (2016): e236–e255.

240 *According to a study of 8- and 9-year-olds published in* Pediatrics: Hillman, Charles H., et al. "Effects of the FITKids Randomized Controlled Trial on Executive Control and Brain Function." *Pediatrics* 134, no. 4 (2014): 1063–1071.

241 *A hot topic in youth sports:* Jayanthi, Neeru, et al. "Sports Specialization in Youth Athletes." *Sports Health* 5, no. 3 (2013): 251–257.

242 *Tiger Woods is more of a statistical outlier than the norm:* Epstein, David. "Sports Should Be Child's Play." *New York Times,* June 10, 2014. https://www.nytimes.com/2014/06/11/opinion/sports-should-be-childs-play.html?ref=opinion&_r=1.

242 *Most research does* not *support early specialization:* Wojtys, Edward M. "Sports Specialization vs. Diversification." *Sports Health* 5, no. 3 (2013): 212–213.

242 *suffer emotional burnout:* McMahan, Ian. "Introducing Your Kids to Triathlon." *Triathlete.* January 9, 2015. http://triathlon.competitor.com/2015/01/features/introducing-kids-triathlon_111208.

242 *three sports rolled into one:* Shaw, Jene. "Parents: How to Raise Future Triathletes." *Triathlete.* March 4, 2016. http://triathlon.competitor.com/2016/03/training/raise-future-triathletes-kids_128819.

PROFILE. JESSICA CAPPELLA

For Further Reading
Coté, Julia. "Believe in a Way Back: Completing a Triathlon After a Spinal Cord Injury." *Philly.com.* August 4, 2014. http://www.philly.com/philly/blogs/sportsdoc/Believe-in-a-way-back-Could-would-should-DID.html.

CHAPTER 18: QUEEN OF THE HILL

264 *what Elysa Walk of Giant Bicycles said:* Walk, Elysa. "The Joy of Two Wheels." TEDx Vail Women. Uploaded January 6, 2014. https://www.youtube.com/watch?v=GK_rmt-OEdY.

Acknowledgments

I could not have written this book without the invaluable support that came from the Mullica Hill Women's Triathlon Club. I am indebted to Maureen Brigham, Lydia DelRosso, Colleen Fossett, and Michelle Powell. You four, and the club you built with such love, served not only as the inspiration for this book but as an inspiration in my life. Safe to say, inspiration in many lives. I am grateful beyond words for what you have done for the women in this town, and beyond.

A huge thank-you to everyone at VeloPress, especially to Casey Blaine, who took a chance on a new author. I have had the best job in the world interviewing triathletes and writing this book. The triathlon community is the most fantastic, caring, supportive group of people you will find, and I'm constantly blown away by the ongoing displays of enthusiasm and assistance with this project. I am blessed to have crossed paths with some incredible, humble women whom I will never forget. Many heartfelt thanks go to Erin Briggs, Jessica Cappella, Tara Emrick, Linda Garrett, Lisa Hallett, Barbara Mockford, Debbie Niemann, Andrea Peet, Jenn Sommermann, Nancy

Stevens, Chrissy Vasquez, Winter Vinecki and her mom, Dawn Estelle, Terry Woods, Theresa Roden of i-tri girls, Cindy Quitzau of Gals for Cal, and one of the strongest kids in the world, Cecilia. You are all my personal heroes. Thank you for sharing the intimate stories of your lives with such tenderness, strength, and candor.

Special thanks to Nancy Reinisch, Celeste Callahan, Julie Marchese, Moira Horan, Jenny Thullier, Mark Dirga, Miranda Hauser, Amy Dillon, every last amazing member of the Mullica Hill Women's Tri Club, and all the triathletes who contributed their stories to make this book come alive. I am also grateful to Gretchen Cooney, Mitch Greene, Katherine Calder-Becker, Larry Creswell, Jesse Moore, Meredith Atwood, Sarai Snyder, and Benjamin Caldwell for their expertise and insights. You gave generously of your time and spirit to help me, and your input made this book better than I could have ever mustered on my own.

To my mom, Jan Clarke, thank you for always valuing creativity and self-expression. To my dad, thanks for all the pep talks and for believing in me. To my extended family, particularly Dr. Alberta Montano-DiFabio (who celebrated every one of my milestones with sweet gifts, pomp, and circumstance), Antonio DiFabio, Miriam Solomon, Bill Gross, and Anselmo DiFabio, I appreciate your constant encouragement and excitement throughout this journey. Kaye and Orville Varnell and Ralph and Dora Cohen, I miss you tremendously, and I know you all would have been very proud.

Thank you to my writer's group, the Moonwriters. Julie, Regina, Caroline, Jennifer, Taralee, and Traci, the enthusiastic support you all have shown me since day one has kept me going in my moments of doubt. I'm especially appreciative of Julie Knapp and Jennifer Cannon, who read many early, terrible drafts. Thank you to Brooke Warner of Warner Coaching, and April Wilson for your editorial help in those beginning stages.

My non-writer friends may not have understood why I was constantly holed up in my house but couldn't have been more supportive. There are too many to thank by name, but I'm thanking you all in my heart.

A huge shout-out to Crescent Moon Coffee and Tea in Mullica Hill for providing all the sweet nectar of the gods that aided in the writing of this book. Apparently, creativity requires an abundance of caffeine.

To my girls, my four little heartbeats and constant source of inspiration, I'll never forget how excited you were when I told you Mommy is going to publish a book. Seeing how happy you were for me was the best part.

Above all else, I could not have written this book and stayed sane without the unconditional love and support of my husband, best friend, and soul mate. In fact, there are a great many things I couldn't do without him. Anthony, thank you for always believing in me, making me laugh, listening to me ramble for hours, and supporting my dreams. Even when it means the house is a wreck and we eat pizza for days. My life is infinitely better with you in it.

About the Author

Alicia DiFabio, Psy.D., is a member of the Mullica Hill Women's Tri Club, the largest all female triathlon club in America, and sits on its board of directors. She earned her doctorate in clinical psychology from Loyola University Maryland and worked as a clinician in the field for over a decade; she is currently staying home to raise her young children. Her articles and personal essays have appeared in various newspapers, magazines, and literary journals. *Women Who Tri: A Reluctant Athlete's Journey into the Heart of America's Newest Obsession* is her first book.

Dr. DiFabio lives in New Jersey with her husband and four girls, one of whom has multiple disabilities. She chronicles her adventures in motherhood, running, triathlon, surviving breast cancer, and parenting a child with special needs at her blog, *Lost in Holland*.